# Election, Barth,
*and the* French Connection

# Election, Barth, *and the* French Connection

How Pierre Maury Gave a "Decisive Impetus"
to Karl Barth's Doctrine of Election

SECOND EDITION

*Pierre Maury*

EDITED AND TRANSLATED BY *Simon Hattrell*
FOREWORD BY *Suzanne McDonald*
AFTERWORD BY *John C. McDowell*

☙PICKWICK *Publications* · Eugene, Oregon

ELECTION, BARTH, AND THE FRENCH CONNECTION
How Pierre Maury Gave a "Decisive Impetus" to Karl Barth's Doctrine of Election
Second Edition

Copyright © 2016, 2019 Wipf & Stock Publishers. All rights reserved. Except for brief quotations in critical publications or reviews, no part of this book may be reproduced in any manner without prior written permission from the publisher. Write: Permissions, Wipf and Stock Publishers, 199 W. 8th Ave., Suite 3, Eugene, OR 97401. First published under the title "Election, Barth and the French Connection: How Pierre Maury Gave a 'Decisive Impetus' to Karl Barth's Doctrine of Election" © 2016.

Translation copyright © 2019 by Simon Hattrell.

Second Edition, revised and expanded.
Pickwick Publications
An Imprint of Wipf and Stock Publishers
199 W. 8th Ave., Suite 3
Eugene, OR 97401

www.wipfandstock.com

PAPERBACK ISBN: 978-1-5326-6718-3
HARDCOVER ISBN: 978-1-5326-6719-0
EBOOK ISBN: 978-1-5326-6720-6

*Cataloguing-in-Publication data:*

Names: Maury, Pierre, author. | Hattrell, Simon, editor and translator. | McDonald, Suzanne, 1973–, foreword writer

Title: Election, Barth, and the French connection : how Pierre Maury gave a "decisive impetus" to Karl Barth's doctrine of election; second edition / Pierre Maury.

Description: Eugene, OR: Pickwick Publications, 2019 | Includes bibliographical references and index.

Identifiers: ISBN 978-1-5326-6718-3 (paperback) | ISBN 978-1-5326-6719-0 (hardcover) | ISBN 978-1-5326-6720-6 (ebook)

Subjects: LCSH: Maury, Pierre | Barth, Karl, 1886–1968 | Election (Theology) | Predestination

Classification: BT809 M459 2019 (print) | BT809 (ebook)

Manufactured in the U.S.A.                                    OCTOBER 30, 2019

All Scripture quotations, unless otherwise indicated, are taken from the Holy Bible, New International Version®, NIV®. Copyright ©1973, 1978, 1984, 2011 by Biblica, Inc.™ Used by permission of Zondervan. All rights reserved worldwide. www.zondervan.com. The "NIV" and "New International Version" are trademarks registered in the United States Patent and Trademark Office by Biblica, Inc.™

All photographs © Maury family, Paris.

Election et Foi © Foi et Vie, La Revue de Culture Protestante, 83 Boulevard Arago, 75014. Used by permission.

Le Grand Œuvre de Dieu © Edition «Je Sers,» Paris 1937. Public domain.

Predestination © Labor et Fides, Rue Beauregard 1, 1204 Geneva, Switzerland. Used by permission. Original translation © Edwin Hudson, 1960, published simultaneously in the United States of America © John Knox Press, Richmond, Virginia and in Great Britain © SCM Press Ltd, London.

Dedicated to the great company of French preachers
of the Reformed family both past and present,
of which Pierre Maury was an illustrious example.

# Table of Contents

*List of Illustrations* xi
*Photo Montage of Excerpts of Pierre Maury's Life* xii
*Foreword—Suzanne McDonald* xv
*Acknowledgments* xvii
*Abbreviations* xix
*Contributors* xxi

1 Introduction—Simon Hattrell 1

**PART 1: Concerning Pierre Maury**
2 Jacques Maury's Tribute to his Father 23
3 Gustave Monod's Tribute to Pierre Maury on the Occasion of his Death in 1956 25
4 Jean Bosc's Tribute to Pierre Maury on the Occasion of His Death in 1956 28
5 Robert Mackie's Memoir of Pierre Maury 30
6 Karl Barth's Foreword to Maury's *Predestination* 35

**PART 2: Pierre Maury on Election**
7 Election and Faith—Pierre Maury 41
8 The Ultimate Decision—Pierre Maury 60
9 Predestination—Pierre Maury 80

**PART 3: Contemporary Reflections on the Theology of Election in the Work of Karl Barth and Pierre Maury**
10 Pierre Maury, Karl Barth, and the Evolution of Election—Mark Lindsay 123
11 Harmony without Identity: A Comparison of the Theology of Election in Pierre Maury and Karl Barth—Matthias Gockel 146
12 Serious Joy of the Ultimate Decision—John Capper 159

13 Karl Barth's Influence on Contemporary Christian Universalism—Damon Adams  172

14 The Human Election of God—Leo Stossich  195

15 The Light of the Gospel: Election and Proclamation—Michael O'Neil  213

Afterword: Being and Becoming in Gratuity: Barth After Maury—John C. McDowell  235

Index  259

# List of Illustrations

1. Karl Barth and Pierre Maury in 1936, front cover.
2. Pierre Maury toward the end of the 1920s.
3. Pierre Maury and Karl Barth, Boulevard Arago, Paris, 1934
4. Pierre Maury Karl Barth and Willem Visser't Hooft (see pp 13, 14, 16, 31, 33 & 34), May 1934, during a student conference at La Chataigneraie Switzerland
5. Pierre Maury with French delegates preparing for the Oxford "Life and Work" Conference at Bièvres outside Paris in March 1937. Amongst those present with Maury (4th from the left front row) are W. A. Visser't Hooft (2nd from left front row), and in between them the celebrated French Philosopher, Jacques Maritain; Suzanne de Dietrich; Robert Mackie (2nd and 3rd from the left in the 2nd row). Jean Bosc is directly behind Maury. A young, 29-year-old Daniel Thambyrajah Niles Ceylonese pastor, evangelist, and eventually president of the Ceylon Methodist Conference, can also be seen on the extreme left hand side in the third row.
6. Pierre Maury receiving an Honorary Doctorate at the University of Chicago, 1954. This was awarded two years prior to his death. Pierre is third from the right. Daniel Thambyrajah Niles, who was greatly influenced by Maury, can also be seen in the photo, fifth from the right.
7. Pierre Maury, 1955.

Pierre Maury toward the end of the 1920s

Pierre Maury and Karl Barth, Boulevard Arago, Paris, 1934

Pierre Maury, Karl Barth and Willem Visser't Hooft (see pp 13, 14, 16, 31, 33 & 34), May 1934, during a student conference at La Chataigneraie Switzerland

Pierre Maury with delegates preparing for the Oxford "Life and Work" Conference at Bièvres outside Paris in March 1937. Amongst those present with Maury (4th from the left front row) are W. A. Visser't Hooft (2nd from left front row), and in between them the celebrated French Philosopher, Jacques Maritain; Suzanne de Dietrich; Robert Mackie (2nd and 3rd from the left in the 2nd row). Jean Bosc is directly behind Maury. A young, 29-year-old Daniel Thambyrajah Niles Ceylonese pastor, evangelist, and eventually president of the Ceylon Methodist Conference, can also be seen on the extreme left hand side in the third row.

Pierre Maury receiving an Honorary Doctorate at the University of Chicago, 1954. This was awarded two years prior to his death. Pierre is third from the right. Daniel Thambyrajah Niles, who was greatly influenced by Maury, can also be seen in the photo, fifth from the right.

Pierre Maury, 1955.

# Foreword

## Suzanne McDonald

IT IS MY DELIGHT to offer the foreword for the second edition of this important volume. The first has already been of immense significance, and this revised and expanded edition will continue to make a valuable contribution to scholarship on Pierre Maury himself, on Karl Barth, and on the doctrine of election more generally. The translation of Maury's work, "Election and Faith," has been revised, thanks to the collaboration of Professor Pierre-Sovann Chauny, of the Faculté Jean Calvin (Institut de Théologie Protestante et Evangélique, Aix en Provence), and there are three new essays in addition to revised versions of the essays in the first edition.

Many who have an interest in Barth studies have heard of Pierre Maury, and know that it was his account of election that became one of the catalysts for Barth's monumental re-working of the doctrine. Few know much more about Maury himself than is contained in the excursus that Barth devotes to Maury's lecture, "Election and Faith," from the 1936 International Calvinist Conference, in *Church Dogmatics* II/2.

Who was Pierre Maury? What was Maury's own understanding of the doctrine of election? What was the nature of his relationship with Karl Barth, and the extent of their influence upon each other?

Here we have a volume that sets out to help us answer those questions and more. In so doing, it offers a contribution both to Barth scholarship and also to twentieth-century historical theology more generally, by allowing us to hear the distinctive voice of Pierre Maury on his own terms, as well as in relation to Barth. This is possible thanks to the new, and now revised and corrected, translations of Maury's key works on election found here, most of which are otherwise unavailable in print or very difficult to obtain.

This volume also provides significant insight into the personal and theological relationship between Maury, Barth, and Charlotte Von Kirschbaum, who corresponded with Maury and translated Maury's works on election into German. As such, it casts light on a noteworthy friendship that has been somewhat neglected in comparison to Barth's relationships with more widely recognized theologians. Given the significance of Barth's account of election in *Church Dogmatics* II/2 for the remainder of his theology, it could be argued that this connection with a relatively obscure French pastor-theologian is of more moment for Barth's theological development and his legacy than any of his more famous theological friendships.

Fruitful intersections with contemporary issues in Barth studies also abound within the essays that engage both Maury and Barth, and there are some significant glances towards aspects of the fraught historical context in which both men were working on their respective doctrines of election, from the mid 1930s through the early years of World War II. The essays also explore some of the implication of both Maury's and Barth's approaches to election for contemporary accounts of the doctrine, and for proclaiming the gospel. Maury's pastoral and preaching focus in his treatment of the doctrine remind us that this is an exploration of election not simply for those of us in the theological academy, but also for those of us whose priorities are preaching and teaching in churches.

While Maury's account of election will inevitably remain in the shadow of Barth's, and will always be interpreted in relation to Barth's, as this volume indicates, Maury offers a re-appropriation and development of the Reformed tradition which merits more than simply a footnote explaining its role in the origins of Barth's mature exposition of the doctrine.

Suzanne McDonald
Professor of Systematic and Historical Theology,
Western Theological Seminary in Holland, MI.

# *Acknowledgements*

I AM INDEBTED TO those who have continued to make an invaluable contribution to this project in its second edition: firstly to Wipf & Stock for their belief in the value of this work, especially Matthew Wimer and Robin Parry for their positive encouragement. I am also very grateful for the input of those who have once more given their time in a spirit of generous collaboration. While John Capper and Mark Lindsay's essays remain as in the first edition, they have always been willing to give advice and moral support, as have John McDowell and Matthias Gockel, who have revised theirs. Even though oceans separate some of us, the fellowship we have enjoyed has been rich. I am still hopeful that Suzanne McDonald will visit our island state one day! In what has now become an updated and expanded edition, Damon Adams, Leo Stossich and Michael O'Neil, have enriched this contribution to Barth scholarship. I would particularly like to thank Professor Pierre-Sovann Chauny of the Faculté Jean Calvin (Institut de Théologie Protestante et Evangélique) at Aix en Provence in France, for his willing and gracious help in improving the translation of Pierre Maury's seminal 1936 work "Election and Faith." Nevertheless, I hasten to add that any remaining deficiencies are mine alone.

This has been a true *theologia viatorum*.[1] I particularly remember the late much esteemed Professor John Webster of St. Andrews University, who gave me his valuable time during a visit to Scotland in 2013. I read him some of my draft translations and he was later to say that "in providing an entry into Maury's theology and its relation to Barth, the translations and interpretive essays of the first edition prompted fresh thought about the content and place of the doctrine of election." John's irenic approach to Barth studies was a great help to me as, I am sure, it was for many others. My wife Barbara, faithful companion of the last 50 years, sat down with me and helped to complete a final edit of Pierre

1. Literally a theology on the way or of fellow travellers/pilgrims.

Maury's French texts. Professor Frédéric Rognon, Director/Editor of *Foi et Vie*, the journal that originally published Pierre Maury's *Election and Faith*, gave permission to publish my translation. Thanks must also go to *Labor et Fides* in Geneva, who published Maury's *Predestination* in 1957, for their generous permission to publish my revised translation of Edwin Hudson's original work and to use part of Jacques Maury's tribute to his father in a wonderful biography of Pierre Maury by Françoise Florentin-Smyth, a greatly respected and distinguished Old Testament scholar in France and Switzerland. She graciously introduced me to Jacques Maury and his immediate family in 2013 during a visit to Paris. Their photos which you see in this book give us a sense of the man that was Pierre Maury and the rich texture of his earthly life. Bernard Reymond's work (1985) of editing and compiling Barth and Maury's correspondence, with many of the details of their enduring friendship has added so much to the human dimension of this amazing theological partnership which was always more than a meeting of great minds.

Pierre Maury has left a lasting legacy: his clear exposition of scripture, the warmth of his devotion to the Master he served, his pastoral heart and the stimulus of his intellect.

*Quand les montagnes s'éloigneraient,*
*quand les collines chancelleraient,*
*mon amour ne s'éloignera point de toi,*
*et mon alliance de paix ne chancellera point,*
*dit l'Éternel, qui a compassion de toi.*
Ésaïe 54:10

# Abbreviations

| | |
|---|---|
| CD | Barth, *Church Dogmatics* |
| EF | Maury, "Election and Faith" or "Élection et Foi" |
| EG | Maury, "Erwählung und Glaube" |
| GD | Barth, *Göttingen Dogmatics* |
| KD | Barth, *Die Kirchliche Dogmatik* |
| UD | Maury, "The Ultimate Decision" |
| PD | Maury, "Predestination" |

# Contributors

**Damon Adams** originally trained as a Presbyterian minister and lectured in Historical Theology at John Knox Theological College, Sydney; Theology, Biblical Studies and Church History at Tabor College, Tasmania; and is currently Senior Lecturer in Theology, Biblical Studies and Church History at Alphacrucis College, Hobart Campus, Tasmania. His lectures are always stimulating and his teaching style is greatly appreciated by many students. Additionally, Damon is presently the national History Subject Coordinator at Alphacrucis. Damon holds a PhD in Theology.

**John Capper** is Director of Learning and Teaching at the University of Divinity, Melbourne. Working with the Colleges and teachers of the University to nurture excellence and develop world-class courses, John brings a quarter century of experience in theological education. A former College Dean within the University and other Colleges, he is a Council member of the Australian College of Theology and member of various Higher Education boards, as well as the Board of Tintern Schools. An ordained Anglican, John has experience in rural, urban and suburban ministry in Australia and UK, and mission experience in Asia. He is regularly involved in interim ministry assignments. John's PhD is from the University of Cambridge, and his ongoing research is in joy, contemporary theology and ministry practice, and theological education, particularly the use of web-based technologies.

**Matthias Gockel** teaches Systematic Theology at the University of Basel, Switzerland, as he formerly did at the Friedrich-Schiller-University in Jena while also serving as Project Coordinator for the Jena Center for Reconciliation Studies (JCRS). He received his PhD from Princeton Theological Seminary and is the author of *Barth und Schleiermacher on the Doctrine of Election* (Oxford University Press, 2007). He has published widely on topics related to nineteenth- and twentieth-century Protestant theology. Recently, he co-edited, with Martin Leiner, *Barth und*

*Schleiermacher. Zur Neubestimmung ihres Verhältnisses* (Vandenhoeck & Ruprecht, 2015). His current research focuses on the doctrine of God's attributes, Protestant theology in the German Democratic Republic, and political ethics. He is an ordained pastor in the Evangelische Kirche im Rheinland.

**Simon Hattrell** is an Anglican Priest who has spent 50 years of his adult life actively involved in various local church ministries ranging from student outreach, church planting, evangelism, children's work, pastoral oversight and preaching. He and his wife Barbara lived for ten years in France serving alongside French churches. On their return to Australia in 1989 they were involved in the development of what has now become Alphacrucis College, Hobart Campus, a tertiary Christian college offering undergraduate and postgraduate courses in Theology, Ministry, Leadership and Christian Counselling. Simon taught Bible, Ministry and Theology. In his retirement he has helped coordinate distance education and training within the Diocese of Tasmania and has been regularly involved in interim ministry assignments in local parishes and interstate.

**Mark Lindsay** is an historical theologian, with over 20 years of experience teaching, researching, and providing senior academic leadership in Australian and overseas universities. His specific areas of interest are Barthian and post-Holocaust theologies, Patristic and modern European Church History, and Anglican Studies. He is a priest in the Anglican Diocese of Melbourne. He serves as Deputy Dean and the Joan F. W. Munro Professor of Historical Theology at Trinity College Theological School, Melbourne. He has taught at universities in Melbourne, Perth and Cambridge, and worked for seven years as the University of Divinity's Director of Research. Mark is widely published, with an international reputation for his work on the theologies of Karl Barth and Dietrich Bonhoeffer. His published works include *Covenanted Solidarity: The Theological Basis of Karl Barth's Opposition to Nazi Antisemitism and the Holocaust* (Peter Lang, 2001); *Barth, Israel and Jesus* (Ashgate, 2007); and *Reading Auschwitz with Barth: The Holocaust as Problem and Promise for Barthian Theology* (Wipf & Stock, 2014). His work on the doctrine of election is soon to be published by IVP Academic. He is currently President of the Australian and New Zealand Association of Theological Schools and is a Fellow of the Royal Historical Society.

**Suzanne McDonald** is an Australian by birth, who did her theological training in the United Kingdom, and is now Professor of Systematic and Historical Theology at Western Theological Seminary in Holland, Michigan. Prior to joining the faculty at Western, she taught theology for seven years at Calvin College in Grand Rapids, Michigan. She is an ordained minister in the Christian Reformed Church in North America, and is the author of *Re-Imaging Election: Divine Election as Representing God to Others and Others to God* (Eerdmans, 2010), *John Knox for Armchair Theologians* (Westminster John Knox, 2013), and numerous articles and essays, especially on the doctrine of election, and on John Owen.

**John C. McDowell** Since 2015 John C. McDowell has been the Director of Research for the University of Divinity, and based in Melbourne, Australia. His published writings cover twentieth-century German theology, in particular the work of Karl Barth; theological ethics; the philosophical theology of Donald MacKinnon; theology and the tragic; neoliberalism and higher education; and hope and violence in popular culture. Among numerous articles and book chapters on theology, higher education, and popular culture, he has authored *Theology and the Globalized Present: Feasting in the Presence of God* (Fortress, 2019); with Scott Kirkland, *Eschatology: Christian Hope* (Eerdmans, 2018); *The Gospel According to Star Wars: Faith, Hope and the Force*, 2nd edn. (Westminster John Knox, 2017); *The Ideology of Identity Politics in George Lucas* (McFarland, 2016); *The Politics of Big Fantasy: Studies in Cultural Suspicion* (McFarland, 2014); and *Hope in Barth's Eschatology: Interrogations and Transformations Beyond Tragedy* (Ashgate, 2000). He has edited a special issue of the journal *Religions* on "Hope in Dark Times" (2019); two special issues of the journal *Colloquium* on "Beyond Education" (2015) and "Engaging Karl Barth" (2018); *Kenotic Ecclesiology: Select Writings of Donald M. MacKinnon*, with Ashley Moyse and Scott Kirkland (eds.) (Fortress, 2016); *Correlating Sobernost: Conversations Between Karl Barth and the Russian Orthodox Tradition*, with Ashley Moyse and Scott Kirkland (Fortress, 2016); *Philosophy and the Burden of Theological Honesty: A Donald MacKinnon Reader* (Continuum/T&T Clark, 2011); and *Conversing with Barth*, with Mike A. Higton (Ashgate, 2004).

**Michael O'Neil** is the director of Vose Research and head of the Christian Thought Department at Vose Seminary (Baptist) Perth, Western

Australia. He has studied at, and been an active member of, Vose since the late 1990s. Michael has also served in various churches large and small for over twenty years, in team pastor, sole pastor, and senior minister roles. He believes that theology must not be an arcane academic pursuit reserved only for a few super-nerdy types. Rather, theology exists for the sake of the church and its mission. It exists to assist ordinary believers read and enact Scripture in authentic ways, together, and in their own locale, as a local body of faithful disciples of Jesus Christ. In 2013 his first book was published: *Church as Moral Community: Karl Barth's Vision of Christian Life, 1915–1922* (Paternoster, 2013).

**Leo Stossich** is a qualified teacher, ordained minister and has planted several churches. Leo pioneered and served as senior minister at Kingborough Family Church (affiliated with the Apostolic Church of Australia) for over 20 years. He gained his doctor of ministry at Tabor College of Higher Education in Adelaide, Australia. His dissertation was *The Healing Spirit: An Investigation of Spiritual Healing for Christian Survivors of Childhood Sexual Abuse*, which has now been published by Wipf & Stock (2019). He has lectured at the Tasmanian College of Ministries and Tabor College in Hobart. He currently pastors at Trinity Life Church, Blackmans Bay.

# 1

## *Introduction*

### SIMON HATTRELL

JUST AFTER MY THIRTIETH birthday, my wife and I took our three young children to live and work in France during the 1970s and 1980s. There I had the privilege of ministering amongst a large congregation in the university city of Montpellier, and was also involved in student ministry. I then engaged over several years in church planting and evangelism in the *Massif Central* region bordering the famous Cevennes mountain ranges and the plateaus of the *Grands Causses*.[1] In various contexts over the years during this time I often had the privilege of listening to some of the finest preachers I have heard in fifty years of active adult Christian discipleship and ordained ministry. So it is not surprising that I have the greatest respect for the erudition and evangelical warmth of someone like Pierre Maury. While this book is not a biography of Maury, his personality and influence are such strong factors that we cannot but throw the

---

1. Any missionary/church worker who has served in France, particularly in those regions that became bastions of the Reformed faith, such as the Cevennes, cannot remain unmoved by the example of those who stood firm for nearly a hundred years up until the revolution of 1789, during a period which became known as *L'Église du desert*—"the Church of the wilderness." In this region many brave men and women were martyred or imprisoned for their faith, particularly after Louis XIV in 1685 revoked the Edict of Nantes, which was an edict of religious tolerance instituted by Louis's grandfather Henri IV in 1598. From Calvin onwards, French Protestants were forced into exile all over Europe and to the four corners of the earth. The spiritual descendants of those who survived that terrible period of persecution have kept the flame burning. Whilst that era has long passed, it still remains a significant backdrop of the life of Protestantism in France and has left an indelible mark.

spotlight on this amazing man, who gave such a *decisive impetus* to Barth in his famous reconstruction of the doctrine of election.[2]

Having retired from active ordained pastoral ministry at the end of 2012, I was able to continue reading Karl Barth's rich theology that I had begun to chip away at in 2002, when I engaged in postgraduate studies in ministry. In the intervening years, though absorbed by pastoral demands, I had managed to read much secondary literature, which helped to reframe certain aspects of the theological "grid" to which I was exposed during my time at a ministry training college in the early seventies. Many critiques of Barth at that time tended to dismiss him as not worthy of consideration.[3] Much of what I learned during that time of preparation for pastoral ministry was very helpful and constructive, but subsequently treading a path between what was considered *off limits* on the one hand and on the other a somewhat rigid approach to Christian revelation, was at times a rocky road until I read Bernard Ramm's 1983

---

2. In November 1950 Karl Barth wrote a moving letter to Pierre Maury, which reveals not only how much he esteemed him but also how strong was his emotional attachment to his French friend. "Unforgettable the day that I saw you for the first time with such a strong impression: that face, and what a character, a man whom I love! . . . The expectation of that day has never failed: I have been the reason for many disappointments and caused you many worries. . . . But I have always found you to be compelling, remarkable, exasperating (in the best sense of the word) and always faithful to the Cause as well as to your friend with and despite his outrageous thoughts, words and attitudes" (Reymond, *Karl Barth—Pierre Maury*, 225 [my translation]).

3. Hunsinger in countering various critiques of Barth observes that "reading what the critics have to say of Barth's theology is usually like looking at an old map, the kind drafted before the dawn of modern cartography in the eighteenth century. Certain basic aspects of the theology may be present, but the distortion factor is high. Topographic features may be lacking in detail. Whole promontories may be absent or diminished. Monsters, lions, and squash lines may do duty for factual content. The task of responsible criticism presupposes a more reliable depiction of the overall terrain, as well as of the proportional relationships among the various segments, than has usually been the case. A quest for better cartography would seem to be the place to begin" (Hunsinger, *How to Read Karl Barth*, x). Nearly ten years later, he also observed that "Barth has set the terms for debate in a field where almost everyone seemed to disagree with him, even though they could not ignore him, and even though, as was also often the case, they had only just begun to understand him, if at all" (Hunsinger, *Disruptive Grace*, 253). Perhaps he had in mind works such as Van Til's *Christianity and Barthianism*, whose critique was far from superficial but comprehensive in its scope and in its day had a marked influence, engendering a cautious attitude toward Barthian theology. However, Van Til, while censuring Barth for his many "errors," respected his scholarship: "The *Church Dogmatics* is a truly monumental work. In reading it one's admiration for Barth knows no bounds. . . . In the *Church Dogmatics* we have the ripe fruition of arduous reflection and research" (Van Til, *Christianity and Barthianism*, 2).

book *After Fundamentalism* in the early 2000s, in which he wrote that he had come to the conclusion that "Barth's theology is a restatement of Reformed theology written in the aftermath of the Enlightenment but not capitulating to it,"[4] I found his at times cautious yet generally positive assessment quite persuasive. Like Donald Bloesch in his *Jesus is Victor*, Ramm had reservations about aspects of Barth's corpus and took issue at various points, but remained an appreciative critic. It goes without saying that many Evangelicals in particular have a strained relationship with Barth, but I concur with the irenic attitude of a theologian such as Mark Thompson, who, while also parting company with Barth in some areas, observes that we should engage with him "not as an enemy but as a fellow disciple of Jesus Christ."[5]

Once anyone begins to engage seriously with Barth's massive corpus, it demands a herculean effort of time and energy. His work represents a lifetime of hard work and indefatigable single-minded attention to his task.[6] It was during a three week study retreat in 2013 that the link between Barth and Maury and its significance for the doctrine of election came into sharper focus for me. In the last week I set myself the task of working through Bruce McCormack's *Karl Barth's Critically Realistic Dialectical Theology: Its Genesis and Development, 1909–1936*, which challenged the traditional view of the evolution of Barth's theology from dialectic to analogy espoused in particular by the late Roman Catholic theologian Hans Urs von Balthasar.[7] It wasn't until I had read all 467 pages of this outstanding piece of historical theology, which the British theologian Graham Ward, Regius Professor of Divinity at Oxford, described as a "major intellectual achievement and interpretative act of great courage, in which Barth studies will never remain the same,"[8] that I discovered how significant the contribution of Pierre Maury was. Naturally I was intrigued. I had discovered a *French connection* in Barth's theological development!

4. Ramm, *After Fundamentalism*, 14.
5. Thompson, *Witness to the Word*, 196.
6. A leading Australian Uniting Church minister friend told me of his visit to Basel many years ago and standing outside Barth's old home. An elderly gentleman enquired about the purpose of his visit and shared his memory of often seeing the light from Barth's study in the night hours. He said that he told his sons, "So you want to succeed in your studies? Look at Professor Barth. Follow his example!"
7. Von Balthasar, *Theology of Karl Barth*.
8. Ward, "Review of Karl Barth's Critically Realistic Dialectical Theology," 88–89.

A major focus of this book's second edition is still Maury's famous 1936 paper "Election and Faith" and on the impact of this paper on Barth's subsequent reworking of the doctrine of election in *Church Dogmatics* II/2 (1942),[9] where Maury's "impressive treatment" of this theme is acknowledged.[10] However, it is important for us in this study, as Suzanne McDonald stated in her foreword to the first edition, to understand who exactly was Pierre Maury, the man, Karl Barth's close friend and confidant, the one who was instrumental in introducing Barth's theology to the church in France in the twentieth century.

Many authors have taken into account Pierre Maury's seminal influence on Barth's doctrine of election,[11] but in the English speaking world he is often neither known nor appreciated for who he was in his own right, despite the fact that he was awarded honorary doctorates by the universities of Budapest, St. Andrews, and Chicago. His groundbreaking paper, "Election and Faith," often gets a mention in the literature for its significance, but until the first edition of this work had never been translated into English. Meeting Pierre Maury's biographer, Françoise Florentin-Smyth,[12] and some of the Maury family in Paris in September 2013 heightened my sense that here was someone and something that needed to be brought to the attention of a wider readership. Hopefully this work will again encourage more readers to reflect on what it was that Maury

---

9. Barth wrote in 1956: "At an important stage in my theological journey, when I was concerned with the doctrine of election, he gave me a decisive impetus." This was part of Barth's tribute to Maury, in a letter titled "Un homme libre [A Free Man]," written to Albert Finet, director of the weekly *Réforme* [*Reformation*] journal, on February 18, 1956 (Reymond, *Karl Barth—Pierre Maury*, 249 [my translation]).

10. "The Christological meaning and basis of the doctrine of election have been brought out afresh in our own time, and with an impressive treatment of Jesus Christ as the original and decisive object of the divine election and rejection. This service has been rendered by Pierre Maury in the fine lecture which he gave on *Election et Foi* at the *Congrès International de Théologie Calviniste* in Geneva, 1936 (published in *Foi et Vie*, April–May 1936, and in German under the title "Erwählung und Glaube" in *Theol. Studien*, Heft 8, 1940). That Congress dealt exclusively with the problem of predestination, and its records will easily show how instructive was Maury's contribution, and how it stood out from the other papers, which were interesting historically but in content moved entirely within the circle of the traditional formulations, and were almost hopelessly embarrassed by their difficulties" (*CD* II/2:154–55).

11. McCormack, *Karl Barth's Dialectical Theology*, 455–63; Gockel, *Barth and Schleiermacher*, 158–64; McDonald, *Re-imaging Election*, 31–37. "Barthian theology and that of Maury were made to meet each other" (Maillot, "P. Maury Prédicateur," 26).

12. Florentin-Smyth, *Pierre Maury*.

gave to Barth not just in terms of a fresh insight into a Christological focus in the doctrine of election but to explore how an amazing friendship helped to foster a different approach to what has been described as a "vast dogmatic minefield!"[13] The essays that follow the translations of Maury's works attempt to address some of these issues. Maury's work merits serious attention on its own, especially as he writes from the perspective both of a pastor and a preacher, which remained a strong focus of his life up until his untimely and much regretted death. My hope is that not only theologians will find inspiration in these extracts from Maury, which are transcripts of addresses that he gave often in the midst of a very busy life. He said that his famous paper on Election and Faith was hastily put together in just two days.[14] They have an immediacy that is often difficult to convey in translation. Many phrases have been reworked and retranslated in this edition.[15]

We first encounter Maury in the seminal paper he gave at the Calvinist Congress at Geneva in 1936. This was an initiative of young neo-Calvinists of that time to celebrate the 400th anniversary of the publication of the first edition of Calvin's *Institutio Christianae Religionis* (*Institutes of the Christian Religion*). Then, from a year later we engage with a sermon ("The Ultimate Decision," 1937), part of a Lenten series

---

13. Gunton, *Election and Ecclesiology*, 220. Similar sentiments are shared by Migliore: "Few doctrines in the history of Christian theology have been as misunderstood and distorted, and few have caused as much controversy and distress, as the doctrine of the eternal decrees of God, or double predestination" (Migliore, *Faith Seeking Understanding*, 87). Fernandez-Armesto and Wilson succinctly canvas the dilemma that has confronted theologians down through the centuries: "If the bestowal of grace is absolute, it must be predestined; if the individual soul can neither attract nor resist it, God must be supposed to have made up his mind about it independently of the behavior of the person saved or condemned" (Fernandez-Armesto and Wilson, *Reformation*, 87).

14. "Between you and me confidentially (and I am not very proud of it) I can tell you that I put together the outline and wrote the text in 2 days! It's disgraceful. Naturally since then I discover all sorts of things that should have been said and others that I could have been able to develop and put differently" (Reymond, *Karl Barth—Pierre Maury*, 102).

15. For this second revised edition Professor Pierre-Sovann Chauny of the Faculté Jean Calvin, Institut de Théologie Protestante et Évangélique (Aix-en-Provence, France) has helped to improve the translation of "Election and Faith" and I thank him for his assistance. As Garrett Green observed in his preface to his translation of Barth on the topic of religion in *CD* I/1, "translation is as much an art as a science, requiring not only linguistic expertise in two languages but also a sense of style and tone in both" (Green, *On Religion*, vii).

(The Great Work of God), preached at the Reformed Church of the Annunciation at Passy, Paris. Lastly we meet Maury as pastor/theologian in a revised translation of his address on Predestination to delegates at the Second World Council of Churches Assembly at Evanston, Illinois, in 1954, just two years before his death.

In "Election and Faith" Maury grounds his view of election in Paul's letter to the Ephesians, giving it a very strong Christological focus:

> Election is really an election initiated by God, that is to say, before the foundation of the world, in God's eternity. Because it is election in Christ and by Christ, the One by whom and for whom all things have been made, it is a choice whose origin is elsewhere than in our time, a decision taken outside of all the sequences in which we are without end enclosed.[16]

The uniqueness of Maury's contribution is found in this Christocentric grounding of election, a focus of hot debate in Barthian studies[17] and seeing election as part of the doctrine of God and not so much as part of a subjective soteriology. Election, for Maury, is a theological, not an anthropological, doctrine (as seen in the title of a chapter in *Predestination*).

These three works of Maury are outstanding examples of original, biblically-grounded exposition in the Reformed theological tradition. Maury seeks to be faithful to Calvin but is not bound by him.

We see the significance of these two orientations in a letter Barth wrote to Pierre Maury on August 21, 1936, in response to "Election and Faith"[18]:

---

16. See page 44.

17. This raises the issue of Barth's "Christomonism," which H. Richard Niebuhr named "a new unitarianism of the second person of the trinity." The "Christocentric concentration" in Barth's whole corpus is reviewed by Henri Blocher, who gives instances of the use of such words as "panchristism" and "Jesucentric" to characterize Barth's thinking (Blocher, "Karl Barth's Christocentric Method," 26–27), and says that "some attempt must be made to sound the strength of its foundations and to probe the durability of its cement and linkages" (Blocher, "Karl Barth's Christocentric Method," 43). Berkouwer claims that Barth developed an extreme Christomonism (see Berkouwer, *Triumph of Grace*), but Colin Greene says that this "would be analogous to an imploding star: the sheer power of the Christological gravitational forces would eventually drag everything into the 'black hole' of the eternal person and being of Christ." However, in striking prose, he believes that it is more accurate to speak of a "Christological prism, where the iridescent light that shines from the person of Christ is refracted through that prism to illuminate the landscape of Christian theology in a way not previously attempted" (Greene, *Christology in Cultural Perspective*, 288).

18. Reymond, *Karl Barth—Pierre Maury*, 99–101 (my translation). Reymond, the

My dear friend Maury! I have just read, no, worked on your lecture on predestination and I hasten to say how much I approve and admire these pages. I am in the process of doing some research on this subject for the lectures which I have to give in Hungary, so I am at this time competent to pass judgment. I have to admit frankly and without wanting to flatter you that it is the best presentation on this question that I know, much better than that which I myself gave seven years ago in my Dogmatics course. The direction in which I was seeking—you know my interpretation of Romans 9–11—was the same, but you were so right to insist much more energetically on the "in Christ" and the way in which you did it is very clear and revealing and still gives me a fresh line of thought. I will need to take a lot of trouble to attain and to maintain in my Hungarian lectures the high standard where the problem is laid out after your "elucubrations"[19] and intensive efforts. . . . Besides, I wonder if you see clearly enough the enormity of the change of the character and the importance of the doctrine of predestination, if it is understood as on page 216 of your work.[20] Would Calvin recognize himself here or would he not mount proceedings against us similar to what he did with the unfortunate Bolsec? Do you not find it also quite astonishing, that, despite his assertions on the "mirror" etc., his own explanations on the role of Christ in this matter are—different from yours!!—rather thin and obscure: repeated propositions rather than explanations? You are quite right to say that the disagreement is secondary. It is also secondary as far as the question of natural theology is concerned. Only, we should not hide the fact that while being good disciples of the Reformation, we are perhaps moving away, further than our

---

editor of the correspondence, writes, "This letter from Barth presents a special interest: it gives his warm reaction before a text of Maury, which we know had influenced him, but concerning this we were only aware of the preface that Barth wrote for the posthumous edition of Maury's study on Predestination (Geneva, 1957). Barth took the trouble to write this letter directly in French" (Reymond, *Karl Barth—Pierre Maury*, 99).

19. Latin—elucubrare, elucubrate—to work at night by lamplight. Lucubration is laborious study especially at night or as in this instance "lucubrations"—a solemn literary work.

20. The page reference referred to here is in *Foi et Vie* (1936), where Maury's study first appeared. Reymond comments, "These are the pages where Maury insisted on the fact that it is Jesus Christ who is at one and the same time both the object of the election and the condemnation of God, different from Calvin, who distinguished between the elect on the one hand and the condemned on the other, independently of Jesus Christ" (Reymond, *Karl Barth—Pierre Maury*, 100).

liberal predecessors, from their way of thinking. There really is no "Calvinism"![21]

It needs to be kept in mind that the evolution of Barth's mature doctrine of election was part of an ongoing conversation that went back many years. Barth recalled this in 1956: "Pierre Maury and I had of course often spoken of this problem."[22] We have another hint of this in a recent work of Satyaranjan about the great Sri Lankan Methodist preacher, D. T. Niles:[23]

> In 1935 Niles attended the General Committee of the World Student Christian Federation at Sophia, Bulgaria, as a delegate of the SCM of India, Ceylon and Burma. This marked the beginning of his entry into the ecumenical world outside his native confines and opened doors to meet with the world's great theologians and spiritual leaders. At Sophia, Niles found a "guru" in Pastor Pierre Maury of France, a spiritual guide who led the Bible study. Niles met Karl Barth, the great theologian, at Basel the same year after the first Missions Conference of the World Student Christian Federation, and asked Barth his opinion of Pierre Maury's understanding of predestination. Niles later reminisced about Barth's reply: "[Karl Barth] underlined the point that Pierre Maury makes, that predestination is a mystery of light and not of darkness, a mystery of grace even when one is speaking about the judgment of God . . . [Pierre Maury] helped me to understand between going to the Bible for answers to questions we ask and approaching the Bible with our answers to the questions it raises. Pierre Maury would say 'Only God has the right to ask questions' (Niles, *Karl Barth*, 5, 7–8).[24]

Another indication of an anterior grappling and ongoing conversation around this issue is also borne out in Barth's lecture cycle at Göttingen, published as *The Theology of the Reformed Confessions*, in which he was treating "Reformed doctrine as a whole" and within this broad overview looking at what he called "the positive doctrine of Christianity." On

---

21. This was, of course, Van Til's assertion—that Barth was not true to the Reformation heritage.

22. See Karl Barth's original foreword to Maury's *Predestination* in this volume.

23. Daniel Thambyrajah Niles (1908–1970) was a Ceylonese/Sri Lankan pastor, evangelist and president of the Ceylon Methodist Conference. He once famously defined the task of an evangelist as "one beggar telling another beggar where to get food."

24. Satyaranjan, *Preaching of D. T. Niles*, 24.

June 21, 1923, fourteen years before his Gifford Lectures of 1937–38,[25] he was focusing on the Scots Confession of 1560:

> It is truly regrettable that in the seventeenth century the Scots Confession became obsolete and today only has historical significance.... We note how clearly the meaning of the doctrine of predestination is handled. This doctrine treats of what God does, not what happens to the human person.... We see how the unclassical problem of the assurance of salvation, this problem whose very emergence is an indicator of confusion and wrong questions, never commands any attention in this context. That is certainly the best thing that can happen to it. It is my opinion that, because of all of this, the Scots Confession, like a few others, may speak to us as a normative and model confession for our pursuit of the question of the positive doctrine of Christianity.[26]

So it would appear that predestination had been a longstanding topic of conversation between Barth and Maury over many years before 1936, and that Barth himself had seen certain "flaws" that troubled him. He considered, as he was to say in his 1937 Gifford Lectures, that Article Eight of the Scots Confession, "Of Election," seemed at first sight to be of a purely Christological character, something which he considered to be a noteworthy innovation in the way the subject matter was ordered:

> By this arrangement its authors have made it known unambiguously that they wish the whole body of material which is called the doctrine of predestination to be explained through Christology and conversely Christology to be explained with the doctrine of predestination.[27]

He concluded his lecture on *God's Decision and Man's Election* by claiming that

> The Scottish confession is right in principle in the position it takes. God's eternal decree and man's election and thus the whole of what is called the doctrine of predestination cannot but be misunderstood unless it is understood in its connection with the truth of the divine human nature of Jesus Christ.[28]

---

25. Barth, *Knowledge of God*.
26. Barth, *Theology of the Reformed Confessions*, 133.
27. Barth, *Knowledge of God*, 69.
28. Barth, *Knowledge of God*, 80–91.

In the present volume I have included selections from five witnesses, concerning the man that was Pierre Maury. Firstly, Jacques Maury, Pierre's son, shares his testimony to the impact of this beloved pastor/theologian as an evangelist. Secondly, Gustave Monod, a senior French government official and past Chief of Staff of the Minister of Education and Inspector General of Education gives a moving personal tribute. Thirdly, a much loved and respected fellow French Reformed Minister and theologian, Jean Bosc, who, with Albert Finet, founded the journal *Réforme*, speaks of Maury's bi-partisanship in matters theological. Fourthly, Robert Mackie, a contemporary and close collaborator of Maury, shares his memories in an abbreviated introduction to the original English translation of *Predestination*. Fifthly, Karl Barth in the same edition just mentioned gives a moving and eloquent testimony to the strength of his friendship with Maury and the enormous respect that the Professor of Basel had for his "never-to-be-forgotten friend."

Following these tributes, we have three of Pierre Maury's works. In the chapters that follow these, seven theologians all engage with Maury and Barth from historical, textual, pastoral, and theological standpoints, and seek to draw conclusions for us in our contemporary setting, sixty to eighty years from their original composition.

In "Pierre Maury, Karl Barth, and the Evolution of Election," Mark Lindsay outlines the major aspects of Barth's articulation of election, describing the political-rhetorical context in which Barth's reflections on this subject were made. Having written in some detail[29] on Barth's theology in the light of the Holocaust, he also shows how the particularities of Barth's doctrine of election stand in self-conscious resistance to the National Socialist hatred of God's ancient people.

In "Harmony without Identity: A Comparison of the Theology of Election in Pierre Maury and Karl Barth" Matthias Gockel takes a closer look at Maury's thinking on election in comparison with Barth's view. He maintains that, despite their principal agreement about the need to put the doctrine on a new Christological basis, minor differences remain. He canvasses a number of subtle changes of the French text in the German

---

29. Mark Lindsay's works include *Covenanted Solidarity: The Theological Basis of Karl Barth's Opposition to Nazi Antisemitism and the Holocaust* (2001); *Barth, Israel and Jesus: Karl Barth's Theology of Israel* (2007); and *Reading Auschwitz with Barth: The Holocaust as Problem and Promise for Barthian Theology* (2014).

translation, which was undertaken by Barth's confidante Charlotte von Kirschbaum, as well as the most significant translation changes raising the vexed question of interpretation in the task of translation.

John Capper's paper "Serious Joy of the Ultimate Decision" focuses on Maury's 1937 sermon "Ultimate Decision." What he finds profoundly troubling from a pastoral perspective is that many who hear the good news of the Gospel do not come to know the saving gift of God. Therefore, pondering election and its polarities in predestination is a means of making sense of this reality, and a step to encouraging steadfastness in the lives of the faithful. This points to some connections between the theological and pastoral aspects of both Barth and Maury.

Damon Adams in "Karl Barth's Influence on Contemporary Christian Universalism" argues that "attached to Barth's newly formulated doctrine of election came explanations that have left many a reader of Barth to conclude that he was effectively teaching a form of Christian Universalism."[30]

The next two essays by Leo Stossich, "The Human Election of God," and Michael O'Neil, "The Light of the Gospel—Election and Proclamation," take a more positive view of Barth's reworking of the Reformed doctrine and classical understanding of election. Stossich draws our attention to the rich theology of the Holy Spirit in Barth and the issue of human freedom and, I would add, *the balancing of divine and human agency in the economy of salvation*, while O'Neil explores "the relation between election and proclamation in Barth's doctrine, in hope of highlighting more explicitly Barth's pastoral and homiletical orientation."[31] Does Barth hold together *the objective and subjective poles of salvation* and is his logic inevitably leading in the direction of universalism?[32] A not

---

30. See page 173.

31. See page 215.

32. Zahrnt observed that "Whenever Barth came to speak of Apokatastasis, he denies it. He skirts it by appealing to the same freedom of God which makes his grace so unlimited. Grace forbids faith to *turn* the open number of the elect in Jesus Christ into a closed number, on the pattern of the classic doctrine of predestination. But to reckon with the redemption of *all* men would equally result in a *closed* number" (*CD* II/2:421–22). Zahrnt also picks up on the theme of O'Neil's essay on the relation between election and proclamation: "The fundamental openness of the number of the elect has to be reflected in the 'open situation of proclamation.' Consequently, Barth answers the charge that he teaches an Apokatastasis by constantly referring to preaching: The Church's mission is not to define and contemplate the divine choice, but to preach it, thereby perfecting the destination of the elect. Predestination is not an object for inquiry and discursive description, but for faith and personal address: 'It is

unsympathetic critic Donald Bloesch is quite categorical in this respect: "It is our contention that Barth does not finally succeed in holding the objective and subjective dimensions of salvation in true dialectical relation. It seems that not only is the objective prior to the subjective but that the real decision has already been resolved and actually accomplished in the eternal will of God."[33] Both Stossich and O'Neil answer some of these concerns in developing the place of the Holy Spirit in Barth. Readers will notice that there are at times some overlaps in all these essays, as they weigh up the various proposals and research put forward.

Finally, in a comprehensive concluding afterword, John McDowell develops many rich themes in "Barth after Maury." He shows that Barth "had not only developed and deepened in his own work that which he appreciated about Maury's *Election et Foi,* but . . . he had pressed this material in all kinds of quite distinctive and theologically rich directions."[34]

---

meant for you!'" (Zahrnt *Question of God,* 110). Ten years after the publication of *CD* II/2 in 1952, Barth published his *Christus und Adam nach Römer 5,* in which he stated that "The very existence of this individual (Christ) is identical with a divine righteous decision which *potentially* includes an indefinite multitude of other men so as to be manifest and effective in those who believe in Him in a way that is absolutely decisive" (Barth, *Christ and Adam,* 12 [emphasis mine]). Barth's use of the adverb *potentially* reveals a certain caution. He was specifically dealing with verses 12–21 of Romans 5, in which, as Morris has clearly pointed out: "There is an objectivity to this section that we should not miss. In verses 1–11, and again in 6:1–9, the pronoun "we" is constant, but in 5:12–21 there is not one 'we.' *Paul is concentrating on objective facts, irrespective of our participation*" (Morris, *Epistle to the Romans,* 228 [emphasis mine]). In a similar vein Barrett concurs in his commentary on verse 19, stating that "Adam's disobedience did not mean that all men necessarily and without consent committed particular acts of sin; it meant that they were born into a race which had separated itself from God. Similarly, Christ's obedience did not mean that men did nothing but righteous acts, but that in Christ they were related to God as Christ himself was related to his Father" (Barrett, *Epistle to the Romans,* 117). See also Barrett, *From First Adam to Last,* 68–119. Bloesch seems to echo Barth's position on the scope of salvation: "In my view the victory of Christ over the powers of darkness benefits all, but it does not liberate all. *It makes their liberation and reconciliation viable but not inevitable*" (Bloesch, *Jesus is Victor!,* 123 [emphasis mine]). This is an issue that still haunts the church in our day. However, Ramm's discussion in his chapter on *Barthian Universalism* in *After Fundamentalism,* draws attention to something that he senses is at the heart of Barth's concern with the "significance of people who are not Christian." He says that what Barth is essentially asking us is "Does the Gospel consign to meaninglessness all those people who have never heard it or never believed it? *Are non-Christians the waste products of the plan of salvation?*" (Ramm, *After Fundamentalism,* 165–72 [emphasis mine]).

33. Bloesch, *Jesus is Victor!,* 106.

34. See page 244.

The great British Methodist preacher W. E. Sangster once reputedly said, "Behind the message, the man." The five moving tributes that follow this introduction give us a sense of what Maury gave to so many. It is not surprising, therefore, that Barth and Maury enjoyed such a unique and significant partnership and friendship, marked by strong mutual respect. This was the hallmark of Maury's relations with so many. As the book of Proverbs puts it, *"As iron sharpens iron, so one man sharpens another"* (Prov 27:17).

The five testimonies and especially the twenty-eight years of correspondence between Pierre Maury and Karl Barth, between 1928 and 1956, reveal an intense friendship of two very different men. This type of friendship calls to mind biblical examples such as David and Jonathan and Paul and Barnabas, along with the tensions that often existed. Church history, too, is replete with records of people growing and sharing ministry together: Luther and Melanchthon, Calvin and Bucer, and the Wesley brothers. Bernard Reymond recounts the beginnings of this unique friendship:

> In the summer of 1931, Maury had already thought of the idea of visiting Barth in Bonn, along with Visser't Hooft.[35] Circumstances obliged them to put off this visit until March 1932. Many years later, Barth himself still vividly remembered that time: "The two of them came to see me at my mother's house in Bern where I was on holiday. It was of course Pierre who led the discussion. I can still see him before me and feel the fresh air that he brought with him."[36] From then on the ice had been broken; their letters abundantly bear witness. The reciprocal attraction must have quickly given place to an ever-growing friendship, especially from the moment when they stopped using the more formal *vous* and adopted the intimate *tu*, when Barth went to Paris in April 1934. "We understood each other so well," Barth recalled in his article in 1956 for *Réforme*. "We were so naturally in agreement on all the great and important things, and yet also so sharply in disagreement on secondary questions, that our coming together could never have become unfruitful or boring.

---

35. Visser't Hooft was the first General Secretary of the World Council of Churches from its foundation until his retirement in 1966.

36. *Réforme*, February 18, 1956. Barth mentions this visit in a letter to Thurneysen, March 24, 1932.

We never wondered what to talk about as we were always so eager to exchange our ideas."[37]

Willem Visser't Hooft is a name that has already been mentioned in connection with Maury and Barth. He says of his own significant friendship with Maury:

> Of the men and women with whom I worked over the years none had a deeper influence on me than Pierre Maury.... For us, as for so many others, Pierre Maury became the pastoral friend and the friendly pastor. He saw my weaknesses and did not spare his criticisms, but he saw more in me than I saw in myself, and so he gave me courage to do things which I would not have done without him.... This man combined in a unique way the deep passion for the discovery of the great objective divine truth with an equally deep interest in persons and in all manifestations of human life.[38]

Barth's own testimony concerning what Maury brought to their friendship is striking not just for the intellectual stimulus but for the warmth of his personality. Maury was that kind of person.[39] Joan Chittister has observed that "differences ... broaden us ... (and) make us bigger people than we could ever have been had we stayed locked in our tiny little intellectual ghettoes."[40] In a discussion of the place of community in the pilgrim life, Eugene Peterson goes further, stating, "We mediate to one another the mysteries of God. We represent to one another the address of God."[41] John Macmurray, the Scottish philosopher (1891–1976), showed the self in proper existence within a community of relational beings and asserted that "there can be no man until there are at least two men in communication."[42]

---

37. Reymond, *Théologien ou prophète*, 54 (my translation).

38. Visser't Hooft, *Memoirs*, 36.

39. Suzanne de Dietrich wrote of Maury and Visser't Hooft, "For three years they shared the same office.... This partnership between an expansive Southern Frenchman and a reserved tenacious Dutchman must have been very amusing at times" (Dietrich, *50 ans d'histoire*, 93).

40. Chittister, *Uncommon Gratitude*, 34.

41. Peterson, *Long Obedience*, 165.

42. Macmurray, *Persons in Relation*, 12. Macmurray claimed that if we "isolate one pair as the unit of personal community we can discover the basic structure of community as such. The relation between them is positively motived in each. Each then is heterocentric; the center of interest and attention is in the other, not in himself. For each, therefore, it is the other who is important, not himself. The other is the center of

When we consider the interpersonal dynamic of this friendship, we also discover an interesting parallel between Barth's doctrine of Creation in *Church Dogmatics* III, the second volume of which appeared three years after the end of the Second World War in May 1948, and Maury's Lenten sermons of the same year.[43] After volume 1 of *CD* III, in which Barth famously integrates creation and redemption, he explores the theme of "being in encounter" in volume 2:

> Being in encounter consists . . . in the fact that we render mutual assistance in the act of being. . . . In the very fact that he lives a man is summoned by his fellow-man. The latter does not wish to be left alone or to his own devices in his action. I cannot represent him. I cannot make his life-task my own. He cannot expect this from me. He must not confuse me with God. And he will certainly have no reason to do so. I must try to help myself, and he will have to do the same. But as he tries to do so, he has the right to expect that I shall be there for him as well as myself, that I shall not ignore him but live with him, that my life will be a support for his, that it will mean comfort, encouragement and alleviation for him."[44]

So in the same year that Barth's discussion of the theme of "being in encounter" appeared in print for the first time, one of Maury's sermons, "To know Jesus Christ is to know man," expressed concepts markedly similar to Barth's development of an anthropology based on a Christologically determined doctrine of creation. For Barth, being in encounter involves human beings looking each other in the eye, where there is mutual speech and hearing, and where we render assistance to each other in the act of being, all of which occurs in reciprocal gladness. Maury declared in his Lenten sermon:

---

value" (Macmurray, *Persons in Relation*, 12)

43. Maury, *Jésus Christ, cet inconnu*.

44. *CD* III/2:260, 263. In 1956, Barth mentioned his interaction with Maury in a letter to Albert Finet. Was he alluding to an ongoing mutually beneficial conversation possibly at the First Assembly of the World Council of Churches in Amsterdam 1948 from the 22nd of August to the 4th of September? He remembered that "It was always refreshing for me to be with him one or two times every year for several hours or several days. It did not matter where, in Switzerland, or in Paris, sometimes at a conference, *in a particularly fruitful way in Amsterdam in 1948*" (Reymond, *Karl Barth—Pierre Maury*, 249 [emphasis mine]).

> Without Jesus Christ, I am without you. More than that, I am without myself.... In any event, for Jesus Christ, to be human, is to understand and love what is "the other."[45]

Not only is this similarity of expression interesting as the joining of two great minds but it bolsters Visser't Hooft's sense that Maury gave him the courage to do things which he would not have done without him. Could not the same be said about Karl Barth? Wolf Krötke, in a discussion of Barth's anthropology, claims:

> If we take seriously the fact that the eternal God has here bound himself with a man, then the history which here takes place is to be understood as a history really grounded in the eternity of God. Barth set this out in an interpretation of the doctrine of election, one of the most genuine accomplishments of his theological thinking, and at the same time a place at which essential decisions about the structure of theological anthropology are taken.[46]

In a subsequent discussion of humanity as co-humanity, he also postulates that

> In Barth's understanding, in the light of faith in Jesus Christ, it is evident that it is no accident that the human creature exists structurally in relations.... The human person is human only in relation to fellow human beings. Human "existence with fellow humans" is the basic form of humanity in which a person is "the parable of the existence of his creator."[47]

I would suggest that perhaps the most significant factor in this story of a unique friendship is this interpersonal dynamic of companionship and mutual encouragement. But let Barth have the last word in a letter to Albert Finet, director of the weekly *Réforme* [*Reformation*] journal, after Maury's death:

> We were great friends. *In all likelihood he underestimated what he brought to our friendship.* If he learned this or that from me, he never in any way became my student. At an important stage in my theological journey, when I was concerned with the doctrine of election, he gave me a *decisive impetus.* Very often he led

---

45. Maury, *Jésus Christ, cet inconnu*, 51, 54.
46. Krötke, *Humanity of the Human Person*, 163.
47. Krötke, *Humanity of the Human Person*, 168. Krötke's quotations are from *CD* III/2:203.

me much further, simply by his questions, his reservations or his objections. He was a legend, when some considered him as my blind partisan. He was too good a Frenchman, and a Christian, to be someone else's passenger. Besides, I didn't have either the intention or the capacity to do that with him. Read his writings and his publications and you can see to what degree he thought everything through and expressed and defended it in his own way. And he had such gifts that I never possessed, which I could only admire in him.[48]

---

48. Reymond, *Karl Barth—Pierre Maury*, 249.

## BIBLIOGRAPHY

Barrett, C. K. *The Epistle to the Romans*. London: A&C Black, 1971.
———. *From First Adam to Last*. London: A&C Black, 1962.
Barth, Karl. *Christ and Adam: Man and Humanity in Romans 5*. Translated by T. A. Smail. Eugene, OR: Wipf & Stock, 2004.
———. *Church Dogmatics*. Edited by G. W. Bromiley and T. F. Torrance. Translated by G. T. Thomson, et al. Edinburgh: T&T Clark, 1936–77.
———. *The Knowledge of God and the Service of God According to the Teaching of the Reformation: Recalling the Scottish Confession of 1560*. Translated by J. L. M. Haire and I. Henderson. The Gifford Lectures, University of Aberdeen 1937–1938. London: Hodder and Stoughton, 1938.
———. *The Theology of the Reformed Confessions*. Translated by D. L. Guder and J. L. Guder. Louisville: Westminster John Knox, 2002.
Berkouwer, G. C. *The Triumph of Grace in the Theology of Karl Barth*. Grand Rapids: Eerdmans, 1956.
Blocher, Henri. "Karl Barth's Christocentric Method." In *Engaging with Barth: Contemporary Evangelical Critiques*, edited by David Gibson and Daniel Strange, 21–54. London: InterVarsity, 2008.
Bloesch, Donald. *Jesus is Victor! Karl Barth's Doctrine of Salvation*. Nashville: Abingdon, 1976.
Chittister, Joan. *Uncommon Gratitude: Alleluia for All That Is*. Collegeville, MN: Liturgical, 2010.
Dietrich, Suzanne de. *50 ans d'histoire: la fédération universelle des associations chrétiennes d'étudiants, 1895–1945*. Paris: Editions du Semeur, 1945.
Fernandez-Armesto, Felipe, and Derek Wilson. *Reformation: Christianity and the World 1500–2000*. London: Bantam, 1996.
Florentin-Smyth, Françoise. *Pierre Maury, Prédicateur d'Evangile*. Geneva: Labor et Fides, 2009.
Gockel, M. *Barth and Schleiermacher on the Doctrine of Election: A Systematic-Theological Comparison*. Oxford: Oxford University Press, 2006.
Green, G., and Karl Barth. *On Religion, the Revelation of God and the Sublimation of Religion*. London: T&T Clark, 2006.
Greene, Colin J. D. *Christology in Cultural Perspective: Marking Out the Horizons*. Eugene, OR: Wipf & Stock, 2003.
Gunton, Colin. "Election and Ecclesiology in the Post-Constantinian Church." *Scottish Journal of Theology* 53.2 (2000) 212–27.
Hunsinger, George. *Disruptive Grace: Studies in the Theology of Karl Barth*. Grand Rapids: Eerdmans, 2000.
———. *How to Read Karl Barth: The Shape of his Theology*. Oxford: Oxford University Press, 1991.
Krötke, Wolf. "The Humanity of the Human Person in Karl Barth's Anthropology." In *The Cambridge Companion to Karl Barth*, edited by John B. Webster, 159–76. Cambridge: Cambridge University Press, 2000.
Macmurray, John. *Persons in Relation*. Vol. 2. The Gifford Lectures, 1953–54. London: Faber, 1961.
Maillot, Alphonse. "P. Maury Prédicateur." *Foi et Vie* 90.3–4 (1991) 13–34.

McCormack, Bruce. *Karl Barth's Critically Realistic Dialectical Theology: Its Genesis and Development, 1909–1936*. Oxford: Clarendon, 1995.
McDonald, S. *Re-imaging Election, Divine Election as Representing God to Others and Others to God*. Grand Rapids: Eerdmans, 2010.
Morris, L. *The Epistle to the Romans*. Grand Rapids: Eerdmans, 1988.
Maury, Pierre. "Election et Foi." *Foi et Vie* 27 (1936) 203–23.
———. *Le Grande Œuvre de Dieu*. Paris: Je Sers, 1937.
———. *Jésus Christ, cet inconnu: six allocutions pour le carême 1948*. Strasbourg: Oberlin, 1948.
———. *La Prédestination*. Geneva: Labor et Fides, 1957.
———. *Predestination and Other Papers*. Translated by Edwin Hudson. London: SCM, 1960.
Migliore, Daniel. *Faith Seeking Understanding: An Introduction to Christian Theology*. Grand Rapids: Eerdmans, 2004.
Peterson, Eugene. *A Long Obedience in the Same Direction*. Downers Grove, IL: InterVarsity, 1980.
Ramm, Bernard. *After Fundamentalism*. San Francisco: Harper & Row, 1983.
Reymond, Bernard, ed. *Karl Barth—Pierre Maury, Nous qui pouvons encore parler . . . Correspondance 1928–1956*. Lausanne: Symbolon, Éditions l'Age d'Homme, 1985.
———. *Théologien ou prophète: Les francophones et Karl Barth avant 1945*. Lausanne: Symbolon, Éditions l'Age d'Homme, 1985.
Satyaranjan, Dandapati Samuel. *The Preaching of Daniel Thambirajah (D. T.) Niles: Homiletical Criticism*. Delhi: ISPCK, 2009.
Thompson, M. "Witness to the Word: Barth's Doctrine of Scripture." In *Engaging with Barth: Contemporary Evangelical Critiques*, edited by David Gibson and Daniel Strange, 168–97. Nottingham: Apollos, 2008.
Van Til, Cornelius. *Christianity and Barthianism*. Philadelphia: Presbyterian and Reformed, 1962.
Visser't Hooft, W. A. *Memoirs*. London: SCM, 1973.
Von Balthasar, Hans Urs. *The Theology of Karl Barth*. San Francisco: Communio, 1992.
Ward, Graham. Review of *Karl Barth's Critically Realistic Dialectical Theology*, by Bruce McCormack. *Expository Times* 107.3 (1995) 88–89.
Zahrnt, Heinz. *The Question of God, Protestant Theology in the Twentieth Century*. London: Collins, 1969.

# PART I

*Concerning Pierre Maury*

# 2

## Jacques Maury's Tribute to his Father

THE CHARACTERISTIC IDENTITY (OF an evangelist) was such a profound part of who he was that it was evident in all the dimensions and contexts of his life. . . . So we see this in all the activities to which he gave himself with such great passion and so little concern about his own welfare that as a result his life was most certainly cut short . . . his multiple institutional commitments in the Reformed Church of France and more generally in French Protestantism, its youth movements and associations; his important participation in the World Council of Churches and in particular his constant relations with Germany and notably with the significant persons of the Confessing Church; finally, and of course it is not for chronological reasons that I only mention it in the last instance, his being Professor of Dogmatics at the Protestant Faculty of Theology in Paris (1943–1950). . . . He was a theologian in all his activities. However much he was stirred into action, he always lived in a manner that was consistent with his theological convictions and he consecrated a large part of his energies to their development. In order to gain some idea of this, just consider the huge part that his friend Karl Barth played in his life, and the energy with which he persistently passed on this message in his journal, *Foi et Vie* (*Faith and Life*), or the occasions that he facilitated for the Professor

---

1. This is an extract from Jacques Maury's foreword to Francoise Florentin-Smyth's book, *Pierre Maury, Prédicateur d'Evangile* [*Gospel Preacher*] (Geneva: Labor et Fides, 2009), 7–9. Used by permission. This is my translation. Jacques is a very distinguished churchman, having served for many years as a pastor of the Reformed Church. He had a strong national profile as President of his denomination (1968–1977) and the Féderation Protestante (Protestant Federation) (1977–1987) as well as being strongly committed to the welfare of immigrants and asylum seekers, which began when he worked in support of Jewish internees during the Vichy Regime.

of Dogmatics from Basel and the voice of the Confessing Church, giving him the opportunity to speak directly with the French, as was notably the case during three theological seminars held at Bièvres, just before and after the war. Just like his famous friend, he was concerned about a genuine doctrinal rigor, and, like him, lived with the ancient Fathers as well as the Reformers. On top of this he was concerned about the church as a place where the Word of God was proclaimed, in accordance with her roots and her unity, and this always steered him away from any temptation to deride her.

But this huge part that he gave over to theological activity always bore the stamp of the primacy of preaching, including his role as Professor of Dogmatics. I was particularly struck by this during my last year at the Faculty of Theology when I was able to take part in his lectures. Most of them, often inspired by Karl Barth, finished with a free exchange with his students. He showed himself to be even more pastoral in these very lectures, and was in fact much more Professor of Practical Theology than of Dogmatics, always concerned about unravelling the impact of revelation in the history of this world and in each of our lives. There as well, as in all the dimensions of his life, he wanted to be first of all, and has been, a "preacher of the Gospel"—a Gospel that never let him rest, and whose flame he always kept burning, not only in his public ministry, but also in all his personal or broader relationships, with his parishioners, his friends and all those, here and there, that he rubbed shoulders with. Whatever peoples' social background, religious or political, his interest was constantly awake to all human situations. As was, for example, the case with his military comrades of the two wars.

I learned from him—and I think, many others like me—that the Gospel must be shared with everyone, that is to say, listened to and testified to. Even more, most certainly, when its testimony is shared with the strength of conviction articulated as Pierre Maury did, who knew full well that when the Gospel reaches its actual preacher, it becomes liberating Good News.

# 3

## Gustave Monod's[1] Tribute to Pierre Maury on the Occasion of his Death in 1956[2]

THERE WAS, IN THE friendship that he brought, something definitive, which stood the test. It was much more than faithfulness: permanent, solid, an abundance always readily available. His generosity went beyond virtue, but was rather a whole hearted radiance and self-giving of mind and heart. He was generous in this other sense that he had "the passion of humanity," as he told me one day. It was, without doubt, love in the Christian sense of the word—but also the respect and emotion in front of each person's "drama." And certainly, he interpreted that in the light of his faith,–but deep down, there was in him, by spontaneous impulse, that sense which sets all humans apart.

I hardly dare speak about his thought. I was present during certain stages of his development. I can still hear, around 1920, in the streets of Rheims in ruins, Maury outraged with certain strict styles of worship, which tend to put God on our level and more accessible to us, a

---

1. Gustave Adolphe Monod (1885–1968) was a teacher and senior French government official. Like Maury he was drafted in 1914. He served as a nurse under conditions which earned him five citations and (also like Maury) the *Croix de Guerre*. He was seriously injured at the end of the war, and lost a leg. In 1933, he became Chief of Staff of the Minister of Education Anatole de Monzie. Then in 1936, he was appointed deputy director of secondary education. In 1940 he was dismissed from his rank of inspector general for refusing to apply the anti-Jewish measures taken by the Vichy government. As a parting gesture he wrote a brilliant letter of denunciation of Vichy policies. After the liberation he was made national director of secondary education and contributed to many significant reforms. He was very much involved in the Scout movement.

2. "Bulletin d'Information de l'Eglise Réformée de France." Also appeared in *Foi et Vie* (May 1956) 283–85. Translation from the French by Simon Hattrell.

comfortable God responsive to all, when our first instinct should be one of worship and humility before the divine glory and majesty. I hear him speaking of the honor of God: the fundamental theme of his theology, which he was to later develop and expand. I remember our discussions seven or eight years later in Marseille and Geneva. Through his contact with Karl Barth, his thought had matured: he put it to the test by the very practice of his ministry. As a hardened Cartesian I tried to resist him. I wasn't up to it. I didn't like the fact that his testimony contained a pathos that both seduced and brought me low. He had a way of making his thought so penetrating, charged as it was with references to biblical and theological reflections. That gave it a wonderful eloquence, which expressed itself in a simple language, but with an astonishing richness and fullness.

And that wasn't the only greatness of Pierre Maury. I use that word deliberately: I believe that Maury has been one of the exceptional men of our generation. There was in literature, in humanity, in his time, a wealth of information which few of his contemporaries were able to acquire, but he did due to his huge output and powers of assimilation. And he was able to draw from so much accumulated wealth thus bringing so much that was new and personal in his works, his sermons, and his private conversations.

But it was perhaps the drama of Pierre Maury to carry within himself much more than he was ever able to express or give. He suffered cruelly the double treachery of the setting in which he lived and the state of his physical health, both working together to limit and compromise the respite and silence indispensable to work, meditation and creation. That was the "drama" of Pierre Maury, of all the great ones, thinkers or artists, who carry with them much more than they have contributed, and whose lives have been corroded by the feeling of what might have been. We were surprised to see that Pierre Maury at certain times had that far away absent air about him, where you could detect a flicker of impatience and sadness: he mused about what was essential, what there would be to think about and do, and time slipped away, undermining his strength and dissipating it in doubtful obligations.

All this, aggravated by the Parisian context in which he lived which excites and dissipates, and which finishes by enslaving until burnout, overtaken by oppressive tiredness. This burnout got the better of Pierre Maury: it is with bitter regret that one thinks about the work that he could have given us and which it has denied us.

But I see the smile of Maury, that is if he heard such sentiments, that smile in which he put all the warmth of his heart, that smile—and that look—which so often reassured us, each of us for whom the memory remains a viaticum[3] for our lives. In his smile he would say to us that the essential thing was not the knowledgeable commentary of Saint Paul, Luther or Barth, but it was to have been able so many times to extend a helping hand to those who faltered, and to help them to continue on their way by showing them, on the horizon, the light which shall never fade away.

3. A last rite and blessing, lit. a provision for our journey.

# 4

## Jean Bosc's[1] Tribute to Pierre Maury on the Occasion of His Death in 1956[2]

HE WAS A FRIEND. It might seem to be strange to those who had never met him that I first say that about him. However that's what he was like. He had an extraordinary and admirable capacity for friendship. Nothing which was human remained unfamiliar to him. He loved life with a magnificent vigor, curiosity, ardor and sensitivity which showed itself in the most varied ways. However, he had no illusions about the world and humanity; neither about himself nor others. He knew the evil, miseries, worries and distress which can live in a human heart. That's why he understood and two hours spent with him gave you a sense of extraordinary intimacy because he knew how to come alongside of you. . . .

But he was a friend while always remaining a pastor. The passion which he put into everything was first and foremost a passionate attachment to Jesus Christ, to his gospel and to his church. His understanding of man was always a dynamic understanding which, while respecting others, sought to place them before their Lord. And if his authority asserted itself with a strength which some could find excessive, that was not to set aside or put down the freedom of others, but in appealing to their sense of responsibility.

---

1. French Reformed Minister, theologian and co-founder with Albert Finet of the journal *Réforme*, Jean Bosc was a close collaborator of the famous French lay theologian and sociologist and author Jacques Ellul. Along with Maury and De Pury, Bosc began translating Barth's works in 1934. He was strongly committed to social, civic and pastoral action in a variety of national leadership roles and also taught systematic theology at the Protestant Faculty of Theology in Paris.

2. *Réforme*, January 21, 1956. Translation from the French by Simon Hattrell.

He was a great spiritual director and preacher, not firstly because he would have had an uncommon mastery of psychology and eloquence, but because his profound human understanding wanted to seek with others the way prepared for them by Jesus Christ and because in preaching, he always had the double preoccupation of being faithful to the Christian truth and the hearts which received it. He loved to proclaim the word of God to one man or a thousand; he was always ready to do it, for he did it with joy. . . .

He has been since 1930 with a few other men, amongst them Auguste Lecerf, one of the artisans of the Protestant theological renewal in France and without doubt the one who has made the greatest impact upon it. He did not hide the fact that his greatest inspiration was, with Luther and Calvin, Karl Barth. He was the one who introduced the theologian from Basel to the French and often said that one of the great joys of his life had been to know Barth and to be his friend.

He shared Barth's thought and constantly worked to spread it, not in an exclusive way, for he was too open minded and bi-partisan and wanted to keep the Reformed church of France united. But that which was, here also, particularly meaningful as far as his personality was concerned, was that his theological activity was inseparable from his pastoral preoccupations and his love for man. He was desperate to understand and to help others understand what he had believed, but he wanted to understand it with all his being and to help others understand it with their whole being.

# 5

## A Memoir of Pierre Maury 1890–1956[1]

ROBERT MACKIE

French Protestantism makes little impact upon British Christianity. Even Scotland recalls a common ancestry only on historic occasions. We speak of Huguenot blood as a proud memory of a lost cause. And so we come to imagine that the Protestants of France today are a negligible, even a scarcely justifiable, minority . . .

Why then is there this misunderstanding and neglect? Language is a major factor. Our stumbling German is better than our stumbling French. Theological merit apart, students will choose a German faculty with a little more confidence. . . . It is admittedly far more difficult to turn a French speech into effective English than to give a tolerable version of a German one. And so our nearest neighbor church is largely unknown to us . . .

Pierre Maury was a rare Frenchman who broke the language barrier in middle life, and was increasingly holding the attention of English-speaking people in World Council meetings since the war. His death has greatly impoverished theological discussion conducted in English, because for the time being France is silent. It was characteristic of Pierre Maury that he was prepared to use in public his rough English or German for that matter. What had to be said must be said, and his use of the unexpected word, even the wrong word, often brought attention sharply to the point he had to make. No matter was too serious for the sudden

---

1. This extract is from Mackie's introduction to the first English translation of Maury, *Predestination and Other Papers*, 7–14.

illumination of humor. He could caricature himself without any touch of vanity. If you still disagreed with him your knowledge had been widened, and your affections awakened . . .

Pierre Maury could only act and speak in intimacy. He broke through not only language but reserve, and brought the family spirit into every group he entered.

He was a personality rather than a theologian. Perhaps we should say he was a theologian whose medium was a personal encounter rather than published writings. What has been translated here will at once give the impression of a fine mind, but the real quality of that mind may be lost without some knowledge of the man himself as his friends knew him. Who was this able and delightful man?

Pierre Maury was born at Nimes in November 1890. By 1912 he was a promising graduate in theology. . . . After military service in the war of 1914-18 he became general secretary of the French Student Christian Movement from 1919 to 1925. From that date until 1931 he was pastor of the Reformed Parish of Ferney-Voltaire on the very edge of Geneva and became deeply involved in the interests of the World Student Christian Federation. In 1931 he joined the staff of the WSCF and continued more directly his close partnership with his friend W.A. Visser't Hooft. In 1934 he was called to be a pastor in the parish of Passy in Paris as a younger colleague to Dr Marc Boegner. These two men worked side by side in a remarkable way for over twenty years, being ministers of a large congregation and at the same time giving outstanding leadership to their Church, to Protestantism in France, and to the ecumenical movement. Amongst Pierre Maury's wider responsibilities were those of being a Vice-Chairman of the World Student Christian Federation from 1935 to 1938, Professor of Dogmatics in the Protestant Theological Faculty of Paris from 1943 to 1950, and President of the Reformed Church of France, in succession to M. Boegner, from 1950 to 1953. His health, his inclinations, and perhaps his gifts, made the last post a difficult one for him. He seemed glad to be released from it and to be his own free incomparable self until he died in January 1956.

My first clear memory of Pierre Maury was at a Whitsun weekend conference of leaders of the European Student Christian Movements nearly thirty years ago.[2] This meeting took place at Bad Boll,

---

2. Dr. Mackie was General Secretary of the British SCM (1929-1938), and General Secretary of the World Student Christian Federation (1938-1948). An excellent biography written by Nansie Blackie, *In Love and in Laughter: A Portrait of Robert Blackie*,

the Moravian center near Stuttgart, which was to become well known later for its "evangelical" academy. For me it was a notable occasion. I was a new general secretary of a national movement and I stepped in amongst giants. Berdyaev was the most striking speaker. But the only talk I remember was from Pierre Maury at the closing service. We had been much obsessed with problems. And no wonder. Between the hotel and the garden-room where we met ran a country road, and along the road passed companies of excited young people on their first spring hike, carrying banners, sometimes with the Nazi emblem, and sometimes the hammer and sickle! We had scarcely found ourselves after one war and a new conflict seemed to be blowing up like a thunderstorm. Reinold von Thadden, already a leading German layman, took the service, and Pierre Maury spoke on being "more than conquerors." His complete confidence in "the over-plus of victory" took me by surprise and lifted me on to a plane of spiritual certainty to which I could never have climbed by myself.

The next encounter I remember was at the meeting of the General Committee of the WSCF at Channcoria in Bulgaria in 1936. When the Sunday came round the officers had the idea—and it seemed to me a very poor idea!—of asking Pierre Maury and myself to speak in our own languages on the same text (was there a German sermon also?) The text was from Romans: "We are saved by hope." How I wrestled with that passage under the great pine trees, and nothing came of my wrestling! But Pierre Maury handled hope as a substance, not an abstract quantity, a substance more concrete than any material one. Again I was ashamed and uplifted.

Pierre Maury communicated faith. I remember the story of a café in Madrid to which he was taken by two or three members of the Spanish SCM, which had then a precarious existence. He was asked to gather his own audience. And he did, not by any of the tricks of the individual evangelist, but by drawing men into conversation, real conversation, on issues which they cared about but on which they were out of their depth. Intellectual ability and camaraderie are not often found together. Pierre Maury loved good talk, and through his passionate, dogmatic, and entertaining contributions shone the radiance of his personal conversation with Jesus Christ.

This natural gift for conversation was perhaps the key to Pierre Maury's evangelistic and pastoral power. He was one of the few people who could write a theological article in the manner of a play, with characters

---

was published by Saint Andrews Press, Edinburgh, in 1995.

speaking from different angles, and all of them seeming to be real people you had met. In the pages of *The Student World* there are a number of these illuminating contributions. The secret, of course, was Pierre Maury's sympathetic understanding of other points of view, no matter how inadequately formulated or expressed. He had the gift of knowing what was in men, and therefore of talking with them rather than at them. No wonder that you can meet so many individuals today who will say simply: "I am a Christian because of Pierre Maury." These conversions were not technical successes; these people were simply new members of the astonishingly varied circle of his intimate friends.

All the published tributes to Pierre Maury speak of his friendship. Karl Barth writes movingly: "I miss him. I have had, and still have, good friends. But there has been in my life only one Pierre Maury." Suzanne de Dietrich records his own comment once in jest: "I am the best friend of eighty other people." And she adds, "The figure is certainly an understatement." I was one of those to whom Pierre Maury gave his friendship. I never knew why. It always came upon me anew like an act of grace. A ring on the telephone in Geneva and a word from Visser 't Hooft: "Pierre is here and is coming over to see you." In he would walk and sit down and draw me into telling him all my problems. He was in Geneva for a few days' much needed rest by the lakeside he loved so much. Latterly he was in poor physical shape, and burdened with all sorts of responsibilities. But he could never pass through Geneva without an hour or two of friendly and invigorating conversation with his friends. How many of us kept our real difficulties to air them some day with Pierre Maury! Not long ago I lunched with a fellow countryman who had only recently come to know him. "I think I should like to discuss this difficult question with Pierre Maury," he said. "But Pierre is dead," I replied in dismay. I shall not forget the look of loss that came into my friend's eyes. It is a great gift of God to be able to carry the hearts of many other men as well as your own.

Being a friend of Pierre Maury's was not always an easy business. He himself had to be explained and defended in ecumenical circles. He was very French, but that is the delightful thing about the French; they never become uprooted personalities. They will never become good Europeans or good world citizens, because they are the essential salt, which is always different. And Pierre Maury could speak out. He hated humbug. An ecclesiastical stuffed shirt made him see red, and say the most dreadful things! . . . His advice on political matters would frequently have got us into trouble, though sometimes afterwards we may have regretted a little that we had avoided it . . .

I suppose this uncomfortable challenge of Pierre Maury may be attributed by some people to his Barthianism. At least that is the conventional comment to make. He was devoted to Karl Barth, and was his chief interpreter to French Protestantism. But there was nothing pedantic or rule-of-thumb about his theology. Karl Barth has been the liberator of the minds of many of my friends. And that liberation through Visser't Hooft and Pierre Maury (for I always think of the two men in association) has been mediated even to those of us who are theologically illiterate. It is surely this liberation which makes Pierre Maury's brief study of predestination so alive, so energizing. The grace of God is not a concept for him; it is a fact. Indeed, it is the basic fact from which all life begins, and from which all truth can be freely explored. There are some words towards the end of this study which describe vividly the man I knew, and which give me courage: "Having nothing themselves, they possess all things in Christ. Able only to ask forgiveness, they have received grace to render thanks. Mocked by the world, troubled in their consciences, they can nevertheless say: "I know whom I have believed." In the peace and joy to which the divine mercy daily brings them back, they fear "neither death, nor life."

Pierre Maury's own death confirmed his radiant assertion of the grace of God. He had been in North Africa, for which the rest of the world is apt to find simple solutions, but which has been such an agony to thoughtful Frenchmen, not least to French Protestants. Pierre Maury had been there because the Reformed Church needed the help he could give, because this was the place of strife to which the grace of God must be brought. No doubt he had been excited, and talked too much, and, above all, listened too much. On the Sunday he preached on the text "My times are in thy hand." Then he flew home, lay down to rest, and did not move again. Sorrow at the passing of a friend, dismay at the loss of a leader—these we knew. But on the next Sunday over the French radio came his own recorded words: "My times are in thy hand." Nothing untoward had occurred, nothing to weaken the influence of his life. For his friends, as W. A. Visser't Hooft has finely said, there is "a sense of continued conversation with Pierre Maury." Perhaps even these brief published fragments will introduce those who did not know him to a conversation on the things of Christ, which has been for so many a gift beyond price.

# 6

## Karl Barth's Original Foreword to Maury's Predestination[1]

IT IS NO SMALL joy to me to write these few lines of introduction to the little book which my never-to-be-forgotten friend, Pierre Maury, devoted to the subject of predestination. I was unaware of the existence of the manuscript, but when I read it I was convinced that it ought to be published—not only in order to recall the memory of its author, who was so suddenly taken from us scarcely more than a year ago, and to whom we owe such a great debt of gratitude, but also because these lectures, delivered in the United States in 1954, will assuredly serve to stimulate the thoughts of all those who are preoccupied with such a subject, whether they are simply believers, Bible readers, pastors, or theologians.

As long ago as 1936 Pierre Maury had delivered an address entitled "Election and Faith" on the occasion of the Geneva Calvinist Congress; that address, which appeared in the same year in the review *Foi et Vie*, was published in German in 1940 in the Theologische Studien series. Most of those present at the Calvinist Congress were neither prepared, nor apt to receive in their hearts, nor even just simply to register in their brains, what Pierre Maury was saying to them then. There were but few who had any idea of the implications of his thesis in the course of the years that followed, when preoccupations of a political nature loomed so large that they scarcely left time or energy for theological reflection of this sort. But I remember one person who read the text of that address with the greatest attention: myself! It so happened that in the autumn of the same year, 1936, I had to give a course of lectures on the subject

1. Maury, *La Prédestination*, 5–7 (my translation).

of predestination (in Hungary). Pierre Maury and I had of course often spoken of this problem; nevertheless, his 1936 address at once made a profound impression on me. And when a few years later I had occasion to return to the subject in a wider context, I did not merely refer to Pierre Maury's pamphlet, but stressed that it ought to be considered as one of the best contributions made towards the understanding of the problem. That is why, as I said at the time,[2] Pierre Maury must be ranked with the rare theologians of the past who, because of the Christological basis of their doctrine, seem to me to have remained here on solid ground (such were Athanasius, Augustine, John Knox, and Johannes Coccejus). One can certainly say that it was he who contributed decisively to giving my thoughts on this point their fundamental orientation. Before I read his study, I had met no one who had dealt with the question so freshly and boldly.

In the present work, written eighteen years after the Geneva lecture, we find a Pierre Maury no less lively, not to say overwhelming; but his thought has matured, and his exposition is richer and more ample in its scope. He, for his part, had assimilated the substance of the bulky volume which I published in 1942 on the subject. But it is blindingly obvious that he has borrowed nothing from me which he has not recreated and made his own, plumbing the Scriptures on his own account; further, in the way he puts and answers his questions, the way he applies and comments upon the biblical text, as also in the implications and developments which he advances, he has remained entirely faithful to himself. But I think that there is no need for me to say more of the book itself; the subject of which it treats and the manner in which the author deals with it suffice to show its importance. I should like simply to be allowed to add a few personal words.

Pierre Maury's great gift, to which every page of this book bears witness, was his ability to ally the keenest and most objective theological curiosity with an undeniable feeling for the human and "personal," and his constant concern to use this double insight in preaching the Gospel to the parish, in both the narrowest and the widest sense of the word. Of all the conversations which I had with him, and of which there are echoes in the present study, I retain a very vivid memory, because he never tried to cover up the difference between what he knew and what he did not know or between what he absolutely insisted on knowing and what, for all sorts

---

2. *CD* II/2:154–55.

of reasons, he wished to know nothing of! And also because every time I saw him afterwards, often tired, overworked, care-worn, this man never struck me as indifferent or resigned. I found him, as ever, full of the same passionate interest (at once both positive and critical) in the questions which preoccupied us both. How well he could tell a story! And how well he could listen and contradict! And how well (at the right moment) he knew how to stop talking and declare himself satisfied—until the next time! I miss him. I have had, and still have, good friends. But there has been in my life only one Pierre Maury.

It is to be hoped that the audiences who had the privilege of hearing him develop the arguments set down here, were able to discern something of the personal genius of this exceptional man—and more, something of the power of the witness which it was given him to bear among us with an ardor which was his both by nature and by grace. And it is to be hoped that both his witness and his person—they are inseparable—will speak in the same way to the many readers of these pages.

# PART 2

*Pierre Maury on Election*

# 7

## Election et Foi (*Election and Faith*)[1]

### Pierre Maury

It is always difficult and it is also always a formidable task to speak of *election*, or predestination, or double predestination. It seems that we can only do it in order to defend it or attack it. Around it we see theological disputes, objections, indignations, and mockeries, or knowledgeable constructions of a far too humanly based logic. Concerning this subject, which evokes sovereign freedom, the incomprehensible mystery of God, all human freedoms confront each other, as well as all human wisdoms which assert themselves, and at the end of the day, not the *ultimate* decision without appeal, of the Lord, but the weak preferences of our reasonings. Considered thus, election is a labyrinth, as Calvin said, a *labyrinth with no exit*.[2] One can only speak of election as a revealed truth, concretely as a *biblical* truth.

Indeed what would we be able to say *by ourselves* about a subject which is strictly the mystery of God, of the God whom no eye has seen, whom none can see without dying? And what would we be able to say

---

1. First appeared in *Foi et Vie* 37 (1936) 203–223. Translation from the French by Simon Hattrell. Any footnotes in this paper of Pierre Maury are inserted by the translator in order to either clarify or expand an issue of translation or give English speaking readers the exact reference of either the original French text or an equivalent English language translation to which Maury refers. In the original French text there were no footnotes or bibliography.

2. Calvin, *Institutes* 3.21.

about a subject where it is our *elusive* reality that is at stake: that is to say, our human destiny, not as we see it, but such as is our lot, our *ultimate* reality, that which is beyond all explanations and which bears the true name of life or death. We did not give ourselves life nor will we be able to avoid death. We have not chosen to live; we cannot choose to *not* die. It is therefore not a question here of *our* choice, the one that we make, but the choice of which we are the object, that which is made (or not made) of us. These are those insurmountable limits, which are *imposed* on us, which election calls to mind. Because this is about *God*—and not the idea of God—because this is about *us*, really about *us*—and not our ideas, our feelings, even our theology—we would not know how to speak of election as just some other interesting topic of discussion. So it is never something to satisfy our "curiosity." As Calvin said, "The curious will find no way out of the labyrinth; they will only find an occasion for dread or blasphemy."[3] And he adds that predestination is "a reason to worship, worship of the high wisdom of God more than understanding of things that God wanted to be hidden and of which he has withheld knowledge."[4]

So if that is the way it is, one will object: would it not be better to be quiet about such an inaccessible problem, to leave it with the secret counsel of God, and in order to avoid the risk of talking superficially, to humbly keep silence? All those who have truly dared, even by the door of Scripture, to penetrate the labyrinth, know very well that such is our temptation. But as Calvin has again said, "However much this modesty seems to be praiseworthy, we need to remind ourselves that, as nothing in Scripture has been omitted which is salutary and useful to know, so nothing is taught which may not be expedient to know."[5]

*Led by Scripture*, that is to say, by revelation, let us therefore try to penetrate within the labyrinth with just the connecting thread of Scripture. We will, above all, be careful not to go beyond biblical moderation. We will not shut out some solutions there where *our* logic would do so,

---

3. Calvin, *Institutes of the Christian Religion*, 608.

4. Calvin, *Institutes of the Christian Religion*, 608. Depending on which translation of the *Institutes* one is working with, it is not always easy to find the exact reference.

5. Calvin, *Institutes of the Christian Religion*, 608. This is an inexact quote from Calvin, in which Maury appears to be giving the sense of what Calvin was saying. Only the sentence, "As nothing in Scripture has been omitted which is salutary and useful to know, so nothing is taught which may not be expedient to know," is an exact citation. It needs to borne in mind that this was a hastily constructed address given to an audience, who, nevertheless, should have been very familiar with the Institutes and especially the chapter in question.

we will not open up some passages there where *we* could derive some human pride. We will therefore not deal with these dilemmas where we are claiming to shut out the electing God—all those which Calvin knew and Paul before him (the dilemma of God's justice and the injustice of the election of this one or that one; the dilemma of the divine decision and responsible human freedom; the dilemma of the love and the wrath of God and however many more, I do not know?). We will no longer try by these arguments to *justify* the unjustifiable divine decree, that is to say, to defend predestination, to explain it, to render it acceptable. If we were able, extraordinarily, to achieve that, how would it still be *God*'s election? It would have become the abominable theory of our so-called human justice—the hardest, the most revolting, the most damned of systems. In all this we would only end up by *subjugating* God, which is blasphemous and contradicts election itself. We would make of God and his secret counsel a sophist's[6] enigma. We would be great sinners.

How, therefore, will we speak with biblical moderation? Not by treating the Bible as a work of logic, even dogmatics; not in haggling over biblical *arguments*, that is to say, in arguing *about* faith. But, if it pleases God, in reflecting *with* faith, that is to say as believers. Scripture will be "guide and master" (Calvin) but guide and master *of faith* and not teacher of philosophy. It will lead us in some points to not follow what Calvin heard in it. But that will not be being unfaithful to him; on the contrary, that will be truly Calvinist. Besides, how would we not remember, even concerning secondary divergences, that it is above all to him that we owe so much for having discovered this depth of divine revelation, to which out of joy and in humble faithfulness he kept coming back for reassurance?

We will therefore speak of election as *believers*. For faith and election are indissolubly linked. Election is known *by faith*—not by unbelief; so all our objections and arguments are only ever the sign, the testimony of our unbelief. The real problem of election is not there where we would expect to find it, that is to say, in our questions, our theories, our resistances, but elsewhere, there where we are not arguing, but where we believe, there where it is not *we* who are speaking of God but where *God* speaks to us (or does not speak to us), there where it is really a matter of *our* election or of *our* rejection, and not of our theories about election. Outside of this *real* context, it is just hot air, even if it is very knowledgeable and skillful.

---

6. A sophist was a paid teacher of philosophy, a specious reasoner or a moral skeptic.

In this domain and as long as we remain there, we know irrefutably that election is real, but the last word in all this is God's alone to say, and for us to hear it and believe it.

∽

In order to determine the real link between election and faith, we need above all to avoid speaking *abstractly* of either one or the other of these terms. So, only one possibility of not focusing on this abstraction is offered to us: the concrete possibility where clearly election and faith join each other, that is to say God and us, God in his wrath and in his grace, us in our adoption and in our condemnation, the concrete living possibility who is called Jesus Christ. Election is election in *Christ*; faith is faith in *Christ*.

Paul wrote to the Romans, "For those God foreknew he also predestined to be conformed to the image of his Son, that he might be the firstborn among many brothers and sisters" (Rom 8:29). And to the Ephesians: "For he (God) chose us in Christ before the creation of the world to be holy and blameless in his sight. In love he predestined us for adoption to sonship through Jesus Christ, in accordance with his pleasure and will, to the praise of his glorious grace, which he has freely given us in the one he loves" (Eph 1:5–6). In the same way it is Christ who is not only the object but "the author and the finisher[7] of our faith" (Heb 12:2). We will take our stand, therefore, in speaking of predestination, on this solid ground, where the hidden mystery of God becomes the revealed grace which is offered to us. We can truly say that outside of Christ, there is neither election, nor knowledge of election—and I mean the word in its strongest sense, the sense of a sovereign choice, free and with no strings attached on the part of God, having a double aspect which has the character of both rejection and welcome. Outside of Christ, we know neither who the God who elects is, nor those he elects, nor how he elects them.

What is there to say? We will deduce from the great text of Ephesians this triple affirmation:

Firstly, Election is really an election accomplished by *God*, that is to say, accomplished before the foundation of the world, in God's eternity. Because it is "election in Christ" and by Christ, the one by whom and for whom all things have been made, it is a choice whose *origin* is elsewhere

---

7. "The pioneer and the perfecter" (Heb 12:2, NIV).

than in our time, a decision taken outside of all the sequences in which we are without end enclosed. In the same way that Christ exists before everything and before his own incarnate existence, so in the same way *in him* each of us is someone else, not only what we see and know—a divine thought, a divine will, a divine vocation. What does this *eternity* mean if not that independently of us—may thanks be given to the master of eternity!—we are a reality, we have a destiny, we live. To the unending questions about the eternal decree that theology has debated, in which we lose ourselves, we can very simply reply as has M. Neeser:

> What is the thesis of the eternal decree saying? It says this: from all eternity and therefore before the fall itself, God destined a certain number of humankind to salvation. Take this notion further, develop it completely and you will manage to seize the deep meaning. *Before the fall*, therefore before history and actual human history; *before* your personal sin, that is to say, since your sin goes back as far as and therefore even further than your memory, before the beginning of your personal story, God decided concerning your salvation. . . . Instead of *before*, try to say *independently of*; that will be more correct, for it concerns an eternal decree, and eternity is less a period of time prior to time than independence with regard to time. Therefore, concerning what has just been said, you need to use the adverb *independently of*. The thesis of the divine decree will mean that which is understandable in a religious sense: that which is seen independently of your spiritual story, independently of your personal spiritual efforts and those of your human milieu, that God decides to save us. And happily, since these efforts are powerless in the face of what is irreversible. God alone saves, not because humankind would merit it, but because it pleases God to save.[8]

So this "before us" of the eternal decree, this "independently of us" has a name, the name of our baptism: Christ.

Secondly, "In Christ" means too that this eternal election has not only as its origin but also its *ground*, the eternal Christ and the incarnate Christ as well. It is because of him that God chooses and marks out—because of him, and only because of him. Because of him, who is the well beloved Son, because of him, who is the Son abandoned at Calvary, the Son sovereignly raised at Easter and Ascension, the Son who will sit in judgment when he comes back. Because of him, that is to say, because of God, for he is *the Son*. All revelation, even when it still does not specify

---

8. Neeser, *L'Église qui sauve*, 91–96.

the Christ, affirms that all that God has done, he does because of him, who is God. "I will give you a new heart and put a new spirit in you; I will remove your heart of stone and give you a heart of flesh. And I will put my Spirit in you and move you to follow my decrees and be careful to keep my laws" (Ezek 36:26–27) . . . "*It is not for your sake*, people of Israel, that I am going to do these things, but for the sake of *my holy name*, which you have profaned among the nations" (Ezek 36:22). This divine name, because of which God creates, calls, condemns and repents of his wrath, remains silent and extends grace. We know who this is: once again, Jesus Christ.

Thirdly, predestination is *in Christ*, because it marks us out as belonging to Christ. Because he is the origin, the ground, he is *the goal* of the divine choice. It is in order "to become like Christ," to reproduce his image, to become by him adoptive sons, that this eternal decision is made. There is no need to insist here about what the whole Bible has never stopped saying, that grace has been freely extended, not that we should despise it in remaining in sin, but to live in grace according to the Spirit so that "Christ is formed in us" (Gal 4:19).

So the election of God is nothing else than the eternal and temporal existence of Jesus Christ, our mediator. And because it is *in Christ* it is truly *our* election. For it is in him, in him crucified, in him alone, that God has met us. Because it is in Christ, we know that election is not some unfathomable eternal caprice,[9] a game played out in the infinitely distant idleness of eternity but a concrete reality, our reality. It bears the marks of the historical and real life of Jesus Christ, living, dying, rising for us.

But it needs also to be spelled out what the presence of Christ in election means *negatively*, and let us be clear, outside of this presence there is no election, and no knowledge of the origin, the cause, or the end of our election. So it is quite simply that election is *in Christ*, because there is not *in us* any possible source of this election, any ground which could engender it, any end to which it could reach out. Calvin never stopped insisting on these numerous texts (that I am not going to enumerate) concerning this threefold dashing of any hope for *us* concerning *divine* election.

---

9. Or "whim."

It is not we who are the *origin* of this choice, for without God we do not know God; if we were not chosen by God, we would never have the idea of choosing him, if we were not drawn by the Father, we would never come to Jesus Christ. It is not we who are the *ground* of our election, for in us there is no trace of virtue that would deserve it, there is only an abyss of iniquity, which makes us more unworthy. It is not we who could be the *end*[10] of that election, since that is the glory of God. In his infinite love, he made that glory consist in the fact that *we* are to give him glory and this glory is that he should be *all* and in *all*. So in this way the dominant feature of election is that it is totally free; we have nothing to offer to provoke it, to be worthy of it, or to see it come to fulfilment.

But all this could only be speculation. It ceases immediately to be the case when it is in *Christ* that we know it. Moreover, from where else would we be able to know in any case? In what autonomous examination of our conscience would we be able to be convinced? Who else but he could tell us that we really need election, that is to say, that we really are *lost*? When we look at ourselves, when we count up, by *ourselves,* our virtues and our failures, we would not know how to come up to such a rigorous standard, to the necessity of such a complete gift; we would still think we have some merit in the eyes of God. *In Christ,* that is to say, before his cross, there is only one truth, that is that he dies because of us. This is because we do not love God; this is the cause of our election, not we ourselves, because we too say: Here's the heir, come on, let us kill him! Before the cross, before this sole place in the world, all virtues die, because we see clearly there that it is these virtues as much as vices which cause the death of the Holy and Righteous One. Before the cross we know—and we know it for ourselves—who are the elect and what election truly is: election of enemies of God, of the torturers of Christ. The elect will always be taken from among those who surround the cross, from amongst those who cry out "Crucify!" and amongst those who remained quiet, amongst those who did nothing, those who could do nothing. "It was necessary that the Son of Man be rejected." Before the cross, too, we understand this paradox: the *price* of free election. For if election does not cost *us* anything, for God it cost his Son. For God to extend grace is to give *everything,* to give everything for us who cannot give him anything. There is in this word grace, which we often use very lightly, a frightening aspect. In the cross of Christ we find the mortal pains of the choice that God

---

10. Or "purpose" or "goal."

has made concerning us. Grace, the sheer gift of election, is the agony of Gethsemane; it is the suffering undergone right up to the harrowing cry, "My God, my God, why have you abandoned me?" This is heaven closed. This is the Son who is no longer with the Father, because the Father is no longer with the Son. And this is, in heaven, the Father who has truly *given* his Son, totally abandoning him for us who had abandoned him to death. This is the night of the ninth hour. What does this darkness mean? Revelation says: punishment. And the Son believes it. Punishment, God's wrath. The only one who will understand grace in election is the same one who understands that it is fulfilled in Christ dying, smitten by God, deserted by men. The only one who will understand how election extends grace is the one who, before the cross, does not come with arguments or with good works, with religious emotion or objections, but who stands there speechless because they have nothing to say, nothing to do, nothing to put forward. I know very well that it is not easy to trust. Here too, it is easier to argue or be unbelieving, easier to line up our questions or to say Was it really necessary for this substitution to take place? Let us put aside all these easy solutions so that this cross is not rendered powerless. All our denials will have no hope of changing the word of the Son of God himself: "The Son of man must be crucified!"

So here we are introduced to the first mystery of predestination, but introduced by the true way *which is Christ*: the mystery of the wrath of God. Here, we particularly see that election means *ruin* as much as *salvation,* rejection as much as adoption, that God's choice has a *ring of death* about it. If election was not *in Christ* there would not be any *double* predestination, and we would not know that God is the one who causes death as much as he makes alive in order to give life. We would not know, because we would not have really encountered him, that "it is a terrible thing to fall into the hands of the living God." We cannot speak of perdition[11] concerning the intention of God except at calvary, but there we *have* to speak of it. But what will we come and say, with all our false scales and our theories about divine justice? Did Jesus Christ protest against this justice? Did he accuse his Father? Did he renounce his existence and submit himself there to do the will of God? Did he contest with the God who inflicts *mortal* punishment? Did he doubt the God who abandoned him? Where then is faith? In us, with all our reasonable questions, our pious arguments about the love of God? Is it in us or in Christ?

---

11. Or "ruin."

We can go further here, those of us who say, regarding election, that it is not right that God treats each of us in the same way. *In fact, he does not treat Jesus Christ and us in the same way.* He strikes him, while welcoming us; he causes him to die while letting us off. If he punishes him, it is so that he can extend peace to us. This is the wonder of "negative" election, as we say. It affects the only one who did not deserve it. We are not subjected to it, we will not be subject to what the Christ was subject to and to which he should not have been subject to. The cross is unjust like election, but this injustice is *our righteousness*.

Whoever has understood that, whoever does not speak of this too hastily, can rejoice that such is the secret of God. He can move forward in this mystery and know that, all things considered, election is always *positive* when it is in *Christ*, that it has only been *negative* for him on Good Friday. Before the cross we do not understand and we worship, we do not question, we bless. And whom would we worship if not the one who has extended grace toward us? Why would we not bless, if not because of his *positive* grace? The cross where Christ is condemned does not condemn *us*, it makes us children of God. By it we *pass* from death to life, because the Son has made our death his and here more than ever, as Paul says "There is only yes in him."[12]

Once more, let us say it again, that this is only true *in Christ*, that is to say, before the cross, in faith. Here, here alone, here truly, faith knows that double predestination has become simple and that "God is love." This is because they have known it; this is because they have believed it, which Calvin and so many others have above all sung about, uniquely, the joy of election. Not that they were hard of heart—harder than us—that is to say more knowledgeable and more proud in their chosen discipline. Just simply, that they had understood that *in Christ crucified* there is only cause for the believer to experience a triumphant joy. Believing, from now on believing *here* in their election, cannot be to believe in their own perdition.[13] In the same way, the Apostles Creed does not say, in the third article: I believe in eternal death—but nevertheless it does not say: there is no eternal death—so in the same way, in Christ—without ever denying that one *cannot not be in Christ*—there is no negative election.

---

12. Maury appears to be alluding to Paul: "For no matter how many promises God has made, they are 'Yes' in Christ" (2 Cor 1:20, NIV).

13. Or "ruin."

We have just clarified by Holy Scripture that divine election has no other locus than Jesus Christ. It remains to be seen what is its object, and how we are involved in it. Here we will again say, *the choice for or against Jesus Christ crucified*. Or, if you want, faith or unbelief *in Jesus Christ crucified*. What is there to say?

First, that *we* choose. Really it is we, wholly, completely, without reserve and forever. *Along with God's eternal election* goes *faith with no opt-out clause* as far as we are concerned. But here we have a question which no one can answer in a theoretical way. We have to risk *everything* in our reply. Faith or unbelief are not possibilities that we would be able to discourse about, that would be *before us* and we *outside of* them. "You are already committed . . . it is a wager," as Pascal said.[14] And to wager is not to become someone, tomorrow, presently, it is to be one or the other *right now* and *forever*. A choice must be made. To accept or refuse. First, to accept or refuse that we have nothing to put on the table, nothing to say, that we can only be speechless, made speechless by our helplessness and by the power of God. To accept or refuse that the crucified in the merciful yes, which he says to us, is saying no to all that puts him on the cross—to evil, to sin, to accept or refuse that he takes upon himself what we are, *so that we will no longer be what we are*.[15] To accept or refuse that in him we are radically *condemned*. To accept or refuse that his death means *our death*, death to ourselves, that to be in him is to be baptized into his death, that to be in communion with him is to be in communion with his death, and *therefore to die*. Quite simply to accept Jesus Christ, to be chosen by God, means to choose to turn away from *ourselves forever*. That means to have from now on an absolute Lord, "to offer our bodies as a living sacrifice, holy and acceptable to God." The election of Jesus Christ is not only the means by which he has chosen us, it is also the way in which we choose him, and *no longer ourselves*. In Christ election is the vocation to *conformity to Christ*. This is the personal and sincere reiteration of the great words of Paul, "Christ is my life," or "it is no longer I who live but Christ lives in me," not meant in some mystical sense, where we would have become Christ, but in the totally concrete sense, a mortal

---

14. "Yes; but you must wager. It is not optional. You are embarked" (Pascal, *Pensées* 3.233 [67]).

15. Literally "that we will not be elect."

sense for ourselves, in which like Christ we have said no to ourselves *forever.*

⤳

Such is divine election; such is our choice. Who will be able to honestly say, *if it is a question of that particular choice,* "I have chosen?" None of us. Because all of us, before the cross of Calvary, when it absolves us, do not think that we "really" have a need of absolution and even there we still have a few virtues to parade. When the cross stakes its legitimate claim, all of us still try to resist a little. When it says *no* to what we are, none of us want to agree *with it totally.* So who can be saved? Who is the elect of God? Here it is still a *divine* mystery—a mystery of love—which comes to resolve our paradoxes and in the place of our dumb voice makes the voice ring out which dares to say yes, which *we* cannot say to Christ on the cross: this voice, it is God's, not ours.

Why does the whole Bible and Calvin and all Christians declare that faith is a gift, that grace is totally free, if not because *no one* can risk everything in this way to renounce oneself and accept the Lord. "To make a saint of man (that is to say, not a perfect man, but a man who says yes to Jesus Christ crucified), there grace is needed, and those who do not know it, do not know either what a saint is or what a man is."[16] Pascal knew himself in writing that, and he knew Jesus Christ. But here, by grace, the *miracle* is possible: it is *worked* in us, really in us, this yes, which does not come from us and which is nevertheless *our* yes. We can be and we are believers. This miracle is what the gospel calls being "born of the Spirit," that which Paul calls "the new man." This is the believer, this is the elect. The elect, in their election, accept everything from the cross: condemnation and grace, judgment and forgiveness, demand and promise, renouncement and life. They accept, that is to say, that they no longer have anything, they allow *everything to be given* to them, they know it, they want to receive everything, to wait for everything, to believe everything, to hope for everything.

But here again an obstinate voice, a sincere voice will say: Am I really that man, since I am not *only* that man? Because this voice is obstinate and sincere, because it speaks the truth and says that we are not *only*

---

16. "Grace is indeed needed to turn a man into a saint; and he who doubts it does not know what a saint or a man is" (Pascal, *Pensées* 7.508 [89]).

that sort of person, there we have *double* predestination. Against this self who does not say yes to Jesus Christ crucified, against us, as we know ourselves not to be the new man, the one who accepts grace, the wrath of God "is revealed from heaven." We would not know how to escape it. But, despite everything, in us, in this eternal movement which makes up the life of the believer in the flesh, there is the spiritual man,[17] this strangely new person who *believes* that "if anyone is in Christ, there is a new creation" (2 Cor 5:17). This new man does not go along with the older man, any more than God does; the new man refuses the old man, the new man calls down the judgments of God upon the old man, the new man bows down in trembling under this deserved wrath, he does not raise his voice, he is not speaking anymore about righteousness. He has no more righteousness, he believes in the righteousness of *God*. We know well that this is the case in us believers, when we read chapters seven and eight of Romans, when we repeat, "Wretched one that I am, who will deliver me from this body of death?" and, "Thanks be to God through Jesus Christ. . . . There is, therefore, no condemnation for those who are *in Christ Jesus*," when we know with Paul that our true self, the self that we want to be true, is our inner man and that we are abandoning the outward man to *destruction* by God. In the *miraculous*, incomprehensible presence of this "new man" who believes, the mystery, alien to our reason, of *double* predestination is resolved, *in faith*.

What we are concerned with here in double predestination is unbelief and faith—the unbelief of the believer and the faith of the unbeliever which dogs us still, alas! on this earth, this believer is, if you will, according to the Pauline image, the old man and the new man. As those who do not believe and are hardened, we are rejected by the wrath of God; as those who accept the divine mercy, we subscribe to his judgments and his grace, so God accepts us. I say *us* and not this one or that one, the reprobates and the elect, because we're talking about *us* and no one else. If we do not understand this at all, it is precisely because we would be hardened, given over to condemnation. Predestination is therefore very much *double*, not as if there were two categories of people that it would separate by *sorting*, but *double* because of having two *terms*: election and rejection, grace and condemnation. So we can apply this double decree to *ourselves*, because we deserve the negative verdict in it as much as we welcome the positive grace in it. In other words, double predestination

---

17. Literally, "the person of the Spirit."

is a truth which only the church knows and never philosophy, but also a truth which *concerns the church* and which the church is only able to preach to her members.

Is not this the only answer we can give to those who, concerning election, do not ask theoretical questions at all about God's righteousness but are deeply concerned about what happens to the "others," the rejected, those whom Calvin presented as the necessary terrible counterpart to the blessed elect of God? Are there elect, are there reprobates, all of them sovereignly, incomprehensibly, freely chosen by God? It is not up to us to pose this question; *we* need to hear it asked about us. It is not *our* place to reply. What is more, *we* do not have any choice to make. It is God, or rather Jesus Christ, who reserves the right to pass judgment, that is to say, the authority to put some at his right hand side and some at his left. Moreover, this discrimination has been *prophesied*, that is to say, described as a reality of the last day, hidden until then. There *are not* elect and reprobate, there *will be* elect and reprobate. Down here until the last day, no one is *elsewhere* than around the cross (this is the universalistic sense of the word of Jesus in John 12:32, "When I am lifted up from the earth, I will draw all men to me"). And, around the cross there are no privileged places, that is to say, places where one would *have less need than the others* of the pardon of the cross. Even more: there is no one that the cross cannot save (hence the universalistic sense of Paul's phrase, "God has shut up all men in disobedience so that he may be merciful to all" [Rom 11:32]). Around the cross, there is everyone, because the cross is for everyone, all enemies of God, all loved by God: the godless and the pious believer, the adulterer and the honest person, the lost and the saved, no exception of persons. *In Christ*, the others will always be, for the believer, "those brothers for whom Christ has died," never the rejected which one could despise or pity (even if it were with all one's soul). *In Christ*, when we consider this terrible question of reprobation, there are only two words which concern *us*—the reply of Jesus to Peter's concern about what would happen to John: "What about him?" "What is that to you? Follow me!" (John 21:22), and the exclamation of the disciples when Jesus announced his betrayal by the son[18] of perdition: "Surely not I?" (Mark 14:19).

On this point, one will retort that this is hardly Calvinist doctrine. It is true that the Reformer strongly insisted on distinguishing between

---

18. Maury is referring to Judas Iscariot.

persons in predestination, as if the gratuitousness of the double decree of election and reprobation were linked to him. And, arguably, one can suspect him here of having ceded to the necessities of a very human reasoning, going beyond the limits laid down by biblical revelation. That is why we must not allow ourselves to be held back by the fear of a divergence from the conclusions of the *Institutes of the Christian Religion*. This divergence, which is arguably necessary to emphasize, remains secondary. Because for Calvin also, what he contemplates in the fate of the reprobate is the "mirror" of free election to salvation, as he has said, and not the fate of certain people to which he would have quite easily consented. For him also, the only important thing is to remain in an attitude of faith, in case "*we too* were rejected" and not to be concerned with statistics concerning heaven and hell; the only important thing is to proclaim grace, always *positive,* which is in Jesus Christ and the perdition which could be *ours.*

Whatever the case, we know only one thing, that double predestination exerts a hold on us, that it is the reason for our vigilance, our trembling as much as our joy. The old man and the new man, according to the New Testament, are not two races that never come together, two humanities. It is that in each of us they are the signs of that which God elects, and that which he rejects. Hear me well; these remarks do not at all pretend to soften in an easy universalism the *formidable possibility* of damnation, which would contradict the whole Bible and Jesus Christ himself. It is true that in our Christian life we need to listen, with a holy fear and absolute seriousness, to the prophecy concerning the Last Judgment, and as Christians we are not to erase any of the texts about eternal death; it is true that, in entrusting ourselves to the love of God, we do not deny his judgments, nor the sovereignty of election so as not to worry about our unbelief. We need to be *in Christ,* we need to believe. It really is a question here of life or death.

But here the supreme question is asked, the really *ultimate* one, beyond which we cannot go back, the one which evokes the final decision without appeal. On whom does true election depend? On whom does it depend that *we are in Christ,* or—and it is the same thing—on whom does it depend that *we choose Jesus Christ*?

We know well that this extreme point is the one where everything in us is troubled, or rebels. For many, it is this question, or rather the objections to the biblical answer, which diminishes the "dreadful" mystery, as Calvin put it, of the secret counsel of God. Before repeating the *only* possible answer, because it is biblical, which is quite simply that salvation depends on God alone and on his unique decision, and not in any way at all on us, before saying with Jesus that only the Spirit *who blows where he wills*, causes people to be born of the Spirit, I would like to present two comments.

First, I want to emphasize that instead of arguing about eternal salvation and the ultimate act from which it proceeds, it is necessary to reflect on the origin of faith. It is not without reason that the Bible speaks of justification by faith as much as salvation by grace. And certainly, the two expressions designate the same reality. But in fixing our attention on *faith* we will arguably avoid conceiving of salvation as a sort of beatitude mechanically granted; arguably we will better understand how much our imaginations concerning a capricious distribution of heaven or hell are ungodly. If we have been saved by grace, it is by *means of faith*, by *our* faith, that is to say, in the act where we adhere to the free mercy of God, where we are totally active, committed and truly ourselves. Further, when we reflect on the way we are freely justified, we cannot contradict the mystery of divine freedom *uniquely* at work to reveal the Father to us, so that we are reconciled with him, so that we are made to await with confidence the Judge of the last day. For we know very well, despite the poverty of our faith, that it is by grace that we believe. Calvin, in his congregational Bible study held in the Geneva church on eternal election, specifically declares,[19] "This is where we have to start: knowing that when we believe in Jesus Christ, that does not come from our own working, nor that we have so much the cultivated or sharp spirit to understand this heavenly wisdom contained in the Gospel, but this comes by a grace of God, indeed by a grace which goes beyond our nature." Against this certitude, all the arguments in the world—and even when it is we who express them—are not sufficient; they only shake our unbelief.

But in the second instance, and above all to the question "Who does our faith depend on?" I would like to put forward first a preliminary request and in my turn enquire, "So who is asking this question? Who is looking for this ultimate origin?" Here again let us leave well alone all those who debate about this in the controversies around determinism

---

19. The French title of this book, *Congrégation faite en l'église de Genève par Jean Calvin*, refers to a Church meeting in Geneva on the topic of eternal election. While Jerome Bolsec was troubling the Genevan Church with anti-predestinarian teachings, Calvin gave his exposition of the doctrine of election, which was then transcribed in this book for the ministers of Geneva's Church, while they were gathered for their weekly meeting.

and liberty, the justice and injustice of God; let us listen deep within ourselves. Who *in me* is asking this question? Is it the *believer*, the one who humbly accepts the injustice of Calvary by which they are saved, the gratuitousness of Calvary, the law of Calvary? Or is it the other, the old man who prefers giving and receiving nothing in front of the crucified, preserving ourselves and saving ourselves? Honestly speaking, everything depends on the answer that we give to this preliminary question. And it is very true that inside of ourselves we reply in *two* ways. But only *one* is true. And it is in that reply that we testify concerning our election, because in that response we really are testifying that it is *God's* election. Yes, it is the pardoned believer who is right, the believer who knows that only God decides and it has to be he who decides, if not, nothing is decided; the believer who knows that God always chooses the first, if not, the choice would always be dismissible, and who, far from being outraged, arguing, rejoices and worships; the believer who knows that if God were to abandon them they would no longer believe in God. This believer in us cannot hold it against God that he reserved the right to this ultimate election, because if it were not *God's* election, we would have our doubts about it. Yes, in us, the believer replies: It is God who decides about *my* faith. Thanks be to him for deciding about this, without me as much as for me! In us, yes! always in us, the other, the "old man," the one whom Paul addresses sharply, "O man, who are you to argue with God?" you who rebel and worry. But he is not right *before* God (because he is not before God); he is only right before himself.

There is, to be quite honest, no other answer we can put forward to this question, no other answer than that of faith. And we cannot go *any further*. The *last* word possible: it will always be God.

Before concluding, let us stay with the joy of this *ultimate* response, the great joy that the Reformation knew and which caused it to find the decree as something "sweet," but did not ignore its "dreadful" aspect. Joy of a *sure* election because it is wholly in God's hands, the joy of a *free* salvation, because it is in *Christ*, the joy to be able to repeat, "I am persuaded that neither life nor death . . . nor anything in this world will be able to separate me from the love (not the love that *I* have for God) which God has testified to me in Jesus Christ." Joy that the peace of God goes *beyond* all understanding. Joy to believe all that, joy to believe only that, joy that all we need to believe boils down to that.

One cannot go further than this faith and this joy. Perhaps some will reckon that that is not a conclusion, that we have not got any further than at the beginning. Honestly speaking, there is not any conclusion that *we* can set out. Predestination is the affirmation that any conclusion belongs to *God*. Predestination is not a harmonious synthesis of two divergent terms (whether those terms are human freedom and the divine decree, or the righteousness of God and his love, or time and eternity). It does not foreclose on anything, (because God does not allow himself to be locked up by any limit); on the contrary, it leaves the door wide open, to the inaccessible divine activity. It stops us there. All discourse, all reflection on predestination, can only finish elsewhere than where Paul stopped his testimony: "Oh, the depth of the riches of the wisdom and knowledge of God! How unsearchable his judgments, and his paths beyond tracing out. For "Who has known the mind of the Lord? Or who has been his counsellor?" and again, "Who has ever given to God, that God should repay him? For from him and through him and to him are all things. To him be the glory forever! Amen!" (Rom 11:33–35).

So what shall we do? For God never speaks to us in order to pull us up, so that we gaze emptily up to heaven. I would like simply to set out several markers where the revealed word on predestination arrests us and in which we perceive once again how election and faith are linked.

The elect ones, the believers in election, are those who are truly *on their guard*.[20] Not because they could be robbed of *God's election*, but because there is always a risk, as was the case for Israel, of transforming *God's* election into *their* possession. They do not watch over *their* treasure in a miserly manner, they rather look for the Kingdom of *God* and his righteousness. They make sure that their election is not confused with feeling elected, and that their faith in election does not exempt them from focusing on those things that are *above*. They are really careful, those who stay upright, looking to the God who elects, so as not to fall, looking downward at themselves. They keep watch, and they never cease to be vigilant. "Happy the servant whose master finds them vigilant."

20. Literally " who truly watch."

The elect ones, the ones who believe in election truly *pray*. The last word of election is *in God*. They ask God to deliver his verdict as far as they and others are concerned. Why would they pray if everything did not depend in the end uniquely on God? How would they not pray if they did not *truly* believe in God over whom they have no rights nor any authority? They truly pray. And they know that all true prayer is given to them by the Spirit; they know that all prayer given by the Spirit is so that we can ask for the Holy Spirit. They gain no access to God's counsel apart from their *true* prayer, and the prayer of Jesus Christ who intercedes. But that access is truly *theirs*.

The elect ones, the believers in election, truly *obey*. Not just in singing hymns or by their spirituality, but in a visible concrete immediate manifestation which is a vocation. They only know their election in the call of God to obedience. They only hear the *ultimate* word, the one that belongs to the Lord, for if this word is the word of a *Lord*, it is an order that must be straightaway carried out.

Regarding the elect ones, three times I have used the adverb *truly*—truly watch, truly pray, truly obey. It is in the honesty of this *truly* that God's decision joins ours, that *God's* election is *our* faith.

So on a human level we must not worry, that is to say, to wonder *to ourselves*, "Am I elect or not?" We should not reassure ourselves on a human level, that is to say, to repeat to *ourselves*, "I am elect and I have nothing to do." We need to realize that faith is a pathway on which we *walk* and that this pathway is absolutely *sure*. It is a pathway which takes us toward *joy*, for walking along it, as long as we walk, we look not to ourselves, but to *Christ*.

"Do you want to know if you are elect? Look to yourself in Jesus Christ. Because those who by faith are in communion with Jesus Christ can assure themselves that they are part of God's eternal election, and that they are his children. We do not need to go up on high to enquire about what must be hidden at this time. But look! God comes down to us and he shows us how this is in his Son; as he has said, 'Here I am: look to me and know how I have adopted you as my children.' So when we receive this testimony of salvation, which is given by the Gospel, that is when we know and are assured that God has elected us" (Calvin).[21]

---

21. Calvin, *Congrégation faite*, 64–65.

## BIBLIOGRAPHY

Calvin, Jean. *Congrégation faite en l'église de Genève par Jean Calvin* [*Congregational Bible study held in the Geneva church on eternal election*]. Genève: P. A. Bonnant, 1835.

Calvin, John. *Institutes of the Christian Religion*. Translated by Henry Beveridge. MA: Hendrickson, 2008.

Neeser, Maurice. *L'Église qui sauve: Lettres à une jeune amie* [*The Church that Saves: Letters to a Young Friend*]. Neuchâtel: Paul Attinger, Éditions de la Baconnière, 1934.

Pascal, Blaise. *Pensées*. Translated by W. F. Trotter. New York: Dutton and Co., 1958.

# 8

## Décision Dernière (The Ultimate Decision)

### Pierre Maury

A Sermon Preached in the Season of Lent 1937
in the Reformed Church of Passy, Paris[1]

    1. Maury, *Le Grand Oeuvre de Dieu*, 51–86. Any footnotes in this sermon of Pierre Maury are inserted by the translator in order to either clarify or expand an issue of translation or give English speaking readers a reference of either the original French text or an equivalent English language translation to which Maury refers. In the original French text there were no footnotes or bibliography. First translated into English by Simon Hattrell. Previously translated into German by Charlotte von Kirschbaum (see von Kirschbaum, *Die grosse Tat Gottes*).

    Reymond reproduces several letters regarding the publication of the work from which this sermon is taken:

    From Karl Barth to Pierre Maury, Basel, April 29, 1940: "It is a good thing that we have your work on predestination in German. We hear from all over the place, that this publication is much appreciated. If it was possible would you agree to 'The Great Work of God' also being translated?" (Reymond, *Karl Barth—Pierre Maury*, 175 [my translation])

    From Pierre Maury to Karl Barth, Lyon, January 16, 1941: "I am full of pride to think that Mlle Von Kirschbaum is translating 'The Great Work of God' at this very moment. Tell her thank you!" (Reymond, *Karl Barth—Pierre Maury*, 189 [my translation]).

    From Charlotte von Kirschbaum to Pierre Maury, Basel, June 15, 1941: "The translation of 'The Great Work of God' is finished and is now going to the editor, who will, however, not release it until after the summer months. I do want to particularly thank you once again for this work which I have unfortunately been often obliged to interrupt, too often, but which has given me a great joy, which was renewed and increased as I became more familiar with the whole of this text. I retranslated it three times from one end to the other, being each time more unsatisfied with its shape. This was much more difficult than when I translated Election and Faith; the reason being that your French text had still completely kept the direct sense of the spoken word—a sense that I did not want to spoil, but which one could hardly render in German. I was strongly aware at this time how much our ways of thinking and our languages are different, how you can sometimes discard logical equivalents to which we are so pedantically attached, without this abandonment leaving an arbitrary impression. I hope that this

Our last talk led us to this conclusion: Jesus Christ is the revelation of God in so much as he is the way (John 14:6); he is only the truth and the life if he is first the way, and therefore in so much as we take this way and commit ourselves to it.

Now, in the face of this intellectually scandalous affirmation, deep down inside of us another rebellious movement emerges: dread joined to a sense of the impossible. For to commit ourselves is a serious act, and to desire or dare to carry it through we need serious reasons. In other words, to choose Jesus Christ as the only way which leads to God, it would be necessary to be sure that he really is this way. But to be sure about this would be to have already made that decision. This is an eternal vicious circle of faith so rigorously closed that we are confronted with its limits in every thinking moment of our Christian lives.—For example, in order to pray, we need to believe, and yet if we pray, it is so that we can ask for faith. And further, to seek God is only possible if we have already found him. Or yet again, to become a disciple of Jesus Christ is to be certain that he is the master, and to know that, we need to already be his disciple: has he not himself already said, "Anyone who chooses to do the will of the one who sent me, will find out whether my teaching comes from God" (John 7:17)?

There can be no question of breaking this circle, even if it were with the intention of penetrating by this breach into the rigorously closed domain of faith. For wanting to break it would in reality be refusing to enter into it. That would be saying that we can *by ourselves* accede to revelation, and therefore to have abandoned all thought that it really is *revelation*, that it transmits to us a wisdom which is truly mysterious and hidden, or more simply that it transmits *God himself.* And yet our heart, like our spirit, demands, sometimes desperately, that this access be given to us! What use would this revelation be to us, if it were to come into effect, achieved elsewhere than where we find ourselves, if therefore it did not really become *ours*; it would only be a much greater mystery, a God even

---

work is now reasonably correct. After several surveys, Karl says that he is satisfied, but he still wants to read it all again before sending it to the editor. I've had the same experience as what happened formerly with the text on election: I admire your gift of saying things in a way that is always new, and to say them in such a way that one can read them with a wholly new interest, that one sees them in a new light. You're going to laugh: I believe that, apart from you, only Karl has that sort of ability. You'll recognize, won't you, that that is a great compliment?!!" (Reymond, *Karl Barth—Pierre Maury*, 192 [my translation]).

more distressingly hidden so that we would know that he unveils himself without being able to go where we can see his face! In calling to mind this anguish, I am not only considering just those people who aspire to have faith, those who, despite their desire to know Christianity, suffer with the anguish of not knowing it, and for whom it remains still an unknown quantity; I am thinking of all those double-minded Christians who are unsure either of their questions or their certitude,–unsure because of their desires on the one hand and their obedience on the other,–and all Christians for whom spiritual dryness is devastating, people who live in those deserts where they more often know the presence of the tempter rather than of God, whose faith is undermined and who are so quick to become suspicious of the divine revelation as if it were a mirage! Yes, how can we know God in Christ, how does Christ really become *revelation*, over and over again, or remain so for us? These are not only questions that are asked out of some vain intellectual curiosity, but also the mortal torment of suffering souls.

So in order to respond to this, there is no other possibility than to give up asking them and resolving them *ourselves*; to accept that these are questions which are addressed to *us* and which are resolved *for us* by *another*, by the God who reveals *himself*—and if he himself doesn't reveal himself, he remains hidden, inexorably. This abandonment, this acceptance, is very precisely the way of Jesus Christ, Jesus Christ who has become our way. And this step which commits us, each hour of our Christian life, entails a constant renewal. Certainly, it can and it must be much easier to do this than in the first instance to take the necessary risk; but it must never be easy in the sense that it would become a religious habit, a formalism of the soul.[2] To commit ourselves yesterday would never mean diminishing the seriousness with which today, tomorrow, right until the end, we will be and we will stay truly *committed*. The Christian life, from its beginning to its end, is decision, that is to say, unreserved commitment. It matters not that our wisdom sees in this affirmation a lack of objectivity; we do not need here any other objectivity than that of Jesus Christ, if we want to really know in Jesus Christ the revelation of God. For, Jesus Christ wants to be objective in the sense that he claims to be an unreserved commitment of God on our behalf, and on the other hand he demands that we become unreservedly committed to him. It is this double aspect of his existence that we are going to examine.

2. Or "a human observance of outward forms."

## DÉCISION DERNIÈRE (THE ULTIMATE DECISION)

Here a misunderstanding of grave consequence could come into play: this would consist in forgetting the first sense in which Jesus Christ is a decision, and therefore to define the choice that we make concerning him as one of multiple human possibilities which are offered to us. Becoming the disciple of this master would therefore be one option among others, neither more nor less serious than one in which we are recruited into a political group, or ranked among the faithful of one of the great modern religions[3] (race, class, nation, etc.). There is no lack in the world today of men, of parties, of doctrines, who demand that we choose them exclusively, that we submit ourselves without discussion to their slogans or to their myths. The time has passed where we made freedom of thought and the dignity of the person consist in the refusal of any choice, under the pretext that to choose is to renounce, and to narrow one's future.[4] Our contemporaries hardly worry about safeguarding this state of mind. On the contrary, we see them eager to commit, be they blind or hasty, provided that they are wholehearted, or as we say, *totalitarian*.

If the Christian decision were of this kind, it would not be more solid or more lasting than all these human possibilities of decision. But it is not of this kind! Jesus is "not of this world" (John 8:23), as he himself said, even though he had lived in this world. And that is why we cannot choose him as we would choose a worldly master. Here again, we need to remember that he is *unique*, in the strictest sense incomparable, and that the faith that we place in him does not resemble any other trust, any other devotion that we would be able to consent to here below. We will not try, therefore, to show that we could know Christianity except in total submission, for it is an absolute.[5] For one could say just the same about everything that people think or decree as absolute. We are not going to go on about the necessity of choice with regard to moral considerations. What would be the purpose anyway? These proofs and analyses have never lastingly convinced anyone. It is because he is who he is, that is to say, not *an* absolute, but *the* absolute, the *unique* Son of God, who demands the obedience of faith. In order to choose him, we need to know more than just the motives behind *our* choice; we need to know by him *who* we choose in choosing Him.

3. Literally "cult."
4. Or "prospects."
5. Or "an uncompromising truth."

And here we are immediately constrained not to argue with ourselves about the legitimacy of Christian claims—a tiring and sterile monologue—but constrained to listen to a message. Saint Paul says, "Faith comes by hearing" (Rom 10:17), that is to say, it never comes from what we say to ourselves. What therefore do we need to hear said when someone speaks to us of Jesus Christ? What is the "the mystery of Jesus" of which Pascal spoke in his famous piece?

I think you have all been taken by the uncommon singular transaction which led the author of *Les Pensées*, after having contemplated the agony of Gethsemane, to that dialogue where the Christ disclosed to him the sense of his redemptive work: "Take solace, you would not look for me if you had not found me. I thought of *you* in my agony . . . *your* conversion is my business, don't be afraid, and pray with confidence as if for me."[6] Whatever our opinion on the right of a Christian to cause his master to speak in words we don't find in the gospel, even if they are only paraphrases of sacred texts, one fact is incontestable: as soon as faith is fixed on this person of past history, it is quite naturally brought to discover in him a personal intention; an interaction has begun. This is not a literary procedure here, but the conviction that Jesus Christ, who never exists only for himself, wants to speak to us and wants us to speak to him. Just as long as, like all the heroes of history, he remains for us an object of reflection, of admiration or curiosity, we do not know him; he is not *him*; he is only that which he wants to be, when we sense his scrutiny and "are called by our name" (Isa 45:4). He is, as the Gospel tells us with regard to his conversation with the Samaritan woman, "a man who knows everything that we have done" (John 4:29), and tells us so. This characteristic is decisive. The incredulous can object: mystic exaltation! The fact remains that millions, for 1900 years, have discovered that in Jesus Christ a unique relationship has been established between them . . . and another thing in their favor: the relationship of a dialogue, the "you" and "me." This relationship has such a strength, such a precision, that sometimes, in the most absolute solitude, we can detect a movement of flight, a gesture of repulsion towards this invisible presence: "Depart from me for I am a sinful man," we say, just like Peter (Luke 5:8), or we even cry out, as we throw ourselves at his feet, "My Lord and my God" like the apostle Thomas (John 20:28). This experience is what is designated in advance

---

6. Pascal, *Pensées* 7.552 (150).

by the prologue of Saint John's gospel when he calls Jesus the *Word*, not because this term was current in Greek or Judeo-Alexandrian philosophy contemporary to the gospel to designate an idea or metaphysical being, but because the evangelist, so nourished by the tradition of the Old Testament, knew that God is a God *who speaks*, who speaks to us, and that, when he becomes flesh in this world, it is not in some dumb impersonal reality, but in a living voice. Jesus Christ for the believer is the *Word* made flesh.

Is this to say that only the discourses of Jesus to the crowd and his private interviews are this divine summons which faith receives? Could we reduce that which we need to hear of him, of his teaching, to that which he says in phrases and words? Would he not just be a supreme prophet, even unique? Certainly not! When God speaks to us in Christ it is not in order to display a truth, but to reveal to us our situation before him, and the attitude that he adopts before us. Language more mysterious and more complete than that which exists to express truths susceptible to be taught! *Living* language, not only in the sense that it is spoken by a living man; but also in the sense that it is the language of the whole of the life of this man—yes, of *all* his life, just as he knew it and makes us know it, his eternal and temporal existence, his 33 years on this earth and his presence before the Father "before Abraham was" (John 8:58), and right up until the day of his return and of judgment. It is not the words of Jesus which are the Word of God, it is he *himself*.

I know that this affirmation will always appear to be incomprehensible to those who have not heard the voice of God in Christ; I know that there are very few who are ready to consent to study, to examine the words of Jesus, they declare inadmissible and crazy the pretension of the church to base revelation on his person heard in such a fashion. But the fact is that such is very much the pretension of the church and that it is in this totality of Christ that his work of salvation is involved. Without doubt a mystery! But without him, which is precisely the mystery of Jesus, Christianity is no more than a doubtful and empty religion. In any case, whether we accept this mystery or not, it is worthwhile reflecting on what it sets out to signify, and to look towards the light by which our lives are enlightened.

We will have the opportunity in our next talks to define the multifaceted living relationship that Jesus Christ wants to establish between God and us: in other words, to clarify how he is our mediator. For today we will confine ourselves to emphasizing, as we have only just indicated, the *decisive* and *ultimate* character of his reality. Decisive: that is to say that the reality of Jesus Christ is a decision of God, therefore without any recourse, as far as we are concerned, a decision of one other than ourselves and of which we are the object; and that is to say, in the second place, that Jesus Christ calls for a decision on our part, a final[7] decision. The apostle John and the apostle Paul each bring forth concerning him extraordinary affirmations with a moving simplicity: "In the beginning was the Word, and the Word was with God; and the Word was God. Through him all things were made; without him nothing was made that has been made" (John 1:1–3). "All things have been created through him and for him" (Col 1:16). Prodigious audacity with which, in this man, this man that they knew, who was not to them a myth, they discover this inconceivable existence! In him, according to them, it is not only a question of him, but of the "gathering together of all that exists in the heavens and on the earth" (Eph 1:10). So all that exists, even our short, poor lives, are linked to that life even by the will which created them. It is from all eternity, in eternity, that between Jesus Christ and us a relationship is established. So we are not just that which we believe ourselves to be, ephemeral beings, fortuitous, incidental playthings of circumstances or of blind forces, endless interchangeable links of our race; our course in life does not go from our birth to our death following the desperate rhythm of our years! And neither are we, in the least, one of those innumerable works of an immense creative generosity! From all times, and before we had even opened our eyes before our sun—it being ephemeral also—we existed, we are known in our most personal reality; for in God's view we have a name! "All the days ordained for me were written in your book before one of them came to be"—so cries out the psalmist, who immediately continues his song of praise: "Your thoughts, O God, seem impenetrable to me" (Ps 139:16–17). But this secret that is declared beyond all comprehension ceases to be overwhelming. For it is in him that it is *individualized*. Indeed, it is not in some great book of heavenly accounting that our story is incorporated with all the other stories of this world, as if God were only

---

7. Or "permanent."

the omniscient historian of our adventures, and as if these adventures, mediocre or magnificent, remained anonymous as far as this invisible wisdom was concerned! It is through Jesus Christ, a man that we can know because he has been one of us, has lived like us and amongst us human beings, it is with him that we are linked. Such is the sense of our baptism. Our name, very personal, the one chosen by the tenderness of our parents, is associated very personally with the name of Jesus Christ. And so this sacrament, in declaring us Christian, is the sign, the confirmation of an eternal reality.

Marvelous revelation of an unfathomable mystery! When this child is born in a manger, when this man dies on the cross and rises again the third day, the eve of the Sabbath, it is our whole life that is swept up in this commitment, it is for our whole life that something happens. He is the one by whom—for whom also—we have been created, who is there. He is there, simple and immense, simple as the simplest of the sons of men, immense because the dimensions of his existence contain us all; he is the beginning and the end of our life. In him everything is enclosed, kept, protected. When he cries out, "Come to me, you who are weary and heavy laden" (Matt 11:28), it is all our destinies that he is calling, because they belong to him. When he stretches out his arms upon the cross, he says that it is "to draw all to himself" (John 12:32), because no one has existed without him and outside of him. When he rises and is exalted to the right hand of God, it is in order to present to God—eternally, and in eternity—those who—from all eternity, in eternity—have always been, are and will always be *his*. I have said, I have repeated: *all*. And it had to be that way. For Christ, as God, with God, is love. And when it is he who loves, who loves in creating, in taking on flesh, in dying, in rising, in interceding, and one day in judging, yes, when it is he who loves, it would be impossible for anyone to be less loved. But I must just as importantly say, with the same insistence, each of us: me, and you. For such is his love, that in giving it he gives it totally to each of us.

Yes! Marvelous revelation! But so that it does not remain an unfathomable divine thought, so that the mystery of Jesus is not just something that God knows, but also that those who are in Christ, that is to say, you and me, will overflow with joy, we need to understand how this humble earthly truth, the life of the Son of Man, is a heavenly secret; in other words, how Jesus Christ is *decisive*.

This decisive character, which involves the fact of Christ, so completely surpasses our thought patterns and our knowledge of ourselves that, in order to define it, we need to resort to the testimony of those who knew him in an immediate sense, that is to say, his disciples and his apostles. (But without ever forgetting that, after their time and continuously, other people of all ages and of all countries have received this revelation in the same strong and direct way: since the 3000 on the day of Pentecost, there is an innumerable number who have believed that their whole existence was linked to Christ, or more exactly, was fulfilled in him).

So how do these first witnesses sense this mystery of Jesus to which they had allowed themselves to be so personally committed? Why do they say, like Peter, "To whom else can we go? You have the words of eternal life" (John 6:68)?—and they were talking about *their* eternal life. I will summarize their testimony in three directions: for them Jesus Christ is someone who *comes; he* is someone who *gives himself; he* is someone who *chooses us.*

Jesus Christ is someone who *comes.* His whole life reveals an intention, a direction. It is not like our life—a mixture of chance and of fixed agenda. His life is movement, execution of a well-defined will and which does not weaken. And this movement always has a bias towards others. It is never this huge backward self-obsessed surge, which is so typical of the invincible currents of our soul. When he is there, everyone feels scrutinized, approached, sought out. This is the exact opposite of our human encounters, where we suffer above all from ignorance of our true state, where we are always reminded that the one who is with us will *leave us and go home.* The Son of Man doesn't have a *home; he* "has nowhere to lay his head" (Matt 8:20); he doesn't leave those towards whom he comes, for the sole reason for his existence is to *come to them.* He lives at our place. "We are his house" (Heb 3:6). "He came to that which was his own, and made his dwelling among us" (John 1:11, 14). Ever since the demon-possessed man whom Jesus met at the beginning of his ministry in the synagogue of Capernaum, and who was the first to recognize this mysterious foreigner as the Messiah—"You are the Holy One of God; have you come to destroy us?" (Mark 1:24), right up to the incessant testimony that we find in the fourth gospel, Nicodemus saying, "You are a teacher sent from God" (John 3:2) and Jesus himself saying, "He who comes from God has seen the Father" (John 6:46),—yes, in all the pages of the gospel,

Christ is the one who is looking for something, who looks for a man, not like Diogenes the cynic, but like the shepherd who wears himself out pursuing his lost sheep (Matt 18:12–14). When he is there, each of us knows that he is there for us, each of us knows we are not only looked for but found. There are all sorts of people in the Gospel like the paralytic by the pool of Bethesda; for so many years he had no one to plunge him in the healing water at the right time: and then one day Jesus was beside his bed, come for him, to heal him (John 5:1–9).

Jesus Christ is someone who *gives himself!* We no longer know the meaning of this worn-out expression. We apply it to the smallest gesture of compassion, to the smallest expressions of generosity! But with Jesus of Nazareth, people knew what it meant: to give oneself is not to give *something*, even much, or *nearly* all of oneself; it is to hold nothing back, to refuse nothing, it is to *give oneself* in the strongest sense of the word. They understood what he meant when he affirmed, "I give my life for my sheep" (John 10:15). They really understood it on the day when this life was given completely into the hands of those who thought they were taking it away from him, when in reality they were receiving it as an incredible gift of which they were completely ignorant. They understood why the sacrament of his presence was not first of all their offering of their life to him in recognition of his rights over them, and in recognition of his love, but rather the gift of his flesh and blood which he gave to them, keeping *nothing* back to himself. They understood that with Jesus Christ it is only ever a matter of receiving, of taking, and of being filled with him.

Jesus Christ is someone *who chooses.* The truth is that this characteristic which typifies his relationship with us humans only makes plain the way in which the reality of the previous two aspects are associated: it is because he truly comes to us and because he truly gives himself to us that we know that we are *chosen* by him. It is he who calls his disciples, and not his disciples who come to him; it is he who chooses those to whom he addresses himself: "I did not come to call the righteous but sinners" (Matt 9:13); it is he who enlightens the understanding of those who listened, in explaining his parables to them (Mark 4:11–13). And even when he welcomes all those who crowd around him spontaneously, he doesn't allow them to remain in a vague anonymous state, he notices them. Just like the woman with the issue of blood, who thought that she only needed to touch the hem of his garment, without being recognized; to the great surprise of his disciples, Jesus immediately asked about her story, and identified her miracle: "Take courage, my daughter," he said, "your faith has healed you" (Luke 8:43–48). She too felt that she was personally chosen.

We need to understand this election in its most positive sense, that is to say, as a testimony of his love, and not negatively as a sign of partiality. To love is to identify the one that you love, to adopt them not at the expense of others, but in their irreducible individual reality. A father loves each of his children with a complete and special tenderness, without at the same time setting aside any of them.

But there is an even deeper sense to the choice that Jesus Christ makes of his own. If they sense that they are chosen by him it's because his election makes a total claim on them, they are joined to him, so that it is a *decisive* election. How often did he affirm that when a man was chosen by him, he needed to expect not just to change his morals and his way of life, but to endure more severe experiences: hostility, persecution, even death! How often did he declare to his disciples that, in making them his own, he *made them alive* forever! In choosing someone, Jesus Christ knows that he is deciding their whole life, from the present and into eternity: "To save your life is to lose it; to lose your life *because of me* is to save it" (Mark 8:35).

However, these attitudes of Christ would not be enough to explain his mystery, not even to shed some light on it. The same could be said about any relationship between one of the masters of this world and their disciples. The real mystery of the action of Jesus Christ is that "he does nothing by himself" (John 5:19). That which he does for us, and that which he does in coming to us, in giving himself to us, in choosing us, is what no person can do: it is an act *of God*! When he adopts us, it is not only between him and us that very close ties are formed; in him it is God who works in us "to will and to do" (Phil 2:13), and it is therefore God who reaches us and adopts us. He speaks, commands, absolves, "with authority" (Mark 1:22). And this authority is indisputable because it doesn't come from him. His adversaries are shocked: "How can this man speak in such a way? Who can forgive sins except God alone?" (Mark 2:7). His disciples are astonished: "Even demonic spirits are subject to him!" (Luke 10:17). He knows that; he sovereignly declares, "All authority *has been given to me* in heaven and on earth" (Matt 28:18).

If we pick up the three characteristics that we raised concerning his human action, we will straightaway discover the divine dimensions! Jesus Christ comes, but *from above*; he is a sent one, in this movement of incarnation, which leads us not only to his will, but also to that of another. And what is unique about him is that in *coming* to us, at one and the same time he does what he wants and what the Father wants. He lowers himself, but in lowering himself, he *obeys*.—Jesus *gives himself* fully, freely, totally; but at the same time he is *given* to us, given in such a way that the gospel uses the strongest expression: "given over"[8] (Matt 17:22). And you understand this when you know what men—not only Pilate and the Jews—did with the one who was more than given up, *abandoned* by God, as he himself also said in that terrible cry from the Cross! The one who offers Jesus Christ to us is he to whom Jesus Christ belongs because he is his Son—Jesus *chooses*; but in choosing us he knows that he *receives* us from the very hand of his Father. When he prays for his disciples in his supreme prayer, he calls them "those whom You have given to me" (John 17:11–12). And if he is sure that they will come to him and that he will keep them, it is because he has received them from God: "All that the Father gives me will come to me" (John 6:37).

Such is the true relationship that Jesus Christ has with those who believe in him: a relationship where God himself legally binds himself to us. He says, "Whoever has seen me has seen the Father" and as long as we don't know that, we neither know God nor do we know Jesus. You will remember that scene just before his death: "If you had known me, you would also know my Father, and from now on you know him and have seen him." Philip said to him, "Lord, show us the Father, that will be enough." Jesus said to him, "Don't you know me, Philip, even after I have been among you such a long time? Anyone who has seen me has seen the Father. How can you say 'Show us the Father'? Don't you believe that I am in the Father and that the Father is in me?" (John 14:7–10).

So from now on we can understand why Jesus Christ is an *ultimate* decision, who has intervened in our lives. This has a double sense. An ultimate decision, because it is from *God*, and therefore without appeal. From what other circumstance could our fate be decided when it has spoken? In what other heaven, higher than God's, would we go looking for our destiny?—But this is also an ultimate decision because, coming from God, it is one of *absolute love*. What would there be beyond this love when he has given everything? What could we still expect when we have received everything? Wise decisions are dismissible and conditional. Love alone, *when it is God's love*, does not mean any reserve, any possibility of backtracking . . . and therefore there is no possibility

---

8. Or "delivered."

of losing ourselves, of being rejected because of our lack of love. Listen to the hymn of joy which closes the eighth chapter of the Epistle to the Romans: "What, then, shall we say in response to these things? If God is for us, who can be against us? He who did not spare his own Son, but gave him up for us all—*how will he not also, along with him, graciously give us all things?* . . . For I am convinced that neither death nor life, neither angels nor demons, neither the present nor the future, nor any powers, neither height nor depth, nor anything else in all creation, will be able to separate us from the love of God that is in Christ Jesus our Lord!" (Rom 8:31–32, 38–39).

So, in Jesus Christ, may our whole life be a decision of God. That is what in the final analysis the Gospel of Judgment announces. Let's be clear here: this is the Gospel, the *good news* of the last judgment. For this judgment is *ultimate,* not because it comes at the end of our temporal existence, but because it is Jesus Christ who is there, in the name of God, the supreme judge. For he himself has said how he will judge and the reasons for his sentence: he will not apply the rules of a code, he will not pass sentence according to any moral standard, nor by taking into consideration the extenuating circumstances of any standard of piety—"Not everyone who says to me, 'Lord, Lord' will enter the kingdom of heaven, but only the one who does the will of my Father who is in heaven" (Matt 7:21)—He will judge according to the way that we have treated him, *He,* who, just as he said, is present on this earth; according to the true or false way in which we will have believed in *him:* "Then the King will say to those on his right, 'Come, you who are blessed by my Father; take your inheritance, the kingdom prepared for you since the creation of the world. For I was hungry and you gave me something to eat, I was thirsty and you gave me something to drink, I was a stranger and you invited me in, I needed clothes and you clothed me, I was sick and you looked after me, I was in prison and you came to visit me" (Matt 25:34–36). And here—let's be quite clear about this, here especially—the essential thing, for those who share his likeness in that day when their lives are laid bare, is that the relationship forged from eternity between Jesus Christ and us depends on whether or not Jesus Christ is revealed, for eternity, in *his* verdict as judge and by the reason underlying his verdict: *himself.*

Oh, I know how much this perspective often makes us tremble, how we don't admit that our lives are to be judged, for we dread so much what they will reveal at that final reckoning, condemned without appeal. But why would we have any fear, why wouldn't we be thrilled with joy, because we know *who* will be the judge? The verdict which is waiting for us is not that of an impassive law, it is not even that of God whose ways are inaccessible and whose light is unbearable; it is the verdict of the one who has come, who gave himself—more than that, the verdict of the one who has ascended to heaven at the right hand of God, to be there, right until the end, (up to the day where he will be the judge), the advocate of our lost causes, our defender (1 John 2:1). Praise be to God that he has postponed the irrevocable sentence to which we will have to submit, to the *ultimate* authority. Praise be to God that our judge is the one who has chosen us . . . and who wanted to be chosen by us!

Who wanted to be chosen by us. There is, therefore, another aspect to all that we have just recognized in the mystery of Jesus, and it is the *ultimate* decision that we must make with regard to Jesus Christ. Perhaps many will feel here that they are on more familiar territory. For we must readily admit it: all these affirmations that I have dared to repeat with the apostles, with the Church, are so bold, out of all proportion to what our understanding and our heart know, that they leave us perplexed, if not full of anxieties. If we must not repeat them as formulas of a totally intellectual belief system, but believe practically, concretely, that our daily lives are continuously referred to the life of Jesus of Nazareth; if we must believe that in him, whom we know so little and understand so badly, the supreme will of God is what decides our destiny, then who will be able to know God? This is wisdom too mysterious, too hidden, way above and beyond our reach!

It is true that in order to see "the radiance of the glory of God in the face of Christ" (2 Cor 4:6) an even greater miracle is necessary in order to believe in God himself. So would it be a case of waiting passively for this miracle and, not grasping this revelation, being out of the loop as far as the mystery of Jesus is concerned? Certainly not! For if Christ is *decisive* for us, it is because we can only know him in a decision. And if his decision *as far as we are concerned* is *ultimate,* it is because he demands *of us* a decision *with no holding back.* So let those who only want to know Jesus Christ with their reason or their emotional demonstrations go away, those who study him as if he were Socrates or Napoleon, those who want to argue about him and, after long and wise discussion, accept him on account of arguments of which they are at the same time the masters and the judges. And let those also, go away, who have more or less correct opinions about him, those with the most orthodox or most heretical doctrines, if as far as he is concerned they have only got opinions or doctrines! There is no room in Christianity for spectators of Jesus Christ and far less for teachers of "Christian metaphysics." Jesus Christ is someone that one *chooses,* for whom we decide with our whole life. And we choose him with an *ultimate* choice, we commit ourselves without reservation, because he is *himself.* For no other reason than that.

We need to insist on the uncompromising nature of the essence of Christian decision. All our other human decisions—however wholehearted they may be—consist of one possibility,—however small that might be—that of being annulled, corrected, replaced. We can go back after having given ourselves. For in these decisions, *we* are the ones who have chosen, *we* are the ones who have committed ourselves. We have shown the power we have over ourselves; we have not given it up. As far as Jesus Christ is concerned, it is a completely different affair. If we choose him, it's because he has chosen us first; if we take him up, it is because he has seized us. Such is the seriousness of his coming into our life that it dispossesses us completely. He only comes as *master. He* is the *Lord* Jesus. How could it be otherwise? Therefore, if he has fixed his choice on us, the choice of God, if he has given us all of himself and if it is God who has given him to us, how could we still imagine that he could be content with that which is not *us*: with what is only our opinions, our fervor, our vague desires? If he only obtained from us a conditional adhesion, revocable, like a renewable lease, this would show that he would not have reached our true center, that our destiny would not be at stake. It is necessary that we honestly understand that in Jesus Christ *we* are the ones who are sought out, and not just a part of us, that is to say that he demands our ultimate decision. If we do not give our consent, it's because we haven't been found.

We do not escape this severity of Jesus Christ. Blessed severity! For this laying hold of our lives, where all possibilities of escape are closed except one, this obligation to say *yes* or *no,* and never "perhaps," is the sign, the only one, that the hand of God is truly laid upon our life and that we are held in his grasp, that truly there will no longer be an impasse against which we will stumble, that sovereign love has said to us and forever *yes*! The intolerable, demanding nature of faith is the mark of *grace* which is ours in faith.

I would like to add a comment here for all those who still hesitate on the threshold of Christianity, because for them in Jesus Christ there is too much mystery. So will it be necessary for them to wait for a more complete revelation? Are they still excluded from this divine choice which would be their joy? One only has to read the gospel to be sure that this is not the way that Jesus Christ demands our choice. How many there were amongst those he approached, forgave, accepted, who hardly knew a thing about him except the secret call of his coming! How many who only asked him to be healed, to save a child in danger, to give them a scrap of bread that he broke! And all of them were granted their wish, so differently from what they expected and beyond what they understood. Reread the accounts of their encounters with the Lord. The only common feature that we find in all these men and women in distress is that they all ran toward Jesus of Nazareth, with the same expectancy, with their whole life offered up and reaching out. They didn't consult him like a doctor among so many others; they didn't believe in him while maintaining the right to argue about his decisions and his gifts; they gave up everything in order to come close to him with total human respect without worrying what others would think; they threw themselves on their knees like that chief of the synagogue (Mark 5:22), they climbed up into a tree like that important tax collector from Jericho (Luke 19:4); they surprised him by their naïve, uncompromising faith, like the pagan woman from the territory of Tyre and Sidon (Matt 15:27) or the captain from Capernaum (Luke 7:9). Yes, all of these, he recognized as his own! And those that he sent away, those that he did not want, they are those who nevertheless know a lot more, but who only "know": like Nicodemus, who ardently asks questions about God—alas! just questions (John 3:1–13), like the rich young man, who wanted to give everything . . . except that which Jesus asked him to give, his riches (Matt 19:16–26), like the disciple who still had something to do before following this Master who was passing by (Luke 9:59–62). . . . In the same way, for us to be a Christian, all we need to do, whatever we've understood about him, is to commit ourselves completely with this understanding, that is to say, in complete simplicity, immediately and without reservation, to do what he tells us to do, to believe, immediately and without discussion, all that he tells us. The seriousness with which we accept this "immediately and without reservation" is the recognition that he demands because he is divine. And there is no other way for anybody to confess him.

And now a great, a formidable question remains perhaps an open one for many. How would we be able *today* to know Jesus Christ, to know this ultimate decision of God as far as we are concerned, and how would we be able *today* to choose him without reservation and conditions? If men have therefore been able to be his disciples, it is because they lived with him or because they had, like Saint Paul, the favor of seeing him in an extraordinary appearance. But we don't have that possibility. He does not come to us, we have to go and look for him in the pages of a book. Will we find him there? Can we find him in such a way as to base our whole life on these brief accounts and these few letters? We all know those troubling interrogations, even more troubling as other voices come and amplify them. Wise persons and historians, with legitimate methodological rigor, contest these very pages; they amputate them or declare them apocryphal. After all their labors, how would we know where to meet *our* Lord?

I do not pretend to be able to examine these problems of philosophy or history, still less to argue about them. I do not ignore either their existence or their complexity. I wouldn't think of contesting their reality; it is necessary to grapple with them, and those who do—not everyone!—should address them with a great and striking intellectual honesty. But when it is a question of the *ultimate* decision of God and of our *supreme* decision concerning Jesus Christ, it is truly *another* question that is asked, that we are asked. Jesus Christ is not a person who may be determined, limited or apprehended by our scientific procedures—he would no longer be the mystery of God incarnate. If he were only Jesus of Nazareth, the greatest of the initiates, we would be able to subject him to the rigors of our intellectual disciplines. For it would only be a question of knowing a human being. Following this hypothesis, we could also pass judgment on him with reference to his doctrine and, if need be, reinvigorate it by injecting new blood into it. But we are dealing with a far more serious matter here. "This concerns us, the whole of us" (Pascal). And from now on we must approach him as we would not dare approach any man, any fact, any historical event. We have to come to him with our life, because it is with his life that he has come to us. And we have to decide as we would in a decision where it is a question of life and death.

So once again, we will ask, how is this possible? Here I have only one response: the one that the church proposes. I would not know any others to suggest; for the church is precisely the community made up of those who take Jesus Christ completely seriously, meaning by that, it is a question of life or death. And this response is summed up in one word: the Bible. Where are we going to look for Jesus Christ as our ultimate decision? The church replies: in the Bible.—Let us say this in passing: all the Christian churches profess this certainty, because all of them have accepted a *canon*, a *Holy* Scripture. Some can only recognize there an acknowledged pathway of knowing Jesus Christ, while accepting some other ways; they can extend Scripture through tradition; and some can imagine that this revelation is continuous, completed by other such special revelations of the Holy Spirit. But all refer to the Old and New Testament as a place where Jesus Christ is presented as a decision of faith.—For the churches of the Reformation anyway; and, in an absolutely rigorous manner, it is through the *Bible* alone that Jesus Christ is made our contemporary. If Scripture is *Holy,* it is because it offers us the possibility of knowing the ultimate decision of our life with no looking back.—Only the possibility? For one can read the Bible without deciding anything at all, and therefore without having met Jesus *the Lord.* But one can also, from the beginning to the end of the Bible, hear the living Word of God, hear God speaking of Jesus Christ, and in Jesus Christ, and, having heard him, one can,—no, one *must* decide *for* or *against* him. Who will decide between the two alternatives? Here again, and because it really is a matter of the decision of *God* concerning us and our decision *for* God, the church replies: God himself and Jesus Christ himself; or, in other words, the Holy Spirit. For to whom else does it belong to be the *ultimate authority*? In the Bible, as in Jesus Christ, to whom would it belong "to reveal the Father if it is not the Son" (Matt 11:27), and who could not "come to the Son if the Father does not draw him" (John 6:44)?

So here again, let no one be discouraged. Certainly we need a miracle to believe in the miracle of decision and the joy that Jesus Christ represents, and we need a miracle to understand our Bibles and to recognize Jesus Christ there. But this miracle, when anyone reads,—no, when anyone *listens* to the Bible speaking so that we hear in it not stories, history, or truths, or morality, religion, but rather the supreme choice of life, the last word concerning our destiny, whoever looks in these pages for Jesus Christ *as their Lord,* sooner or later, slowly or all of a sudden, will find what they are looking for. And they will know who he is and who God is; they will hear God speaking to them *today.* "If you then, though you are evil, know how to give good gifts to your children, how much more will your Father in heaven give the Holy Spirit to those who ask him!" (Luke 11:13).

And here as well let no one shy away before this requirement to look for Jesus Christ *only there*! It has always been the intention of God that it would be like this. In the same way that he came to us in the doubtful appearance of a man, in the humility of an exceptional life, in the same way he causes us to understand this unheard of coming by the questionable means of a book—everyone knows how we can argue about books!—a special book, drawn up, finished, without possible addition. Once again, we will ask: Why this book? And the Church replies: "Because it is the book of the prophets and the apostles of *Jesus Christ!*" But why *nothing but* this book, and not other documents so close to the canonical writings of the Old and New Testaments? The Church replies: "Because it is in these *testimonies* that I heard God speak of Christ *as the ultimate decision.*" Faced with these affirmations of the Church, one is astonished and scandalized. But that is because we have not understood that it is a matter of the ultimate decision, of life and death. Those who only have this unique wealth, their life, know that it will end in death, and do not worry about all the arguments and all the objections. They go to the Bible and hear it said, "That which was from the beginning, which we have heard, which we have seen with our eyes, which we have looked at and our hands have touched, this we proclaim *concerning the word of life.* The life appeared; we have seen it and testify to it, and we proclaim to you the eternal life, which was with the Father and has appeared to us. We proclaim to you what we have seen and heard, so that you also may have fellowship with us. And our fellowship is with the Father and with his Son, Jesus Christ. We write this to make our joy complete" (1 John 1:1–4). And those people begin to rejoice.

Can Jesus Christ be this joy? Can he be that joy, because in him and through him we know that God has chosen us in his final decision? And can he be that joy because we choose him? Do we truly choose him, once and for all, with no holding back? Do you want to, can you even choose him in this way, with your double-minded hearts, which in the final analysis only ever succeed in choosing themselves? In other words: are we worthy of God, worthy that God may choose us, and are we fit for God, fit to choose God?

This essential question, which is the very center of Christianity, will be the focus in our next study.

## BIBLIOGRAPHY

Maury, Pierre. *Le Grande Œuvre de Dieu* [*The Great Work of God*]. Paris: Je Sers, 1937.
Pascal, Blaise. *Pensées*. Translated by W. F. Trotter. New York: Dutton and Co., 1958.
Reymond, Bernard, ed. *Karl Barth—Pierre Maury, Nous qui pouvons encore parler . . . Correspondance 1928–1956*. Lausanne: Symbolon, Éditions l'Age d'Homme, 1985.
Von Kirschbaum, Charlotte. *Die grosse Tat Gottes—Sechs Vorträge* [*The Great Work of God—Six Lectures*]. Zollikon-Zürich: Evangelischer Verlag, 1941.

# 9

## *Predestination*[1]

### Pierre Maury

Introduction  81

Election of God by God: Election as a Theological and not an Anthropological Doctrine  88

Elect in Christ  97

The Elect: the Goal, the Manner, the Effects of their Election  108

---

1. From Pierre Maury's *La Prédestination* (Geneva: Labor et Fides, 1957). Translated from the French by Edwin Hudson as *Predestination and Other Papers* (Richmond, VA: John Knox, 1960). Revised translation by Simon Hattrell.

# 1

## INTRODUCTION

I should like to talk to you about predestination, practically, as a pastor, that is to say, without scholastic overtones, so that this great biblical truth may help you in your ministry as it does not cease to help me in mine.

Predestination is a doctrine to which certain persons attach themselves, as much as others refuse to accept it. Among Christians many censure those who have defended it, for example Calvin, while others are surprised that the author of the *Institutes* and his followers should have maintained it with such intolerant rigor.

Outside the Church, there are even more in number who vehemently denounce predestination and accumulate arguments against it; for they see in it only determinism and fatalism, or some other kind of philosophical position.

In the face of all these misunderstandings, I should like to be able to discuss the problem with you, not in conformity with what we know of the ecclesiastical tradition, and even less in conformity with philosophical objections; not as a partisan or an adversary of the doctrine, but as one who, in accordance with Calvin's formula, wishes to submit himself to the school of Holy Scripture, and learn from it all that it is necessary to know.

It goes without saying that to have recourse to Scripture as the sole source of knowledge and the sole authority does not mean using it as a collection of texts which can stand by themselves independently of their context. That context is the whole Bible. It is a constant principle of a truly scriptural method in theology, that we must seek in the relationships between Old and New Testaments, as well as in those we discover between books, the unity and the fullness of the divine revelation. To accept the canonical principle is to accept the authority of the Holy Spirit over and within the Church—but on condition that the canon is not broken up into isolated elements.

I ought to point out to you that in these lectures you will often recognize the thought of Karl Barth. We have, in fact, for many years discussed this doctrine together, and he has propounded it in masterly fashion, infusing it with new life, in his *Church Dogmatics* II/2.

∽

We have recalled that this doctrine arouses strong opposition as well as equally passionate support. And sometimes it is the same people who adopt successively these two attitudes. For a pastor predestination is either too difficult, if not impossible, to reconcile with his conscience, or else too easy and therefore of no significance and very little use.

The first reason for these varying reactions is that most people—pastors as well as laymen—think of this doctrine *in isolation*, as if its truth—or its error—resided in itself. It becomes then the pure and simple assertion of the unfathomable—and, it must be said, crushing, abhorrent—omnipotence of God, irreconcilable with the good news which is the all in all of the Christian revelation.

We have emphasized that in submitting ourselves to Scripture we must not take its different parts in isolation, but accept the whole of its testimony, which furnishes the true exegesis of particular texts; and we shall say, similarly, that in theology it is equally impossible to split up the overall doctrinal content. This is especially true of the dogma of predestination. For it is bound up with all the other truths of the Christian faith. In fact, it qualifies them all, they and it being unintelligible in isolation. We shall come back often, directly and indirectly, to this necessity to avoid cutting up the expression of the Church's faith into a mosaic of separate doctrines with nothing to ensure their coherence and interdependence. And in particular we shall not cease to affirm that it is in their Christology that all these dogmas are related, throw light upon each other, and compel our faith.

Thus you are forewarned that the mystery of predestination will lead us and even oblige us to consider the other great doctrinal affirmations—among them those which are the most difficult to comprehend: I refer to the dogma of the Trinity, that of the two natures in Christ, and eschatology. Once again, I shall try not to give way to the temptation of sterile discussions, and shall make it my concern to show you how this great basic truth about God is, as Calvin used to say, a "practical doctrine."

∽

The second reason for the very hesitant acceptance if not the rejection of this expression of God's absolute sovereignty is that everyone speaks about it, more or less, as philosophers. The result is that we find ourselves beset by dilemmas, and as it were prevented by a sort of paralysis from professing our faith on this point.

Here, for example, are some of the philosophical notions which impose upon us alternatives that are foreign to the thought of the Bible:

(a) The notions of *time* and *eternity*. We search for the relationship between our temporal existence and what has preceded it, and the extent to which eternity determines time and the content of time. We ask how the Lord God can *fix* time (that is, render it unchangeable in advance) and if he wills to fix it. So we end up with one of the classic impasses: Are we still *free* in time if the Lord of time orders our days and the whole of our lives? And if we are free, does the Lord of time really remain Lord?

In other words, what is the significance for our *destiny* of the sovereign *precedence* of God? Does it or does it not irrevocably determine that destiny?

(b) The notion of *mystery* and of *revelation*. We seek the relationship between the mystery of God and what we are able to know. We seek to find out whether God is as absolutely unknowable as he is unknown, or if his decrees are intelligible—conformable, that is to say, with the norms of our intelligence. And we come up against other classic impasses: all those of natural religion, in which God is conceived according to our scale of human measurement, in which we are sure of finding him solely because we seek him (as if he were another human self).

(c) The very notion of *election* as conceived by the mind of man. We seek to know if it is compatible with God's divinity (his being God) that he should choose between his creatures, and thus that he should have favorites at the expense of others to whom he does not give preferential treatment. And we find ourselves in yet another classic impasse: God is not just if he does not treat everyone in the same way, if he does not respect the rights of man, which are the same for all; or in other words, what is the significance of rejection, of damnation, in a doctrine of the God of love?

To these questions I could add others. They are the questions raised by the doctrine of predestination when it is considered from the standpoint of philosophy.

I shall confine myself for the moment to emphasizing that the word *predestination* is falsified if it is used in accordance with philosophic categories of thought. On the one hand, it includes the concept of *destiny*, which, at least in our modern speech, has a completely different meaning from the way it is used in the Bible. In fact, in the thought of the West, which is heir to the Greeks, and in many of the great metaphysical systems and religions of the East, destiny has the character of a blind, anonymous force, to which the divinity is often itself subject, whereas in the Bible the *destination*—not the destiny—of man, of history, and of the universe itself, is the supremely personal work of the wise, free, and sovereign God.

Further, in the word predestination, the prefix *pre* puts well-nigh exclusive insistence on the *prior* character of the decree which destines the persons and things concerned. Now if in the Bible the eternal *before* is the beginning of all history, this is not because it preceded it, but, as we shall see, because it is *Someone* who carries out their purposes.

Even more, eternity, the precedent time, is not a finite time, which would have replaced that which succeeds it; it is a time which is not subject to the succession and annihilation which our time involves. Of the concept of eternity it is written: "The grass withers, the flower fades, but the word of our God *shall stand for ever*" (Isa 40:8). If we wanted to use the language of philosophy, we should say that in reality eternity is the eternity of our time, but if we wish to take the much better course of keeping to the language of the Bible, we shall affirm that it is the relationship, permanent as well as precedent, of the Lord of time with all our time, the presence of that Lord, free, prescient and omniscient, sovereign and faithful, in this fleeting time. Psalm 139, for example, proclaims this eternity of the God of all our days. Jesus dares to say, "Abraham rejoiced to see my day, and he saw it, and was glad." And inversely, "Before Abraham was, I am" (John 8:56, 58). And after his resurrection: "Behold, I am with you always, even to the end of the age" (Matt 28:20).

I have chosen this example of a sound method in theology—a theology which is not to be made into a metaphysic, but is to remain in conformity with God's Word—because reflections on the question of time and history have received particular attention from modern Christian philosophers and theologians.[2] But it is above all because we shall need to

---

2. Maury's footnote: Niebuhr in the United States, and very differently, in the name

consider what has been called the *actuality* of predestination, and all the problems that it raises in classical, and particularly in Calvinist, theology.

To conclude these general remarks on the need to read the Bible and to study theology, not as philosophers or scholars, but as believers, since after all the Bible itself is addressed to believers, let me add that I shall be using the word *election* rather than predestination, without however excluding the latter, since the Bible uses it (infrequently, it is true: twelve times only) and because traditional theology has used it almost exclusively. In this way also our thoughts will be less limited. For the notion of election is certainly wider, as well as more in conformity with the thought of the Bible as a whole and is at the same time more faithful to the vocabulary of the Holy Scriptures.

༄

We shall divide our study into four chapters. We shall examine first the general biblical data concerning election and related or synonymous ideas.

We shall then think about the acts of God who elects, and what they reveal to us of his nature, as well as about the special relationship which is set up in the predestination of the creature by the Creator.

We shall thus be led to examine election as it is accomplished positively and negatively in Jesus Christ.

Having thus studied the characteristics of election as an act of God, we shall consider how that act is accomplished, what are its purposes and its results: the calling of Israel and of the Church, the calling of the elect, the exclusion of the rejected, the witness of positive election, the assurance of salvation, and the proclamation of grace.

In conclusion we shall indicate what it means to believe in predestination and what the life of the elect is.

༄

How is the concept of election presented to the reader of the Bible, even one unfamiliar with theology? In the Old Testament it is applied to God's

---

of biblical theology, Cullmann in Europe, have taken up the problem of revelation and its historical character. You will perhaps recall the way in which Cullmann contrasts the linear time of biblical thought with the cyclic time of Greek metaphysics.

chosen people, whose ancestor is Abraham and all his descendants after him.

Moreover, it must be pointed out at once that other concepts are equivalent to that of election, or almost so, and that they are in all cases indispensable to a correct understanding of the latter. I am thinking in particular of the notions of grace, calling, and—here the word must be used—predestination. These concepts are essential if the election of which the theologians speak is really to be that of the Bible, namely the eternal act whose sole author is God, the act which in its operation distinguishes one man from another, the act which is essentially free and merciful, which has purpose and effects. We shall therefore utilize all these resources of biblical vocabulary.

Coming back to the idea of election properly so-called, in connection with Abraham, we shall observe first that this election is not an end in itself, but that it is for the sake of posterity that the patriarch is chosen and called, and that in his seed all the nations of the earth will share in the blessing of this man, the first of the elect; secondly, we shall note that the election of Abraham incontestably takes its place in a whole series of divine decisions which go back to the creation itself. The first eleven chapters of Genesis contain this prehistory of the election of Israel, and Hebrews 11 enumerates the witnesses of the acts of God which followed upon the calling of the first patriarch, and conceives it to be quite in order to go right back to the formation of the world by the Word of God. It also recalls that Rahab, the pagan prostitute, participated in the election of the people of God because of her faith (similarly Matt 1:5 includes her in the genealogy of Jesus), thus showing that election by God has no foreseeable limitation in history.

But it is obviously in the New Testament that we shall find the most explicit formulation of the affirmation of God's sovereign will. Although the word elect is applied only once to Christ himself—and that by his executioners, calling on him to come down from the cross if he is the chosen (elect) of God (Luke 23:35)—it is obvious that the solemn declarations that came from Heaven at the baptism and the transfiguration—"This is my beloved Son, in whom I am well pleased" (Matt 3:17; 17:5), as well as the many Johannine sayings concerning "the Son, who is in the bosom of the Father," who "came from the Father," and all Paul's Christological sayings, to which I shall return later—are taken by all the New Testament authors as being the fulfilment of the prophecy of the second Isaiah, "Behold . . . my Elect (Chosen) One, in whom my soul delights" (Isa 42:1), and more generally of the whole of the Old Testament, of the promise made to Abraham, tirelessly reaffirmed by the choosing of David, and at the worst times by the voices of the prophets. Truly, in the fullest sense of the word, Jesus Christ is the Elect/Chosen of God.

But it is no less important to emphasize that neither does the New Testament consider the election of Christ as an end in itself. Quite differently from Abraham, Jesus of Nazareth is chosen for the sake of others, and for their sake alone. Even before the Cross, his apostles around him signify the mystery of that life whose only meaning is the existence of others. And, much more, since his Resurrection, his Ascension, and Pentecost, the Church, which is rightly the convocation, the assembly of the elect, finds in Jesus Christ the place of its own election, and bears witness to it before the world.

## 2

## ELECTION OF GOD BY GOD: ELECTION AS A THEOLOGICAL AND NOT AN ANTHROPOLOGICAL DOCTRINE

We have seen that according to the Scriptures Jesus Christ sums up in himself all divine election: the election of Israel, in that he fulfils the promise of the Old Testament, and the election of the Church, in being the very focus of the life of this Church. It is this central affirmation which we shall examine, pointing out how, in some respects, it has been developed by traditional theology and how much in others ignorance has reigned or it has been watered down.

༄

Let us begin by distinguishing the elements of the act of election as we see it manifested in Jesus Christ.

First, quite simply and according to the Gospels, that act is announced by divine, heavenly declarations. "This is my beloved Son" is not just a mental picture, it is an act of God: "in whom I have placed all my affection" (Matt 3:17; 17:5). But this choice from on high—a very exclusive one: "*all* my affection"—is not only a gift and like a favor publicly shown to Jesus of Nazareth by the Almighty (the only One in the Bible who speaks from out of the cloud). This choice has a purpose. Matthew specifies it first by adding to the divine declaration at the Transfiguration the injunction, "Listen to him." The Christ is chosen by God in *order to be heard*, in the very strong sense that this verb has in the Bible: not only hearing, but believing and obeying as well. But, even more explicitly, the evangelist declares that in this man was fulfilled what had been announced by the prophet Isaiah:

> Behold my servant, whom I have chosen, my beloved, in whom my soul is well pleased. I will put my Spirit upon him, and he shall show judgment to the Gentiles. He shall not strive, nor cry; neither shall any man hear his voice in the streets. A bruised reed shall he not break, and smoking flax shall he not quench, till he send forth judgment unto victory. And the nations will hope in his name. (Matt 12:18–21)

We cannot, however, be content with such a summary definition of election: a heavenly choice with a view to a mission. Inevitably a first question arises: Who is this who speaks from the sky? What God is it who makes this choice? And what does the choice mean when it is God who makes it? To find the answers to these questions we must listen to the whole of the Bible. For it may truly be said that it is, in its entirety, the witness borne to the election of Jesus of Nazareth, to the motive and the consequences of that choice, to the revelation of its author.

What, then, do the Scriptures tell us of the God who is at once both proclaimed and hidden by the cloud out of which he speaks?

First they tell us in what manner this God who chooses us exists, what the word "exists" means when it is applied to him. It has, we find, a meaning quite different from that which it has when we apply it to our own human life, or to any other reality in the universe. God exists as *Creator*; everything that is not God exists as *creature*. This is an absolute distinction which no human pride can abolish or diminish. It is emphasized not only by the first few chapters of Genesis, but on every page of the Bible, including, for instance, those great moments of the revelation to Moses of the name of the Lord: "I am that I am" (Exod 3:14), the pronouncements of Jesus concerning the Father, and the apostolic affirmations concerning God who "framed the worlds" (Heb 11:9) and who dwells "in an unapproachable light" (1 Tim 6:16). The distinction is at once made clear, first of all by the indication that the Creator had no need of his creature in order to be himself, but that he saw that it was *good* (Gen 1:12, 18, 21, 25, 31) to bring other beings into existence over against himself, beings capable of loving him in return for his goodness which had given them life.

This is not the place to deal at length with the risk taken by the eternal and perfect Being who, as the doctrine of the Trinity reminds us, is fully self-sufficient in the mutual love which eternally unites the Father and the Son in the bond of the Holy Spirit. The outcome of this risk was the denial of the Creator by the creature, the revolt which the Bible calls sin. For the time being we shall point out only that God did not wish to be the *only one to exist*. It was by his free and sovereign will that this was so. For there is not the slightest suggestion anywhere in the Bible that God in any way needed the existence of the world and of man, whether by an internal requirement of his own nature, or by some law outside and above himself. Similarly, in the government of the world, the Lord is subject to no constraint.

But though God is subject to no compulsion in his creative decision, though it is perfectly free, by this decision he has committed himself, with the same complete freedom, to the work of his hands. He has made a covenant with it. And thereafter he finds in his creation the obligation which he has imposed upon himself. He has made this commitment with man, made in his image, charged with dominion over all created existence. This covenant binds and will bind the Lord with this man. It has and will have the strength of the faithfulness of God.

It is impossible to insist too strongly on this biblical revelation of the action of God. To ignore it is to condemn ourselves to the anguish that is caused by unknown divinities, by hidden and cruel destinies. Above all, it is misjudging the good news of God.

It is a revelation in the fullest sense, for what it announces is, strictly speaking, unbelievable. Is it believable that an almighty God should have accepted the proud rebellion of Adam—the name of all of us? Is it believable that he should have gone on loving this man who rejected his love, and that his covenant should have been capable of modification as a result of that rejection—modification in form, but not at all in the purpose it expressed? Above all, is it believable, because the covenant was made by the act of creation, and renewed immediately after the fall, that God should have linked his own existence to our lowly human existence, for it amounts to nothing less than that? Once more, it is God who freely decides that this should be eternally so. How should we contest his decision, since he has made and goes on making it, and since it is our salvation while at the same time the salvation of the world?

Here I must forestall an inevitable objection. How do we know that this is so? The first few pages of Genesis are impressive in their majestic poetry. But are they anything more than poetry? May we not and ought we not to look upon them as being another of those mythical explanations of the origin of the universe of which oriental theogonies[3] give us so many examples? And are we to take the prophets of Israel as being any more reliable in the matter of historical truth? The objection cannot be sustained: neither the Genesis narratives nor the Old Testament as a whole will by themselves reveal to us this incredible divine act, this covenant between two partners so unequal in strength as well as in love. We know nothing of this great secret until it is unveiled in Jesus Christ. It is he who is clearly the *other* being over against God, other than the Creator,

---

3. *Theogony*: an account of the origin and genealogy of the gods.

and yet not Adam with his opposition and hostility to his Creator, but the one in whom God finds his love answered by grateful love. He is the second, the true Adam, as Saint Paul says, whereas the first—ourselves—is too distorted for us to find in ourselves the knowledge of him who gave us our being. Classic theology, in asserting the full humanity of Jesus Christ in the dogma of the two natures, is not principally concerned to set before us an ethical example, but rather to bring out the very meaning of the creation, namely, an act of love, and the way we joyfully accept it in obedience; much more, it is concerned to show that the destiny of man has become—once more through the free decision of God—the same destiny as his. Here we ought to quote all the synoptic or apostolic texts in which God is linked with Jesus of Nazareth, not only by the prayer of him whom "the Father always hears" (John 11:42), but those which remind us of the complete unity of will between the Father and the Son, although reverence for the Lord never ceases to dwell in the heart of his servant: "Not my will, but yours, be done" (Luke 22:42).

We could summarize these remarks by saying that the first choice of God consists in being *voluntarily* what he is: love—not taken up with love for himself, that which the doctrine of the Trinity would be content with asserting if it were the only doctrine to be derived from the biblical revelation, but love for all those beings which the act of creation has made "other," relatively independent of their author. God chooses to love, which is the same as saying that he loves freely, or even more explicitly, that he loves truly; for could we still call it love if it were not completely free? He chooses to love, in order to be loved himself in return, voluntarily and freely, by his creature. We sometimes wonder why God has allowed us the terrible freedom to sin. And in our pride we reply by extolling our power to be ourselves. That cannot be the true answer. It would, indeed, be nothing more than the very sin that Eve and Adam committed in wanting to decide for themselves alone what was good for them, ignoring the instruction of the Word of God, and when they coveted the excellence of the forbidden fruit. No, the true answer is that God would not have created beings who really loved him if they were under any compulsion to love, if the only response to his creative will had been the acquiescence of automata, the obedience of puppets. What he must have was the wonderful response which he received in the filial obedience of Jesus of Nazareth, the first to call him *Father* in all truth, in order for his first purpose to be fulfilled, that unchanged purpose of him in whom "we live and move and have our being" (Acts 17:28), in order that the tempter of Genesis, and of the desert where Jesus withstood him for forty days, might be shown to be an impotent liar who tries to pervert the work of the Creator, asserting to God's face, as in the prologue to the book of Job, that none loves God "in a disinterested manner" (Job 1:9–11). The fact is that Job, mysteriously prefiguring Jesus of Nazareth, is the man who does really love because he is loved.

∽

Before we proceed further, there is an important point which must be made clear. For if what we have said is true, it is obvious that the decree of election—let us say predestination here if you will—is not, as classic theology has maintained, from Augustine to Luther, Calvin and the orthodox dogmatic theologians from the seventeenth to the nineteenth century—the obscure and impenetrable decision of a divinity who does not, on this point, reveal his purposes. It was because they asserted that the absolute decree of the Creator, anterior to any creation—and even to any fall, as the Supralapsarians[4] held—was the unknowable secret of an absolute power, that predestination appalled even those who defended it with the most unflagging ardor. I think of Calvin, for instance, whom the "labyrinths" of this mystery filled with a kind of holy terror. How can it be otherwise, if we know nothing, and can know nothing, of the grounds which undergird God's creative activity, if the liberty with which he loves us is replaced by the arbitrary decision of pure omnipotence? How can such a God, so far from being from all eternity the God of the covenant, appear in that eternity—and so in time, in which his purposes are worked out—as anything but a capricious tyrant, no longer the God of grace but the wielder of a crushing power who is worshipped only in terror? How can we be sure that he wishes to save the lost?

Of course I do not wish for a moment to detract from the mystery of God's sovereign liberty. He wills to act only in accordance with his good

---

4. *Supralapsarianism:* A Calvinistic view of predestination that maintains that in the "logical order of divine decrees" God decreed the election of some persons and the reprobation of others before allowing the Fall of Adam. Hence the decree of election is "supralapsarian." In supralapsarianism the emphasis is on God's predestination of uncreated and unfallen humans rather than on created and fallen humanity (sublapsarianism). Consequently, the supralapsarian view leads to the idea of double predestination: God has chosen to glorify himself by predestining certain persons to eternal life and others to eternal condemnation. See S. Grenz, et al., *Pocket Dictionary of Theological Terms* (Downers Grove, IL: InterVarsity, 1999), 110.

pleasure (Phil 2:13), but it is a *good* pleasure. His entire revelation tells us so, tirelessly. There is nothing higher than his goodness, nor anterior to it. God *loves always*, from all eternity. And his purpose, before which, and outside which, there is none other, is to ally his life to human life in a reciprocal love. Often, moved by their sense of the worship of the divine majesty, the great teachers of predestination, especially Calvin, have exalted the mystery of the *absolute decree*. But why have they turned it into a mystery as impenetrable as night, the secret of an opaque God? It is not in the darkness of an eternal obscurity that God lives and makes his decision, but in light "unapproachable," yes, but light! Darkness and night are, in the Bible, the abode of the devil, in which he prepares and makes a decision about his "works of darkness." If there is anyone who tyrannizes man, his victim, it is the devil, not the Father "who has delivered us from the power of darkness" (Col 1:15), and "has called us out of darkness into his marvelous light" (1 Pet 2:9).

It is absolutely necessary, then, to maintain the mystery of election—for God's freedom is the sovereign liberty of the Creator, which our liberty may neither dispute nor judge: "O man, who are you to argue with God?" (Rom 9:20)—provided that we know and preach that this mystery is none other than the peace that passes understanding. It is unfathomable because the love of God is unfathomable. And the only act of worship God expects of us is our wonder at a purpose that overwhelms us.

This is all the more so, as we shall see from another (the Christocentric) point of view, since the covenant made and renewed between the Creator and his creation is made at a price—also unfathomable—which is the Cross.

⁓

So the first choice[5] of God is that by which he is himself love, creating and covenanting with his creature. Let us not say that in so doing God is obeying his own nature. Doubtless from all eternity he is love, but this particular manner of loving, which consists in bringing into existence beings which are not necessary, and which are capable of denying the love which God bears them, is nothing else but sheer grace.

---

5. Maury uses the French "élection," not "choix" (choice). In other words he seems to be deliberately using "élection" to convey perhaps the Barthian sense of God's "primal" choice to be God in Jesus Christ for humanity.

We have just uttered a word that is indispensable to every notion of election, and, indeed, of predestination as well: the word *grace*. In the Bible, as you know, it designates the sovereign liberty of God and at the same time his merciful goodness, in particular the goodness of his forgiveness. It is essential always to keep in mind these two meanings. The great theologians of predestination, being as they were theologians of grace, understood this well, and that is why, in spite of all their errors, they always brought the Church back to the very center of her faith. *God is a God who forgives—a God of grace.* And as such he has a right to our praise, our service, and all our acts of thanksgiving. God is a God who acts in grace, and because that is what he is like, we trust him totally. Who will remember our sins if he has blotted them out in forgiving them? "Who shall lay anything to the charge of God's elect? It is God that justifies.... I am persuaded that neither death, nor life, nor angels, nor principalities, nor powers, nor things present, nor things to come ... nor any other creature, shall be able to separate us from the love of God, which is in Christ Jesus our Lord" (Rom 8:33, 38–39).

Here we are brought to that aspect of election in which man comes to the fore, man as the elect—or as the non-elect, as rejected. However, before coming to the second partner in the covenant and his engagement in it or his exclusion from it, I wish to lay further stress on the first contracting party in this treaty compacted by the act of creation itself, and later by the explicit acts of the contract of covenant. This is necessary because one of the most serious errors that we can commit, giving rise to the most dangerous consequences, is the belief that the doctrine of predestination is the doctrine of the *predestined*, and not the doctrine of the God who *predestines*; in other words, an anthropological, not a theological doctrine. Thus it is turned into an agonizing business of selection and sifting, since it takes place not at the Last Judgment, as has been proclaimed, but before all existence, among beings who have not asked to live and on whom their salvation or rejection is imposed by force. Whereas, if election is the expression of the free love of God, then those whom it concerns may turn without fear to that love, and "come with confidence before the throne of grace" (Heb 4:16).

Nevertheless, since it is first of all a doctrine of God and not a doctrine of man and the rights of man, it is essential that it should affirm God's prerogatives[6] without any reservation whatsoever. Now, the

---

6. Literally, "rights."

prerogatives of God are to "show mercy" as he wills; this is expressed in biblical terms as follows: "And the Lord said to Moses... I show mercy on whom I will show mercy" (Exod 33:19). Saint Paul gives us an exegesis of this proclamation which must make us tremble: "Therefore he has mercy on whom he wants to have mercy, and he hardens whom he wants to harden" (Rom 9:18). As I shall have more to say later explicitly on the subject of rejection, I shall not dwell here on the negative aspect of election. But I must insist on the indispensable, positive aspect of what its various opponents call the arbitrariness of predestination. And this positive element is the fact that the divine decision in no way depends upon the man who is its object. It is not even the case, as is claimed by some who try thus to soften what seems to them caprice, that it is because of a foreknowledge by which God would know in advance the faith or virtues of those he chooses by grace. His grace is pure, pure grace. It depends only on his "good pleasure." Such is the divine nature of God. And I know well that against that exclusive deity, jealous of its rights, everything in us rises in revolt. We want God to acknowledge, if not our merits, at least the value of our decisions, whether positive or negative. For, strange as it may seem, it is our right to damn ourselves that we sometimes claim in opposition to the right which God arrogates to himself of saving us in spite of what we are. It is true that these evil speculations—the exact opposite of the "Shall we continue in sin, that grace may abound?" (Rom 6:1), which aroused Paul's anger—no longer occupy our minds and hearts when, appalled by the realization of what we are, we find that all we can do is to ask for God's mercy, to rely on that divine right so that we may no longer fear the passing of the judgment we know we deserve. In any case, the fact is that in spite of every protestation to the contrary, grace is free. "So then it is not of him that wills, nor of him that runs, but of God that shows mercy" (Rom 9:16).

This remark must be supplemented; first, by the recognition that it is this freedom to show mercy independently of man which gives to this same man a knowledge of God. In the text from Exodus 33:19 which I have already twice quoted, it is possible to translate not "I show mercy on whom I want to show mercy," but "I shall show mercy on whom I show mercy" or "I show mercy on whom I shall show mercy." In other words, God pledges the future, his future; he wants man to know him, to trust him (Ps 130:6), to wait upon him, and to hope in him (Isa 30:18; Hos 1:6, etc.).

The second part of this act of trust in God is, if you will pardon this familiar expression, that we should not suppose him to have any ulterior motive, neither after nor before the Creation and the Fall. He remains now what he has always been. And he is what he does. This is important when we remember the distance that always separates our thoughts from our conduct, and the reservations which are always hidden away at the back of our minds even when we are performing our sincerest acts. There is no such distance, no such reservation, in God. He is what he does. He is only what he does. That which he does, he is. It is an assurance of this kind that prompted Melanchthon to say that to know God is to know his benefits.

This is what we are going to study, remembering the second form of God's choice: the choice by which he chooses to be Jesus Christ.

# 3

## ELECT IN CHRIST

### The Second choice of God: the Incarnation

In speaking of the election of Christ, we must realize that it is not enough to say that God chose Jesus Christ, but that he chose *to be* Jesus Christ. This is the second divine election. It was not only the most complete form of the covenant between Creator and creature; it was the very possibility and the reality of that covenant. For in Christ, in his twofold nature, God and man are present: God as the sovereign of free grace, man as that special creature among all others who answers for the whole of creation before the Creator. The "gathering together of all things in heaven and on earth" (Eph 1:10), as well as their reconciliation (Col 1:20), is fulfilled in him.

I am well aware that this dogma, like the dogma of the Trinity, seems totally inconceivable and even against reason. Too often has one heard such propositions as: "Jesus did this in virtue of his divine nature, and that in virtue of his human nature." Apart from the childish oversimplification of such explanations, how is it that those who put them forward do not see that they are gravely compromising the *union* of the two natures, which is as essential to the dogma as their distinction?

However that may be, the clear witness of the New Testament is that Jesus Christ is man, and that he is not "divine" but God, without endangering the unity of his person. Jesus prays *and* forgives sins; Jesus is tempted, *but* the devils are subject to him; Jesus suffers hunger, *but* he can miraculously feed the multitudes. One could point to many other signs of his double nature.

So God chose to be the man Jesus, the Creator to become a creature, the Word to be "made flesh" (John 1), he who was holy and righteous to be "numbered with the transgressors" (Luke 22:37). None of these terms should be considered as an alternative. Each must be maintained fully and strongly so that unhesitatingly we bear the same witness as the Synoptic Gospels do when they say before Jesus of Nazareth, like Peter at Caesarea Philippi, "This man is the Son of the living God" (Matt 16:16), or like John, "The Word which was in the beginning, this man is he" (John 1).

But it is the connection between election and this affirmation of the union in Christ of divine nature and human nature that we wish to analyze, and not the dogma of Chalcedon. We shall say, therefore:

(a) In Jesus Christ all previous historical elections are fulfilled. He is the fulfilment of the promises made since the creation of the world, and especially since the call of Abraham, by the Creator to his creature. With him, the "fullness" (Gal 4:4) of all times has come. He is the son of David, the son of Abraham, as the genealogy in Saint Matthew's Gospel says (Matt 1:1–17); and Saint Luke, going further back in his human family line, calls him the son of Adam, and even—the first form of the covenant—Son of God (Luke 3:23–38).

(b) Such is his full humanity. His divinity is no less evident. It is he whom God has chosen so that in him we may "see the Father" and "come to him" (John 14:6–9), the One who provokes Thomas's cry of joy, "My Lord and my God" (John 20:28).

(c) This is the grace of a choice, an election, in which alone the divinity and humanity of Jesus Christ are known: "Happy are you, Simon son of Jonah, for flesh and blood has not revealed my divinity to you, but my Father, who is in heaven" (Matt 16:17). "No one knows the Son except the Father, and no one knows the Father except the Son and those to whom the Son chooses to reveal him" (Matt 11:27); and again, "No man can come to me, except the Father which has sent me draw him" (John 6:44). One could go on from the witness of the Gospels to quote the Epistles, all of which refer to the election of those to whom it is "given" to know Christ and that which he is. Let this clear affirmation by Saint Paul suffice: "But it pleased God, who separated me from my mother's womb . . . to reveal his Son in me" (Gal 1:15–16).

## Election: Chosen in Christ

But what is much more important than these indications, which might be only a form of words, is the great fundamental fact to which the New Testament bears witness, namely, that the mystery of the life of all the elect resides *in Christ* alone. He himself said, "Abide *in me*, and I in you . . . without me you can do nothing" (John 15:4–5). But the apostolic witness, notably that of Paul, is unfaltering. I should like to go with you through a passage [Eph 1:3–14] which is of cardinal importance for the doctrine of election, and which insists on the fact that this election is centered *in Christ*. "*Blessed be the God and Father of our Lord Jesus Christ who has blessed us with all spiritual blessings in heavenly places in Christ: just as he chose us in him before the foundation of the world*" (this is clearly eternal election, and not some particular and temporary choice in the course of history), "*that we should be holy and without blame before him in love: having predestined us unto the adoption by Jesus Christ to himself, according to the good pleasure of his will*" (as in the act of creation, this is a sovereign purpose which is expressed in Jesus Christ, and for no other reason than that it is good in God's eyes), "*to the praise of the glory of his grace, by which he made us accepted in the beloved*" (once again we have "in" his elect/chosen One).[7] What happens here, *in* this Beloved, is not an arbitrary distribution of happiness and misery, of heaven and hell, but joyful glorification of the merciful liberty of the Almighty. Nothing here is nameless, unknown, the secret of an inaccessible God; all is personal and present: Jesus Christ, the beloved of God; we ourselves, represented by Christ and living in him; God, who in Jesus Christ sees us, seeks us out, and chooses us. "*In (him) we have redemption through his blood, the forgiveness of sins, according to the riches of his grace*" (once again we are placed by election where God wills us to be: in Christ crucified—the place where the wicked life is ended by forgiveness, and where the love of God appears as it really is, free from avarice and full of generosity and grace freely given); "*which he made to abound toward us in all wisdom and prudence, having made known to us the mystery of his will, according to his good pleasure which he purposed in himself, that in the dispensation of the fullness of the times he might gather together in one all things in Christ, both which are in heaven and which are on earth, in him. In him also we have obtained an inheritance, being predestined according to the purpose of him who works all things according to the counsel of his will, that we who first trusted in Christ should be to the praise of his glory. In him you also trusted, after you heard the word of truth, the gospel of your salvation; in whom also, having believed, you were sealed with the Holy Spirit of promise, who is the guarantee of our inheritance until the redemption of the purchased possession, to the praise of his glory*" (Eph 1:3–14).

I am well aware that this "*in Christ*," which recurs like a refrain in all Paul's letters, is quite foreign, not only to our language, but also to our thought, so difficult is it for us to think of ourselves as living except in ourselves. But if we fail to grasp it, if we refuse to allow it the absolutely

---

7. Literally, "beloved" (cf. Matt 3:17; Luke 9:35).

realistic character which Saint Paul, following Jesus Christ himself, meant it to have, the Gospel is nothing but a vague and inapplicable ethical treatise, an unimportant metaphysical musing.

The fact remains that it is by the decision of "divine election" that "in him dwells all the fullness of the Godhead bodily" (Col 2:9). It is also by the divine decision that we are *gathered together in Christ*, not living in sympathy, understanding, communion of thought with him, but in the most objective sense united with him. Does not Saint Paul write, "Your life is hid *with Christ in God*" (Col 3:3), and again, "(God) has . . . made us sit together in heavenly places *in Christ Jesus*" (Eph 2:6–7)?

The fact also remains that it is to Christ that we are destined by the decree of election. This is what we have just read in the text from Ephesians: "[God] predestined us unto the adoption of children by Jesus Christ" (Eph 1:5). It is even more explicit in Romans 8:29, "For whom he did foreknow, he also did *predestine to be conformed to the image of his Son*, that he might be the firstborn among many brethren."

Here it seems clear that it is to the humanity of Jesus Christ to which we are destined to be conformed. What sense, or rather what nonsense, would there be in our claiming to be made divine by our election? It is true that Peter expressly says that we are called to be "partakers of the divine nature" (2 Pet 1:4), but it is the partaking which is total communion, which it was God's purpose to grant us through the covenant, not the transmutation of our creaturely condition. By the Incarnation God became man; by election, man does not become God, but rather the normal creature, submitted, obedient, happy through him, which God had wanted in giving him his life and his vocation.

## Jesus of Nazareth, the Place of Eternal Election

It is important, at this stage, to reflect upon one of the greatest mysteries of the Christian faith. I mean the eternal election of *Jesus*, and in *Jesus* of Nazareth, as being God's eternal choice. We readily accept the idea of Christ through his Incarnation becoming the man of Nazareth, who is then chosen by God. It is to this non-incarnate Christ that we apply the mystery of predestination. And yet in limiting myself to one text—the only one in which, I may add, Christ is spoken of as "foreordained before the foundation of the world" (1 Pet 1:20)—it describes him as "a lamb without blemish and without spot." So therefore, before all existence, before any Fall, he who was crucified on Good Friday is already he in whom the redeemed are chosen. In the same way, Paul had written in the passage from Ephesians with which we began, "In Jesus Christ, God has chosen us before the foundation of the world."

Here we have to meet the objections which we mentioned in our first lecture. It seems inadmissible to us that an historical being, not yet born, should be in his very historicity the focal point and foundation of eternal election. Without going back to the notion of time, which we share with philosophers and scientists, instead of receiving it from the Bible, I wish to stress that this scriptural notion of eternal election *in* Jesus is our assurance. For this Jesus is he who was crucified. To be predestined in him, on that cross, is to have the certainty of grace upon us. Without that cross, the eternal judgment upon our lives and upon all life could only be the awful negative, the perdition to which Saint Augustine saw the whole "human mass" justly condemned. We could no longer look towards Calvary and say with the whole Church, "*Ave crux, spes unica*" ("Hail to the Cross, our only hope") for we should not know whether Jesus Christ died *for us*, or whether he was merely the victim of our damnation, of our negative election—of our rejection.

Away then with our rational objections! Let us recognize that eternal election in Jesus Christ is election in "the Lamb of God, who takes away the sin of the world," who came to be baptized by John (John 1:29), this "lamb without blemish and without spot, who truly was foreordained before the foundation of the world, but was revealed in these last times for us who by him do believe in God" (1 Pet 1:20).

## The Word Who Was in the Beginning

In order to grasp the mystery of this pre-existence—which is more than a pre-existence, rather the foreordaining of Jesus, this man whom God became, and of those who are in him—in order to discover how the doctrine of election and the doctrine of Christ fit together, it is worthwhile to stay for a moment in the first chapter of Saint John's Gospel. (There are several prologues in the Bible which are useful for the precise orientation of our minds in the faith: in addition to the long prologue to the Old Testament—and indeed to the whole Bible—constituted by the first eleven chapters of Genesis, there are the openings to the Epistles to the Ephesians, the Colossians, and the Hebrews.)

How does John's prologue begin? *"In the beginning was the Word and the Word was with God, and the Word was God."* There are three propositions here:

The first is *"In the beginning was the Word."* The Word is the origin of all existence. He is before anything else. We are not told that "In the beginning of God was the Word," for God has no beginning. But we are told, "All that has begun, is beginning, and will begin, has its beginning there." (Similarly, the Epistle to the Colossians asserts, "Christ is before all things, and by him all things consist.") So, since nothing exists before the Word, every decision, every choice, and every initiative is in him. If it is the notion of predestination with which we are concerned, we shall say that all destiny proceeds from that Word. The infirmity of our reason boggles at the inconceivable idea of a "before" which nothing precedes. But the Bible, at the beginning of Genesis as well as at the beginning of Saint John's Gospel, affirms this absolute "before"—"In the beginning."

The second proposition: *"The Word was with God."* It is for that reason that he is the beginning of all things. Because of that co-eternity with God, he is the pre-existence of all existence, the predestination of all destiny, and we can look in him for the solution of the enigma of our existence. God has no other thoughts, no other decisions, than those which he shares with the Word. For the Word was *with* God, he was not some demigod, or some wisdom independent of God. He was ceaselessly and fully *with*.

This, in spite of an apparent paradox, is what the third proposition of the prologue makes clear. The apparent paradox is that after saying "The Word was with God" Saint John goes on to say, *"He was God."* In order to avoid the paradox, we sometimes say the Word was "divine." But neither in this prologue nor anywhere else in the Bible is there any warrant for this weakening of the affirmation, "He was God." It is this mysterious presence together of the Word and God and of God and this Word (which obliges us to say, "He was with God, he was God") that the Church has attempted to explain in the dogma of the Trinity.

We are thus brought to the essential problem: who is this that pre-exists all existence, this God with God, this God in God, if I may make so bold?

Here the prologue, like the first chapter of the Epistles to the Colossians and to the Hebrews, is explicit. This Word is the One of whom, in verse 14, Saint John says, "This Word, who was with God, who was God, is *this man*." Not one of those eternal ideas with which Plato peopled a transcendent world; not some mythological personage. No! This Jesus, of whom the same apostle wrote elsewhere: "That which we have heard, which we have looked upon, and our hands have handled" (1 John 1:1). This man, who was in time and whose existence in time none of his witnesses hid, who lived for thirty-three years, whom therefore we can place in the stream of human destinies with his own destiny, this man is the eternal beginning of all existence, pre-exists it and predestines it. Similarly, in the letter to the Colossians Saint Paul says, "All things were created by him and for him, and he is before all things . . . and he is the head of the body, the Church." And the Epistle to the Hebrews declares, "Upholding all things by the word of his power. . . . You made him a little lower than the angels . . . yet he learned obedience by the things which he suffered" (Heb 1:3; 2:7; 4:8).

## Jesus Christ, the Elect Who Elects

If I have devoted to the exegesis of this passage more space than perhaps seemed necessary, it is only because the chosen one of God is there said eternally to pre-exist his own existence as well as all other existence, and because the elect are those for whose sake God chose to become the man of Nazareth, but also because in that passage Jesus is explicitly presented to us as *electing* as well as *elected*. Not only because he is in the beginning, with God, and himself God, but expressly because those among whom he is to accomplish his election are called his, that is to say, those who belong to him. Note that there is nothing here that indicates that those who are "Christ's" are all humankind. On the contrary, they are specified, distinguished. Throughout the Gospels and the Epistles Jesus is described as calling, choosing first the twelve—"You have not chosen me, but I have chosen you" (John 15:16)—and then all those who have been called by him or in his name (Rom 1:6). And when the calling is not by name, it is through the word of Christ that it comes to us—whether affirmative or negative in form. It is enough here to recall the parable of the Sower (Mark 4:3–20), according to which it is the word of Jesus that performs the sifting—not an eternal sifting, though it may become so of those who have ears to hear, and those who do not listen at all. Because it is his, a word as decisive as is the Word of God, it does not return to him void (Isa 55:11). As such, it rejects as radically as it accepts. Do we ourselves not know something of the mystery of election by God's Word alone, in the mystery of preaching, both when we listen and when we preach to others?

So Christ, the chosen one of God, is he *in whom God chooses*. How could it be otherwise, if the doctrine of the two natures is true? How could we do other than find in him the God who *calls*, as the Gospel of John never stops telling us, and the Brother whose perfect obedience is our best, and doubtless our only response to the election of grace?

## Jesus Christ, the Chosen One Rejected

And so we come to the supreme secret of election, when it is truly, uniquely, exclusively election in Christ, and by Christ. He is not, as Calvin kept on repeating, the "mirror" in which we may contemplate the secret of a purpose formed elsewhere, of the *absolute decree* issued by the Almighty in the obscurity of his majesty. Rather is it in him that everything takes place, in whom the decisions are made as much as applied. Much more, he himself is *the* unique, eternal decision.

But, here at the center of God's revelation, we find the chosen one who ceases to be chosen, or rather who is the non-elect, the rejected one, the beloved Son who is abandoned. None of those around his cross make any mistake about it. The voices cry: "Let him save himself, if he be the Christ, the chosen of God" (Luke 23:35). And he himself knows it well when he utters that awful cry: "My God, my God, why have you forsaken me?" (Matt 27:46). We must not treat lightly either the cry or the powerlessness of the condemned to come down from his cross. There is no illusion here; it is all true and definite reality. Jesus was truly forsaken. Jesus, in very truth, could not come down from the cross. Saint Paul was bold enough to give the explanation of that event which passes all understanding and is beyond all horror. He said that according to the Word of God himself as expressed in the Law, the crucified Jesus was *cursed*, "being made a curse for us" (Gal 3:13). How can we be astonished at this when God himself "made him to be sin for us" (2 Cor 5:21)? For "the wages of sin is death" (Rom 6:23). In short, we may say, we must say, that on the cross Jesus is the rejected one, that predestination is there uniquely negative. Nowhere but there, as long as history lasts, will there be any final decree of death, since, biblically, it is only at the Last Judgment at the end of history that there will take place the sifting against which there is no appeal. But for God history virtually finishes on Calvary. And the other word, "Everything is accomplished" (or fulfilled, John 19:30) formally announces it, for one can legitimately translate this by "Everything is finished."

We must not say that the Resurrection blotted out the curse, as if there had been since the ninth hour on the previous Friday only the appearance of abandonment, or as if on the third day God had rectified a tremendous judicial error committed against his eternal justice. No, the Resurrection did not abolish the Cross nor the punishment it represents. It swallowed them up—with death itself—in a quite other and unimaginable victory. We must say, in fact, that the light of Easter, too dazzling for our weak spiritual sight, lights up before all else the definitive event of Good Friday.

## The Mystery of Total Love

However, all that we have just said would be quite insufficient, falling far short of the meaning of the Cross, if we had nothing else to add.

For in the first place we would have refused to take into consideration that Christ accepted this abandonment. And who will ever be able to fathom the meaning of that acceptance in the heart of him who was truly the Son, always in communion with the Father? Moreover, throughout the Gospel, and not only during that terrible week, not only in Gethsemane, the anguish of the Passion is confessed, as well as its necessity accepted. Jesus said, "The Son of Man must suffer many things" (Mark 8:31). And later, "Now is my soul troubled, and what shall I say? Father, save me from this hour. But for this cause I came to this hour" (John 12:27). The fact that Jesus accepts this obligation ought to stop us from being shocked, as we sometimes are, at what was imposed upon him. If he consented to drink the cup, who are we to withhold it from him?

Also, and above all, we would have refused to accept, at the point where the Father and the Son are separated by the curse, the abyss of that abandonment, as terrible for the one as for the other. (On earth would not the man Abraham have suffered as much and more than Isaac if he had had to sacrifice him?) The secret of God is unveiled. God the Father and God the Son—for we must use these metaphorical names which the Gospel has given us—God himself is truly what he is. He is *love*. He keeps back nothing of his life. He surrenders it; he gives it.

How could we understand? We who do not know how to keep nothing back, even when we give our life, for we do not give it over to our enemies—that would really be to give it up, as Jesus said; at least we receive the friendship of the friends for whom we sacrifice ourselves. But if we do not understand, we can adore this utter emptying, which Jesus spoke of in these words: "God so loved the world, that he gave his only begotten Son" (John 3:16), and which inspired Saint Paul to write his hymn to the Christ who humbled himself and was highly exalted because of his self-abasement and obedience even to the death of the Cross (Phil 2:5–11). That hymn shows us that the Son of God was never so truly the Son and never so truly God as in the moment when he renounced equality with God.

In reflecting thus on the nature of Christ, have we left the subject of election for the domain of Christology? Indeed we have not, for the events of Maundy Thursday and Good Friday are in fact the revelation of *the love which elects*. Indeed here, and only here, contrary to our earlier reflections, the mystery is a mystery of the night. Jesus himself declares that this is the hour of the power of darkness (Luke 22:53). The eclipse which lasted from the sixth to the ninth hour, and the oppressive gloom of Holy Saturday, were the signs that God had given everything, and that the world was no longer living through any of the days of which the book of Genesis said that God saw that they were *good*. But we know that the light of Easter had begun to light up the new world, the old world become new.

## God's Supreme Choice

God's election is precisely that in which the Lord chooses to make alive, whatever the cost to his own life, in which he chooses to be sacrificed for man, in which he takes man's part, in which he justifies him at his own expense. God is thus so seriously and completely in covenant with his creature that he can take upon himself the penalties of the covenant into which he has entered. He loves us enough, "children of wrath" (Eph 2:3) that we are, to make of us, at the expense of his Son, at his own expense, "children of adoption," these children of God of whom John's prologue says that the Word gave them "authority to exist" (John 1:12). Free grace, sovereign and disinterested, is offered there. There is no violation of justice. Love chooses, and pays the price. And we can praise "the Father of lights, with whom is no variableness, neither shadow of turning, and from whom descends all excellent grace and every perfect gift" (Jas 1:17).

# 4

## THE ELECT: THE GOAL, THE MANNER, THE EFFECTS OF THEIR ELECTION

### What Does it Mean to be Chosen?

We come now to the anthropological aspect of election. We are going to speak of the elect, remembering always that God elects Christ, chooses, in the person of the Word, to be Jesus Christ, in order to elect *in Christ* those with whom he has entered into a covenant, of whom John's prologue, calling them "his own," asserts that they did not receive him—remembering also that there is no election, either positive or negative, *except* in this man Jesus.

What then does it mean to be elect, chosen, predestined? It means, first, being the object of an act of God which changes and determines our life, or, to put it even more simply, it means being the object of the divine will which, because it is divine, is sovereign. But it is necessary to define what God's will is as it concerns election. Can we speak of it, as we are apt to do, in the same way as we speak of our own will, merely multiplying it by infinity? Here again we are giving way to the temptation of viewing it anthropomorphically.[8] The truth is that God's will is in no way comparable with any human will. In the first place, because his will is immediate, because there is no gap between it and its object; secondly, because it is exercised without any constraint, and because no power in the world can obstruct its effective action; lastly because it is in no degree capricious, changeable, or unfaithful.

To be elect, therefore, is to be someone whom God *wills* sovereignly to be set in motion by him, to be filled by him with confidence and peace.

### The Unfaithful Elect

Is it true that in the Bible all who are chosen are people of that sort? Are we not reminded of Israel, the unfaithful chosen people, and of Judas, "one of the twelve," as the Gospel repeatedly reminds us, of whom Jesus long before his betrayal said, "Have not I chosen you twelve, and one of

---

8. As having human characteristics.

you is a devil?" (John 6:70). Are we to say, perhaps, that a mistake was made in the choice? In the great texts dealing with election (Rom 9–11, for example) this explanation is in all cases declared to be false: God is not unfaithful to his promise, and when it is given, he who receives it can be in no doubt that it concerns him. Are we then to say that election depends, if not eternally, at least in time, upon the attitude of the chosen—in a word, that the latter conditions the divine choice and can annul it? This would be to ignore the fact that man does not in any way collaborate in the grace which is given to him, that he is altogether the beneficiary, and never, even in the least degree, the author. The Gospel knows nothing of a religion of merits, even when, as Roman Catholicism holds, these are the fruits of grace already granted. Grace, according to the Bible, is a divine act which nothing in man calls for or justifies, an "operation foreign" to man, as Luther said, although it becomes his new and active life. We must then firmly renounce these weak efforts which ruin entirely the election of grace by watering it down in the hope of making it acceptable and more just. We must allow that the mystery is inaccessible to our reason. But, as we have said, it is a mystery of light, the mystery of unfathomable love.

Nevertheless, this respectful and even silent admiration, since the light that blazes forth is too dazzling—such as the sun, which our eyes cannot behold, so blinding is its radiance, though everything is lit up by its rays—even this worship cannot do away with the fact that in the Bible those who are chosen are often tainted by a certain ambiguity, uncertainty, and unfaithfulness.

## Double Election, Positive Grace and Rejection

The Bible deals with two kinds of election: positive and negative. We have already referred to them several times. The time has come to speak of them without dodging the issue, and this I shall try to do as honestly as I can.

But before we enter the "mortal labyrinths" of which Calvin spoke with such anguish, it is important to make certain incontrovertible affirmations, and to point, if I may be permitted to use the metaphor, to the entrance and exit of those labyrinths.

The incontrovertible affirmation is that God wills to save and not to destroy. "Have I any pleasure at all that the wicked should die, says the

Lord God, and not that he should return from his ways and live?" (Ezek 18:25). And, in the New Testament, "God has shut up all unto disobedience, that he might have mercy upon all" (Rom 11:32, RV). There is not, to my knowledge, any text in the Bible indicating a single and eternal will to damnation in the Almighty.

And yet it would scarcely be faithful to the Scripture to speak of universal salvation as being affirmed by the Bible. In the Gospel of love—and not only in the Old Testament—we read that "the wrath of God is revealed from heaven" (Rom 1:18). And Jesus himself speaks of the "everlasting fire, prepared for the devil and his angels," in which the accursed will complete their wicked lives (Matt 25:41).

How then shall we be able to accept these divine sayings which our hearts (and not only our minds) find contradictory? First, by noting that in the Bible there is never any parallelism between negative election, rejection, and positive election, entry into grace. It is true that both depend on God, and on him alone. Paul, in Romans, reiterates this with a rigor that we have already emphasized: "So then it is not of him that wills, nor of him that runs, but of God that shows mercy" (Rom 9:16). And concerning the children of Rebecca and Sarah, he writes, "For the children not yet born, neither having done any good or evil, that the purpose of God according to election might stand, not of works, but of him that calls. It was said unto Rebecca, 'the elder shall serve the younger'" (Rom 9:11–12).

But in spite of their identity of origin and of their utterly different destinies, it must be observed that the life of Esau, the victim of all his brother's trickery, is not presented as the counterpart of that of Jacob, the blessed of God, nor is it suggested that the hardening of Pharaoh's heart is in the same category as the choosing of Israel by God's amazing grace. In fact, none of these accounts (of which I should like to give you a detailed exegesis) is written in order to announce the final judgment upon all those referred to as being rejected. Their sole purpose is to tell the story of God's mercy towards a people—his own chosen people—which is unfaithful to his election and wishes to save itself by its works. And what a wonderful story it is, of the unshakable faithfulness of God to his promises and to his covenant.

That in the course of that long story, patient, urgent, suffering—I say all that of God—in his fervent love used instruments which seem to be the victims of that unwearied determination, Paul does not deny; he affirms it. But to anyone who protests at this "injustice," he answers:

"O man, who are you that reply against God?" (Rom 9:20). This is not, as it is ordinarily interpreted, the brutal order of the sovereign using his power to impose silence. Taking the whole context into consideration, it simply means, "O man, who are you to set yourself up against my mercy, you who belong to this very people whom I suffer and save? And, if you do not belong to this very people, if you are one of those pagans who, like Pharaoh, harden their hearts because of my mercy towards Israel, whatever you are, O man, speak not against the right, which is mine, and which I shall maintain: the right to love." Are we not reminded here of Jesus' parable of the laborers hired at various times, in which the master replies to those who are annoyed at receiving the same wage as those who have toiled for less time than they, "Is your eye evil, because I am good?" (Matt 20:15). Paul develops his argument in a way which shows that this is indeed what he means. For both Gentiles and Jews, in the astonishing dialectic of their individual as well as their common history, by their rivalry and their holy jealousy serve the purposes of God, which are the same for all, the purposes of his goodness: "For God has shut up all unto disobedience, that he might have mercy" (Rom 11:32, RV). The mysteries of history may at present be impenetrable, for "God's judgments are unsearchable, and his ways past tracing out," but that cannot lead us to doubt the riches of his wisdom and his knowledge (Rom 11:33).

Since we cannot spend any more time on this passage, which is without doubt the most explicit on the subject of predestination, let us at any rate note that the will to harden is not in God equivalent to the will to save, that we are not called on to balance the one against the other. The great misfortune, and sometimes the great unfaithfulness, of the classic teachers was that they thought that in this balance, this parallelism, they were asserting the fullness of positive grace. There must be, they thought, some people damned—they dared not say by grace, but nevertheless in the name of the sole unconditional, irresistible sovereignty of God. These must be damned, that the rest might be elect by a positive, certain, and irrevocable grace. I remember a famous professor, a fervent disciple of Calvin, saying to me once, "Let there be one man damned, just one, and all the elect will have their place in the Kingdom because of the absolute, irrevocable decree."

## An Election without Christology

How has it been possible to develop a doctrine full of what Pascal called "false windows"—those windows painted on the facades of some old houses in order to achieve an apparent symmetry? This is what we now need to look into.

We shall see here again the weakness, which we have noted several times, of a doctrine of election that is independent—I mean unconnected to Christology, or rather one that sees in the redemptive person of Christ nothing but the executor of a purpose formed without him in the darkness of the mystery of God.

If Saint Augustine, Saint Thomas, Calvin, Luther, and Pascal had seen more clearly that God has no other thought, no other will, no other action than Jesus Christ, that he dwells in Christ in the fullness of the Godhead, if they had, like Saint John of the Cross, repeated the famous sentence, "God never speaks any word but one, and that is his Son," doubtless they would have given us a description of "the grace that is in Christ Jesus" (2 Tim 2:1) by the decision of God, a description that would not make us tremble, but would fill our troubled hearts with peace. And if they had known more clearly that to be elected is to be elected in Christ, and that this election of which we are the object is as freely sovereign, and as independent of any merit on our part, as the absolute decree whose power they venerated, but could not praise, because it was utterly hidden from them, doubtless they would not have caused so many misunderstandings, nor such anxiety in the consciences it was their intention to reassure, and in the long run such ignorance—relative at least—of the love of God and of his Son.

## Christ the Rejected, Rejected for Us

In Jesus Christ we cannot see a man "fallen from grace" (Gal 5:4). And the reason for this, the only true reason, is that he himself accepted that fall, the dereliction of Calvary, that he accepted it so that no sinner might be deprived of positive grace, that they all might know for themselves and for their fellows that God is love—yes, but strictly and solely in Jesus Christ.

Does this give rise to yet another objection? For, alas, it seems that we always have some objection to raise against unqualified grace. Are we asked how we are to explain those refusals of grace by the elect, of which the Bible—and life!—furnish us with so many examples? How are we to understand the falling, the unrepentant backsliding which runs like a thread throughout the history of the chosen people? We shall answer fully in accord here with the great classic teachers of predestination that no one, on earth, can pronounce a sentence of damnation. It is at the judgment seat of Christ, and only at "the great day," that the irrevocable verdict will be given, and the mystery of election unveiled. The vicissitudes of history are indeed linked to that mystery, for nothing that happens can be hidden from the "secret counsel of God." But they do not exhaust the mystery. To be convinced of this it is sufficient to reflect on the very different occasions when God's choice—his positive election—is manifested. Who would have seen in Saul of Tarsus, on the eve of his journey to Damascus, anything but a persecutor of the Church of God, the very type of the rejected? And yet, from the moment when the living Christ laid hold upon him, from the moment when he met Ananias, he became for the whole Church the example of mercy freely given. History—God be praised!—is not finished.

Is it objected that in any case history is irrevocably fixed, if God is the sovereign author of his grace? Here again we must remind ourselves that predestination does not mean the determination of individual destinies after the manner in which a cause determines its effect in the chain of earthly events. The teachers of the church were well aware of this when they discussed continued predestination, and in particular the actuality of predestination. If we keep to the biblical facts, it is manifest that God is a living God, concerned with everything that happens to those to whom he is bound by his covenant, and not the distant monarch who, having uttered his sovereign command, thereupon allows it to be applied by some minister of his power, with no possibility of anything being changed in his decree. Sufficient proof of this is to be found in the poignant complaints, or the occasional cries of joy, by which, through the mouths of the prophets of Israel, the Lord complains or declares his love as he lives with all his being every circumstance of the life of his people. It is enough to hear how those prophets, certain as they nevertheless are of the eternal knowledge and power of the Lord, use the most naïve and the crudest of anthropomorphisms to describe the part taken by God in the lives of those who are his (for example, the "repentance of God" which so embarrassed those classic predestinarians who believed in the unalterableness of the eternal decree); those prophets who, however, all glimpsed the day when the ungodly, now become "the ransomed of the Lord," will "return and come to Zion with songs and everlasting joy" (Isa 35:5–10). Or take the words of Jesus on the patience of God in history: "Let the fig tree alone this year also . . . and if it bear fruit, well; and if not, then after that you shall cut it down" (Luke 13:8–9); and, on the same theme of patience, the affirmations of Rom 9:22, and notably 2 Peter 3:9: "The Lord . . . is longsuffering toward us, not willing that any should perish, but that all should come to repentance."

Knowing, then, that everything that takes place in Christ is of the very nature of the human life of Christ, who, "though he were a son, yet he learned obedience by the things which he suffered," let us remember also that he becomes "the author of eternal salvation unto all them that obey him" (Heb 5:8–9). Thus shall we receive from him who fulfilled the times on the cross the full evidence that at the last day he will make it appear how, and how closely, time is linked to eternity, in the hands of the good Lord alone.

Does this mean that sooner or later election always becomes positive, and that all we have to do is to wait for the inevitable day when grace will work conviction in everyone? Once again the Bible says nothing of the kind. It takes grace too seriously. But because of that very seriousness we can appeal to the Bible, believe in it, and trust in the Lord.

## The Historical Fulfilments of Election: Israel and the Church

It tells us so by reminding us in the first place that election is not primarily individual, dealing out heaven and hell to isolated lives, but that it is God's way of directing the history of his *people* Israel, and of that *people* of Christ crucified, resurrected, and ascended to the right hand of God, which is the Church. It even makes it clear that it is the historical relationships of Israel, the Gentiles (that is, all those who are not the children of Abraham), and the Church, which are the true "mirror of election." This election is made manifest in the ending of the separation between Jew and Gentile in the positive unity of the Church (Eph 2:18). To be elect is to belong to the new Israel, included in the covenant, the first-fruits of the Kingdom in which finally God will be all in all (1 Cor 15:28).

## Rejection and Grace in the Life of Each of the Elect

We are next told, by being reminded—which is even more important—that the elect and the castaways are not, at least until the end of history, two categories of persons, but two resolutions of God upon the life of each of those whom he calls. Each Christian knows that in Christ his life is rejected, and pardoned by grace; faced with the Cross he sees himself to be the unpardonable executioner of his Savior, and at the same time the pardoned sinner whom nothing can separate from the love of God, which is in his Son (Rom 8:39). This double discovery the Christian never ceases to make and to make anew; it is not double because two simultaneous presences confront each other within us, nor yet because we are at one and the same time, in a sort of immobilized co-existence, both the chosen and the castaway; it is rather the *movement* of faith itself, of repentance and peace, a continual passing from death to life, which leaves with us no false peace "as the world gives" (John 14:27), but lets us "come boldly to the throne of grace" (Heb 4:16).

The seriousness of the Christian life is thus the seriousness of one who does not wish that "the cross of Christ should be made ineffectual" (1 Cor 1:17), to them that perish foolishness, but to them that are saved the power of God.

I am well aware that this interpretation of election, which makes each of the elect the object of rejection and of grace, will shock many as being unscriptural. Doubtless Calvin would have firmly rejected it.

However, I wonder how an attentive reader of the Bible can avoid it. To quote but one formal example, let us recall the text we have already mentioned: "I buffet my body, and bring it into subjection, lest . . . I myself should be a castaway" (1 Cor 9:27). But whose is the hand that writes these words, keeping such strict watch over his Christian life? The same who declared to the Romans that everything, absolutely everything, in regard to his salvation, depends not on man, but on "God who shows mercy" (Rom 9:16). And what does the Apostle Peter say, after speaking of God as "him that has called us by his own glory and virtue" (2 Pet 1:3, RV)? He says this: "Give diligence to make your calling and election sure" (2 Pet 1:10). Does not each of us find quite simply, as we read our Bibles, how justly we are condemned, how truly we are lost? But then when we straightaway ask for forgiveness we receive the witness of the mercy that is shown towards us in spite of everything. So we may say that rejection is not a formal decree of God who is love, but the reverse side of the sincere love which the Father bears towards us, the shadow that is non-existent in itself, yet very real, the shadow which is ceaselessly dissipated on our path by Jesus, the light of the world—or, if I may be permitted to take up again the image I used just now, the exit from the labyrinth in which we lose our way, but which is always the grace which abounds more exceedingly (Rom 5:20).

I would not have any of us make light of these declarations because they seem to be contradictory, or of this constant passing from death to life, life being always stronger than death, life being the calling of God which casts out the devils. It is a serious matter to be tempted, to be a sinner, to deserve damnation. But I am bold enough to say that it is a still more serious matter to be loved by God, to know it and to rejoice at it "with joy unspeakable and full of glory" (1 Pet 1:8).

## The Calling of the Elect

And now, bearing in mind all that we have said and emphasized, let us try to arrive at a definition of the one who is elect.

First, I would not want to say that to be elect is to have discovered the "still waters," but to have been led there by God, who "leads us in the paths of righteousness for his name's sake" (Ps 23:1–3).

So election is always the path by which God leads us towards his mysterious and freely-given righteousness. It is thus also the path to that "righteousness of the Kingdom" (Matt 6:33), in seeking which we are seeking to be like Jesus Christ, which is our family likeness, the path by which those who are justified by grace seek to be righteous towards their fellow Christians in the way God is righteous: not, that is to say, in accordance with some law, but in charity. If, as we have indicated, election and vocation are for the Bible related and almost synonymous words, we shall not be surprised that election is invariably with a view to service. To those who were troubled about their personal predestination Calvin pointed, as the sign and criterion of election, to fidelity to their calling. Moreover, in the Scriptures, election is *always* a call to obedience, thanksgiving, and brotherly love. God chooses in Christ "to the end that we should be to the praise of his glory."

## The Assurance of Salvation

It is only when we have understood the predestination of the elect as being "conformed to the image of his Son" (Rom 8:29), as the conforming of the servant to the destiny of his Master (John 13:16), that it is possible and necessary to stress one of the aspects which are dearest to those who have spoken of it most enthusiastically, namely, the assurance of salvation. Indeed, they were and are right, those who find in the decision of God their only certainty of his grace. Having nothing themselves, they have everything in Christ. Able only to ask forgiveness, they have received grace to render thanks. Mocked by the world, troubled in their consciences, they can nevertheless say, "I know in whom I have believed" (2 Tim 1:12). In the peace and joy to which the divine mercy daily brings them back, they fear "neither death, nor life" (Rom 8:38).

## The Witness of the Elect

Much more, they are, by the very movement of their daily passage from death to life, constrained to witness. It was certainly not by chance that Saint Paul, right in the middle of his great study of election, underlined the necessity of preaching: "How shall they believe in him of whom they have not heard? And how shall they hear without a preacher? And how shall they preach, except they be sent?" (Rom 10:14–15).

## Election in the Pastoral Ministry

Now that I have come to the end of this brief introduction,[9] let me come back to my opening remark. I said that I wished to speak as a pastor. And perhaps you have been thinking that I have allowed myself to be carried away into too many abstract speculations. However, in all that I have been trying to put before you, I have never forgotten that election is concerned with living souls, those which are entrusted to each of us in his own place so that we may assure them that the Father makes them "meet to be partakers of the inheritance of the saints in light, and has delivered them from the power of darkness, and has translated them into the kingdom of the Son of his love" (Col 1:12–13), and also that they may learn

---

9. Was this a "tongue-in-cheek" remark by the preacher Maury with perhaps a smile on his face?

from us what good works God has prepared for them to walk in, since it is by grace that they have been saved, and not by works, lest anyone should boast, for they have been created in Jesus Christ (Eph 2:8-10).

I have not forgotten this. I should like to conclude with three brief points in affirmation of it. We must not preach predestination; that would be the worst error, and also the worst betrayal, I believe, of the Gospel. We must preach Jesus Christ, in whom, from everlasting to everlasting, "dwells the fullness of God," and who "dwelt among us, Living Word, full of grace and truth" (John 1:14). We must preach salvation and not damnation, the forgiveness of sin rather than sin, and call our flocks unceasingly to the renewal which daily manifests our new birth, which is a "birth of God" (John 1:13). We must learn to proclaim the Man of Sorrows, abandoned, rejected *for us*, "who was delivered up for our offences, and was raised again for our justification" (Rom 4:25). And we must dare to do what, in spite of his love—because of his love—he so often dared to do: I mean, to speak of the holy wrath of God who is "of purer eyes than to behold evil" (Hab 1:13), and who "is not mocked" (Gal 6:7), for "it is a fearful thing to fall into the hands of the living God" (Heb 10:31). As we dare to do all this, which does not mean preaching hell, let us remember that, as Jesus did, we cannot but proclaim deliverance from the forces of hell by the victorious Christ.

May I add that one of the greatest joys that the mystery of election in Christ gives to a pastor is that of *believing for others*? Often, in the face of clear evidence of the hardening of one of our parishioners, or even of our whole congregation or our Church, we are discouraged and lose hope. Then let us remember that God's mercy is stronger than the strongest resistance, and that it is "in the heavenly places," which means "far above all rule and authority and power," that his unspeakable love chooses how it will love and save. There is here, I think, a change in outlook, which the doctrine of election authorizes us to make. Let me illustrate this by an example. One day an Indian friend of mine asked me, "Do you believe that Gandhi is saved?" In all good conscience I could only reply, "I do not know if Gandhi is saved. But I know that Jesus Christ is Gandhi's Savior. And I believe in Jesus Christ."

Another way of believing in election in our ministry—although the hardest, it ought to be the sweetest—is to really *pray* for others as for ourselves. If everything depends on the heavenly decision, how could we recognize it except by appealing to it, for others as well as for ourselves?

In short, it was not in order to maintain a theological standpoint that I refused at the beginning to discuss election in philosophical terms. The secrets of God are not for those who delight in arguing about them. The mystery of the Kingdom of God is known only to those to whom it is given (Mark 4:11). And they are not "the wise and prudent," for God hides these things from them, to "reveal them to babes" (Matt 11:25).

Only faith can receive the witness, as the assurance, of election. They belong to the realm of faith, which by this election in which it believes, is itself brought into being, nourished, and increased.

One last word to my dear colleagues in the ministry: our election is also the charge which is entrusted to us. Sometimes it is a crushing burden. And we wonder if we are capable and worthy of bearing it, or even if we have been called to it. At such times let us recall, for our peace, and to make us more faithful in our service, that it is "by God's grace that we are ministers of Jesus Christ to the Gentiles, ministering the Gospel of God" (Rom 15:16). We shall never be pastors except through his mercy, but through his mercy we shall be so with joy.

# PART 3

*Contemporary Reflections on the Theology of Election in the Work of Karl Barth and Pierre Maury*

# 10

# *Pierre Maury, Karl Barth, and the Evolution of Election*

## Mark Lindsay

DURING THE WINTER OF 1942, and with another period of military service with the Swiss Army auxiliary troops imminent,[1] Karl Barth completed the second part-volume of *Church Dogmatics* II. He had started work on it in the summer semester of 1939, as Europe was on the cusp of yet another devastating conflict. Without a doubt, the outbreak of war in September of that year, and the ramping-up of various resistance activities over the subsequent months, influenced Barth's material considerations while he wrote. As Barth put it in a letter to Otto Weber ten years later, everything that was taught in the Basel lecture theatre during this period "had a wartime background."[2] In stark contrast to the caricaturized "other-worldly Barth," whose theology was, so it is claimed, so devoted to the transcendent God as to be of no earthly (and certainly no political) use, the Barth who wrote *CD* II/2 was deeply implicated in a total and unconditional (*unbedingt*) resistance against the Hitler regime.[3] Ingredients to that resistance included his letters of support to churches in war-torn countries, his sheltering of Jewish refugees and provision of

---

1. Barth's duties were to guard bridges and public buildings against sabotage. See Barth, "Current Discussions," 77. He was not, by his own admission, very good at it—on one occasion allowing an entire squad he was leading to desert their posts to a hut where there was a warm fire and hot coffee! See "Witness to an Ancient Truth."

2. Barth to O. Weber, June 20, 1949 (Busch, *Karl Barth*, 301).

3. Busch, *Karl Barths Lebenslauf*, 316.

financial aid to various underground networks in Germany, and, later in 1944, his attempts to secure rescue for Hungarian Jews facing deportation to Auschwitz.[4]

Nonetheless, and despite his hatred of Nazism and unqualified opposition to it, in this second volume of his Doctrine of God Barth exemplifies the principle he articulated in 1933: doing theology "*als wäre nichts geschehen*" (as if nothing had happened).[5] The overtures of global war and the fight against fascism did not intrude directly into his dogmatic work. On the contrary, he continued with his determination to refuse Hitler and Nazism any constitutive theological significance at all. Barth had built this principle into his theological methodology when, in the second volume of his Prolegomena he had insisted that the critical function of dogmatic theology must be the summoning again of the teaching Church to the voice of Jesus Christ alone.[6] Through her dogmatic task, the Church is called to return ever anew to the Word and revelation of God that has been spoken in Jesus Christ, and to which the Old and New Testaments attest. It is vital, that is, that the Church is called by her dogmatic work to return to a Word *already spoken*, and not to try to find a new word for a new day. Barth wrote:

> The requisite modernity and actuality of dogmatics cannot consist in the fact that it speaks to any time, to any political, intellectual, social or ecclesiastical structures of the present, as though this can be the standard of Church proclamation.... In the present, and for the sake of the present, dogmatics will not inquire about the voices *of* the day, but about the voice of God *for* the day.[7]

Consequently, in the lectures that formed the basis of the Doctrine of God and indeed all volumes of the *Church Dogmatics*, Barth felt himself to be constrained by Scripture and not by political events, no matter how tumultuous those events may have been. In this light, the particular emphasis of *CD* II/2 was neither the war that was raging throughout Europe nor the ideological heresies that underpinned Nazi Germany's

---

4. See especially chapter 7 of Lindsay, *Covenanted Solidarity*; Kranzler, *The Man Who Stopped the Trains*.
5. Barth, *Theologische Existenz heute!*, 280.
6. *CD* I/2:812.
7. *CD* I/2:843.

aggression, but, rather, a locus of dogmatic enquiry that gave Barth "much pleasure, but even greater anxiety"—specifically, the doctrine of election.[8]

This is not, however, the whole story. Barth's theology was never as contextually vacant as his methodology might suggest. Notwithstanding his consistency in dogmatically enquiring after the voice of *God* rather than the voice of the *day*, there is nonetheless an undercurrent of political rhetoric evident in Barth's treatment of election if one is prepared to see it. Perhaps, then, Barth's anxiety about this locus was not only due to the evangelical weightiness of the subject, and not only because of how sharply he departs from his Reformed predecessors, but also because of his awareness that in his manner of treating it he *does* say something of specific political intent that stood in opposition to and accusation against the prevailing Nazi racism.

In this chapter, then, I will do three things. *First*, I will outline the major aspects of Barth's articulation of election. *Second*, I will describe the political-rhetorical context in which Barth's reflections on this locus were made. And *third*, I will show how the particularities of Barth's doctrine of election stand in self-conscious resistance to the National Socialist war against the Jews.

## THE OUTLINES OF DOCTRINAL REVISION

Volume 2 of the *Church Dogmatics* was not the first time that Barth had attempted an articulation of the doctrine of election. In his first cycle of dogmatics in Göttingen (1924–1925), Barth introduced the idea of God's gracious election as the counterpoint and correspondent to the dialectical veiling and unveiling of God in his revelation (§18).[9] Election and its "parent" locus of predestination most properly exist dogmatically in the closest possible relationship to the doctrine of God and not, as Lutheran theology typically has it, subsumed within the doctrine of creation as a corollary to justification.[10] We will return shortly to why Barth thinks that this must be the case. In truth, however, his treatment of the doctrine

---

8. *CD* II/2:x.

9. Barth, *Göttingen Dogmatics* (hereafter *GD*), 440–41.

10. *GD* 444. Bruce McCormack argues that it is this placement of the locus of election that exemplifies the classically Reformed stance that Barth takes here (McCormack, *Karl Barth's Dialectical Theology*, 371).

in these early years of his academic life betrays what he knew at that time to be true of himself: that his knowledge of theological texts was limited and that "he had much catching up to do."[11] As he put it in 1927, "I can now admit that at the time I did not even have a copy of Reformed confessions, and I certainly hadn't read them."[12] His way of catching up was to read incessantly. "All day long I am reading pell-mell hundreds and hundreds of pages: Heim, Thomas Aquinas, Fr. Strauss, Alex. Schweizer, Hermann."[13] What he relied on most, though, was a turgid volume of Heinrich Heppe's *Reformed Dogmatics*. His later reflections on this are now well-known: "It was out-of-date, dusty, unattractive, almost like a logarithm table, dreary to read . . . [but] fortunately I did not dismiss it too lightly. I read, I studied, I pondered and found myself rewarded by the discovery . . . of a dogmatics which had both form and substance (*Gestalt und Substanz*)."[14] With this as his primary educative text, and then with two lecture series on John Calvin (1922) and the Reformed confessions (1923) under his belt,[15] it is hardly surprising that his first attempt at an explication of the doctrine of election was thoroughly Reformed in nature.

What it means to say that Barth's early understanding of election was Reformed can be gleaned from the way John Calvin himself approached the matter. "The covenant of life," says Calvin in his *Institutes*, "is not preached equally to all, and among those to whom it is preached, does not always meet with the same reception."[16] In other words, Calvin, who (like Barth) was a preacher at heart, was exercised by his pastoral observation that some people respond to the gospel while others do not. The "primary function" of his doctrine of election is thus to explain this curiosity. As McGrath says, "Calvin's predestinarianism is to be regarded as reflection upon the data of human experience."[17]

---

11. *GD* xvii–xviii.

12. Barth in Busch, *Karl Barth*, 129.

13. Letter from Barth to E. Thurneysen, March 20, 1924 (Barth, *Revolutionary Theology*, 176).

14. Barth, "Foreword." See also Busch, *Lebenslauf*, 167.

15. Barth, *Theology of John Calvin*; *Theology of the Reformed Confessions*.

16. Calvin, *Institutes* 3.21.1.

17. McGrath, *Christian Theology*, 452. See also his very similar comment in *Reformation Thought*, where he states: "Calvin's predestinarianism is to be regarded as *a posteriori* reflection upon the data of human experience, interpreted in the light of Scripture, rather than something which is deduced *a priori* on the basis of preconceived

This is fundamentally the same point that Barth wishes to stress in his Göttingen lectures. Predestination is, "in its strict form," nothing other than the truth that there is a "twofold possibility," according to which there exists "the simultaneous presence and succession of faith and unbelief in different individuals or even in the same individual." One might know or not know, believe or not believe—and whatever the situation may be, it is *God's* work through his eternal election of grace.[18] For Barth, of course, this twofold possibility is inextricably connected to his dialectics of revelation, in which God's self-revealing is always *hidden*. Christ is always revealed only in the incognito—ἐν ὁμοιώματι σαρκὸς ἁμαρτίας ("in the likeness of sinful flesh" [Rom 8:3])—only where it could be explained away as something *other than* the revelation of God.[19] One should note, too, that unbelief—the seeing *only* the incognito and *not* the revelation—is, in Barth's view, the far more reasonable path. It is only *belief* that needs any explanation.

But for the Barth of the Göttingen years, the key point to note is that this twofold possibility is, as it was for Calvin, an utterly real possibility. Rejection, or reprobation, may be accorded an unequal weighting relative to election—God's Yes speaks even out of the No, and his No tends always towards his Yes. Nonetheless, anyone who wishes to hold a Reformed view of predestination must, says Barth, be willing to say both A and B. God's Yes and No are both real possibilities for him to declare over different individuals, or even over the same individual at different times.[20]

And to whom is this twofold possibility spoken? Or, to put it otherwise, who does Barth consider to be the objects of divine election and reprobation? At this place, Barth does part company with Calvin, Heidegger and others of his Reformed predecessors. Against their view that there are two separate and fixed groups of "certain people" who are eternally predestined by God to be *either* blessed believers *or* damned unbelievers, Barth insists rather that "both are both."[21] Exemplifying the

---

ideas concerning divine omnipotence. Belief in predestination is not an article of faith in its own right, but is the final outcome of scripturally informed reflection on the effects of grace upon individuals in the light of the enigmas of experience" (McGrath, *Reformation Thought*, 138 39).

18. GD 443–44.
19. GD 446.
20. GD 452, 455, 461.
21. GD 454.

actualism[22] with which Barth's entire theological method is pervaded, predestination becomes, under this scheme,

> exclusively a basic description of God's dealings with us, of his free and actual use at every moment of the possibility of saying Yes or No to us, of electing or rejecting us, of awakening us to faith or hardening us, of giving us a share in the hope of eternal salvation or leaving us in the general human situation whose end is perdition.[23]

As McCormack notes, Barth's understanding of election in his Göttingen years is thus actualistic and theocentric.[24] The focus is upon the *freedom* of *God's* actions and decisions. Insofar as it is God's determination for any individual that is in play, the doctrine is theocentric. Insofar as those determinations are freely made moment by moment for individuals, and not eternally mandated for fixed groups of people, it is actualistic, and consequently at odds with Barth's Reformed tradition.

What is strikingly missing from Barth's doctrine of election at this time is any substantive reference to Jesus. Indeed, in the whole section there are only half a dozen references to him. One might well also complain that Barth's early view of actualistic election provides no ground for salvific certainty—that according to this view one could find oneself to be in one moment elect and in the next moment rejected. Barth came to recognize that these two problems are not different but are in fact the two sides of the *same* problem. Thus it was precisely by taking more seriously the person of Jesus Christ, by reorienting his doctrine Christologically, that this double-sided deficit was overcome. This, indeed, is what Barth does in *CD* II/2, to which we now turn.[25]

By the time Barth began work on volume 2 of the *Dogmatics*, nearly fifteen years after his first cycle of dogmatics in Göttingen, two things of determinative significance had happened. *First*, Barth had radically reconstructed his theological method on the basis of his (re-)discovery of the ancient doctrine of the *an-enhypostasia*.[26] True, Barth had begun

---

22. See Hunsinger, *How to Read Karl Barth*, 30–31.

23. *GD* 455–56.

24. McCormack, *Karl Barth's Dialectical Theology*, 373.

25. It should be noted that Barth did not address the problem of election at all in his Münster dogmatics of 1927, so it is only possible to compare what he said in Göttingen with his more developed articulation of this doctrine in the *Church Dogmatics*.

26. Editor's note: The human nature of Jesus totally dependent on the divine nature of God.

to orient his theology according to this formula from as early as 1924. When compared with his *Romans* period, for example, Barth's Göttingen theology gave the incarnation as such much greater significance; it was not relegated simply to a mathematical point, as it had been in 1922. Yet curiously, and as we have seen above, this incarnational reorientation did not at the time decisively impact Barth's understanding of election, which remained fundamentally oriented towards the free activity of God.

But *second*, in 1936 Barth travelled to Geneva, where he heard French pastor Pierre Maury deliver a lecture on the topic "Election and Faith" at the International Calvin Congress.[27] In that lecture, in which Barth heard of a very different type of twofold election from that which he had taught previously—one that located both election and reprobation in Christ himself—Barth was provided with the resources he needed to bring his Christology to its logical conclusion. Bruce McCormack and Matthias Gockel have shown that the full articulation of this logic was not presented until the early 1940s.[28] Nonetheless, the foundations of Barth's theological reorientation—in which election was grounded Christologically, or, to put it another way, in which Christology became the fountainhead of the knowledge of the electing God—can be traced back to 1936.

In *CD* II/2, Barth adopts, and takes significantly further, Maury's conception of election. It is not simply that Jesus Christ is the locus of both election and rejection, although he is indeed that. Maury crystallized for Barth the "particularist" nature of the knowledge of election; that is, that "outside of Christ, we know neither of the electing God, nor of His elect, nor of the act of election."[29] But Barth went somewhat further, with his Christologically-circumscribed doctrine of election speaking directly, and controversially, to the eternal being of God himself. In order fully to grasp the revolutionary significance of Barth's doctrine, as well as its utility as a piece of theological resistance, we need to consider both of these aspects.

27. Editor's note: The lecture was later translated by Charlotte von Kirschbaum and published under the title *Erwhählung und Glaube*. The lecture is also translated for the first time into English in this book. Note that Barth in all likelihood missed the delivery of the lecture itself, and had to read the text afterwards. See Reymond, *Karl Barth—Pierre Maury*, 94.

28. McCormack, "Seek God," 263; Gockel, *Barth and Schleiermacher*, 162n14.

29. Maury, "Erwählung und Glaube," 7. EF 44. "Particularism" is one of the four motifs that George Hunsinger uses to construct a hermeneutical framework for interpreting Barth's theology. See Hunsinger, *How to Read Karl Barth*, 32–35.

Consistent with his dialecticism, as well as with what he had gleaned from Maury, Karl Barth's most obvious dogmatic move was to orient both the Yes and No of God's electing will towards the person of Jesus Christ. Jesus is identified as the (only) one in whom both our election to mercy and our rejection to judgment cohere. He is the one truly elected man, and also the only one who is truly rejected. Of no one else can either be said, without this Christological caveat.

And so Barth is led to claim that the particular partner "over against God which cannot be thought away . . . which is so now adjoined to the reality of God that we cannot and should not say the word 'God' without at once thinking of it" is none other than the man Jesus of Nazareth.[30] In particularist terms, Jesus of Nazareth is "not merely *one* of the elect, but *the* elect of God" (*nicht nur ein Erwählter, sondern der Erwählte Gottes*).[31] He writes:

> Of course, the election has to do with the whole of humanity . . . although materially it has to do first and exclusively with the one man. . . . Thus the doctrine of election is rightly grounded when in respect of elected men as well as the electing God it does not deal with a generality or abstraction in God or man, but with the particularity and concretion of the true God and true man.[32]

In order properly to ground our understanding of election, we are therefore to look solely, and at least in the first instance, to Jesus Christ, who is himself "the 'particularity and concretion of the true God and true man' and therefore as such the true elect man."[33]

But by the same token, this Jesus is also the (only) one who is truly rejected. Living by the grace of God, Jesus is also "branded by the wrath of God [*der von Gottes Zorn Gezeichnete*]." He is at one and the same time, and the one because of the other, "*both* the elected *and* the rejected of God [*zugleich der von Gott Erwählte und der von Gott Verworfene ist*]."[34] Both Cain and Abel, Isaac and Ishmael are to be found paradigmatically in him.

Importantly, while this has infinite soteriological benefit for humankind, it also has profoundly devastating consequences for God's own

---

30. *CD* II/2:8.
31. *KD* II/2:125; *CD* II/2:116.
32. *CD* II/2:51.
33. *CD* II/2:58-59.
34. *KD* II/2:403-4; *CD* II/2:366 (emphasis mine).

being. For Barth, God's freely-willed condescension into humanity's own state means that God "has declared Himself guilty of the contradiction against Himself in which man was involved"; that God has taken upon Godself the "wrath and judgment to which man had brought himself; that he took upon Himself the rejection which man had deserved; that He tasted Himself the damnation, death and hell which ought to have been the portion of fallen man."[35] This is not merely a suffering of these things *alongside* humankind, but bearing of them *in humanity's place*. No wonder that Barth calls this a "severe self-commitment"![36] And of course, all this accrues most properly to the one Jesus of Nazareth. As the electing God and elected man, he is also the elected *and rejected* man, on behalf of all. To be genuinely and actually lost and abandoned is in fact the concern *only* of Christ. There is, says Barth, "only one Rejected, the Bearer of all man's sin and guilt . . . and this One is Jesus Christ."[37]

In the first instance, by locating the traditional polarities of predestination—election and reprobation—*in Christ* rather than in individuals or in distinct groupings of people, what this move did was to undercut the existential uncertainty with which this doctrinal locus has typically been infused. Instead of making the determination of election or rejection subsidiaries of, on the one hand, an unknowable *decretum absolutum*[38] (Calvin) or, on the other hand, an unstable actualism (Barth's Göttingen iteration of the doctrine), Barth was able to honor the real seriousness (or the serious reality) of God's righteous judgment and yet at the same time affirm the unqualified scope of God's grace.

In a very real sense, this Christological revision of the old theory of "double predestination" was a thoroughgoing refutation of Reformed orthodoxy, though, as we have seen from Maury, not one that was unique to or even initiated by Barth himself. Remarkably, however, it has not been the most controversial aspect of Barth's understanding of election. As suggested earlier, Barth's truly revolutionary contribution within this particular locus concerns the eternal being of the triune God. Orienting

---

35. *CD* II/2:164.

36. Barth, *Schwerste Kompromittierung*; *KD* II/2:179.

37. *CD* II/2:346, 352. The German original—"*Jesus Christus ganz allein ist*"—renders more sharply the singularity of Jesus's determination as the only truly rejected one (*KD* II/2:382).

38. Absolute decree.

this doctrine with reference to Jesus Christ leads him to posit a fundamentally new way of thinking about God's very nature.[39]

According to Bruce McCormack, who has taken the lead in identifying the inescapable logic of Barth's doctrine, Barth's identification of Jesus Christ as the subject of election means that election is not simply the sum of the Gospel but part of the very doctrine of God itself. Election is not simply something that God does, but is rather intrinsic to God's very being. Indeed, it is the decision by which God constitutes God's own being as triune.[40] In McCormack's words, "God is what he is in the eternal decision of election and not in a state or mode of existence that is above or prior to that decision."[41] That is, the works of God *ad intra* (the Trinitarian processions) find their ground in the first of the works of God *ad extra* (election). This entails a dissolution of the distinction between the *Logos asarkos* and the *Logos ensarkos*,[42] between the *incarnatus* and the *incarnandus*.[43] The *Logos asarkos* never exists—not even within the immanent Trinity—*in abstracto* but only ever in the most complete identification with the *Logos incarnandus*. In the incarnation of the Son, therefore, what happens economically has ontological bearing on what is

---

39. Robert Jenson concurs: "The doctrine of election, of God's choice 'before all time,' is for Barth the center of the doctrine of God's being" (Jenson, *Systematic Theology*, 1:140).

40. See also Eberhard Jüngel: "As the beginning of all the ways and works of God, God's election of grace is not only an *opus Dei ad extra* (external work of God) or, more precisely, an *opus Dei ad extra externum* (external work of God directed outwards); it is at the same time an *opus Dei ad extra internum* (external work of God directed inwards). For election as such is not only a decision made by God and in so far an election which also certainly concerns him; it is equally a decision which affects God himself. . . . If, then, the decision of the election of grace not only affects elect humanity but also at the same time affects God in a fundamental way, then it is dogmatically consistent to treat the doctrine of predestination as a part of *the doctrine of God*" (Jüngel, *God's Being is in Becoming*, 83–84). See also Myers, "Election, Trinity," 121–37.

41. McCormack, "Election and the Trinity," 223.

42. Editor's note: The Second Person of the Trinity pre-exists his incarnate, or creaturely state. He is "without flesh" or asarkos as well as "enfleshed" or ensarkos.

43. See, for example, McCormack, "Grace and Being," 92–110; "Seek God." Note, however, that McCormack vehemently insists that he does not thereby collapse the economic Trinity into the immanent Trinity, as Paul Molnar suggests. "Talk of a 'collapse' makes it sound as though there is only an economy of God, that there is no immanent Trinity 'before the foundations of the world.' On the contrary, to say that God constitutes Himself as the triune God in an *eternal* act is to say that God is already triune before He creates a world" (McCormack, "Let's Speak Plainly," 63–64).

and has been true for God *immanently*.⁴⁴ Importantly, McCormack does not claim this as his own idea, but as the necessary consequence of Barth's own logic.⁴⁵

Paul Molnar and George Hunsinger have railed against this, both from the perspective of their own exegesis of Barth's theology and also on account of the dogmatic implications of such thinking. Paul Molnar has taken issue with McCormack's view that, for Barth, the immanent Trinity is a product of God's will to be *pro nobis* in the economic Trinity.⁴⁶ Rather, Molnar contends that the immanent Trinity is vital to any theological endeavor to retain God's being in freedom. Indeed, if McCormack is correct that (in Barth's theology) God's work *ad extra* determines His being *ad intra*, then His being as triune is dependent upon the world which needs saving. Moreover, if God's being *a se* is predicated upon God's decision and action *pro nobis*, then God is thus constituted anthropomorphically and not in terms of His own free perfection.⁴⁷

Similarly, George Hunsinger has rebutted McCormack's interpretation of Barth, by questioning the dissolution of the *Logos incarnatus* and the *Logos incarnandus*. To say that Jesus Christ is the subject of election does not mean, argues Hunsinger, that the eternal Son had no existence apart from election. On the contrary, a perichoretic Christology would enable one to maintain a distinction between the eternal Son and the Son *incarnatus*, "who mutually coinhere with one another without losing their real distinctiveness."⁴⁸ The decision for election *emerges from* God's perfect triunity, but does not constitute it.

For our purposes here, however, what is more important than the debate itself, and even more important than the (hermeneutical and dogmatic) rights and wrongs of both sides, is the fact that Barth's doctrine of election underwent a foundational and (therefore) material change between its first articulation in Göttingen and its final statement in *CD* II/2. Moreover, it is crucial to recognize that this change was not initiated by Barth's own theological creativity, as though he were reflecting *in*

---

44. Jones, "Obedience, Trinity, and Election," 149–50.

45. Editor's note: The *logos asarkos* means the Word prior to taking on human flesh, whereas the *logos incarnandus* is yet to be incarnated.

46. Dempsey, *Trinity and Election*, 7.

47. See Molnar, *Divine Freedom*. Much debate centers around how one defines, respectively, God's Self-*determination* and His Self-*constitution*.

48. Dempsey, *Trinity and Election*, 10. See also Hunsinger, "Election and the Trinity."

*abstracto*.⁴⁹ On the contrary, it was precipitated by (among other things but perhaps pre-eminently) Maury's lecture in 1936, and then refined in its articulation by the peculiar historical circumstances in which the doctrine was developed. It is to this more contextual matter of authorship to which we now need to turn.

## THE DEVELOPMENT OF THE DOCTRINE IN ITS POLITICAL CONTEXT

As we have already seen, volume 2 of the *Church Dogmatics* was not the first time that Barth had attempted an articulation of the doctrine of election. However, the circumstances in which Barth developed the doctrine for the second time around were markedly different from what they had been in 1924–25. Barth's Göttingen years coincided, of course, with the disastrous Weimar Republic, about which Barth had initially been enthusiastic. As McCormack has put it, "however 'watered down' the socialism represented by the Weimar government.... Barth regarded it as the best hope for Germany in the present."⁵⁰ Yet in spite of his keen observations, his theology was not greatly impacted by the German politics of the day. In part, his initiation into teaching left him little time for anything other than lecture preparation. As Barth himself said, "I had to work in my study." He "simply had no time at this point for entangling [him]self in political activity."⁵¹ What did exercise him somewhat more were the toxic politics of his own university, not least within the Faculty of Theology. Relations were constantly strained, particularly with Carl Stange and Emanuel Hirsch. In early 1924 Barth wrote to Thurneysen that, "my relation to the faculty is now worse than ever.... All of them are now outspokenly unfriendly to me. But that is mutual."⁵² In other words, during his first attempt to write about election, Barth was more occupied with securing his own place in the university than thinking through the doctrine with any great novelty.

During the writing of *CD* II/2, on the other hand, Barth could not fail to be affected by wider issues. There was, indeed, a global seriousness

---

49. From an abstract point of view.
50. McCormack, *Karl Barth's Dialectical Theology*, 200.
51. Barth, *Letzte Zeugnisse*, 42–43; Busch, *Karl Barth*, 148.
52. Letter from Barth to Thurneysen, March 4, 1924 (Barth, *Revolutionary Theology*, 175).

to the context from which Barth could not, and did not want to, escape. The production of this volume, and the lectures by which it was comprised, was bookended by, on the one side, *Kristallnacht* (November 9–10, 1938) and, on the other, by the start of Operation Barbarossa (June 22, 1942), the beginnings of the mass deportation of Jews, and the construction of the Bełżec and Chełmno *Totenlargeren*[53] (December 1941 to March 1942). Far more than internal faculty back-biting, Barth's writing and thinking about the doctrine of election was thus contextualized by the early horror of the *Sho'ah*. Critically, Barth's theological work was affected by this context.

In 1938, Hitler had removed the last voices of moderation from his government. Initially, the Economics Minister Hjalmar Schacht, Foreign Minister Konstanin von Neurath, and Generals Fritsch and Blomberg, had acted as brakes on some of the regime's more extreme policies. But within five years of his seizure of power, Hitler had had enough. With their removal, the way was open for the more radical elements of the Party to enact their ideas. As a result, the Jews

> were attacked simultaneously on all fronts with a fervor unknown since the heady . . . days of 1933. Boycotts were organized, Aryanization was accelerated, legislation was promulgated, deportation was attempted, and for the first time large numbers of Jews were herded into concentration camps.[54]

Then, coinciding with the annexation of Austria, Adolf Eichmann was given chief responsibility for solving the "Jewish problem."

In the midst of all this, Barth was not silent. In March 1938, during his Gifford Lectures, he noted (in agreement with Article 14 of the Scottish Confession) that "under certain conditions there may be resistance to the political power, which is not merely allowed but enjoined by God . . . a resistance which can in certain circumstances be a matter of opposing force by force."[55] He continued this tone later in the year in his *Rechtfertigung und Recht*, in which he made plain that when faced with the specter of an unjust State, the Church's fulfillment of its political duty takes shape in "responsible decision about the validity of laws, responsible

---

53. Death camps.
54. Schleunes, *Twisted Road to Auschwitz*, 216.
55. Barth, *Knowledge of God*, 229.

care for their maintenance, in a word, political action, which may and must also mean political struggle [*politischen Kampf*]."[56]

In the aftermath of *Kristallnacht*, Barth put into practice precisely this action on behalf of the persecuted Jews of Germany. In stark contrast to the rest of the Confessing Church, which stood by wordlessly, Barth perceived the destruction of the synagogues as the tipping-point, after which it was only ever possible for the Church to say an uncompromising No! to Nazism. "The really decisive, biblical-theological" reason for the Church's necessary rejection of National Socialism was its inherent anti-Semitism. "Were this to stand by itself it would in itself justify the sentence: National Socialism is the anti-Church fundamentally hostile to Christianity."[57] But Barth went further. Recognizing that anti-Semitism was an attack not only upon the Jews but upon the Jew Jesus, he condemned it roundly as the sin against the Holy Spirit and, as such, the most damnable blasphemy.[58]

Of course, once the war itself had begun, Barth was back in Switzerland. This, though, did nothing to stop his efforts on behalf of both Christians and Jews in the Nazi-occupied territories. He sheltered Jewish refugees in his own home in Basel, gave financial support to Gertrud Staewen's underground resistance movement, and coordinated an attempt in 1944 to help rescue Hungary's Jews from deportation.[59]

These, then, were the contextual bookends within which Barth was busy writing his revised doctrine of election between 1939 and 1942. Unlike the surrounding circumstances within which the Göttingen doctrine had been prepared, these events did not fail to make their mark upon Barth, both personally and theologically. As we shall see in the final part of this chapter, Barth's articulation of election during the war years, far from being doctrinal abstraction, was in fact itself a piece of theological *Widerstand*.[60]

---

56. Barth, "Rechtfertigung und Recht," 44.
57. Barth, "Die Kirche," 89–90.
58. Barth, "Die Kirche," 90.
59. See, e.g., Lindsay, *Covenanted Solidarity*, 241–70; *Barth, Israel, and Jesus*, 31–35.
60. Resistance.

## ELECTION AS RESISTANCE

To say that Karl Barth's doctrine of election resonates politically as resistance against Nazism is, admittedly, a statement that needs some nuancing. First, it does not mean that Barth was seeking to write this volume as a self-conscious manifesto against Hitler. His intent, here as in all his writings, was to serve the Church by expounding as best he could the biblical witness to Christ and, in so doing, subjecting dogmatic tradition to the scrutiny of Scripture. Neither Barth's doctrine of election, nor any other part of the *Church Dogmatics*, is what we could properly call "political theology."

Nonetheless, that does not thereby render it apolitical. I have argued elsewhere that Barth seems to have been dogmatically unmoved by the Holocaust. At least, it does not rate a mention in any of the places one might expect it to appear, for example in *CD* III/3 where Barth speaks of radical evil in the form of *das Nichtige*.[61] I remain convinced that this constitutes a serious lacuna in Barth's theology. However, I do not therefore claim that Barth was either unaware of or unaffected by the horrors of Nazism. That the geo-political context of World War Two and the *Sho'ah* was not foregrounded by Barth in his dogmatic work does not mean that it was of no material consequence to him.

Moreover, the historiography of the Nazi period provides ample evidence that there was not just one type of resistance to Nazism, but many. To put it otherwise, the grammar of resistance can be parsed in multiple ways. The syntax of that grammar includes Hans and Sophie Scholl's "White Rose" movement and the von Stauffenberg bomb plot of July 1944. But it also includes non-violent resistance, such as the innumerable acts of *Kiddush haShem* (sanctification of the Name) performed by Jewish prisoners in the concentration camps, as well as intellectual dissent like that of Helmut von Moltke's Kreisau Circle. As von Moltke wrote to his wife Freya on the eve of his execution, he and his fellow conspirators were condemned not for what they had done but for what they had *thought*.[62] It is in this context of what we might call "discursive resistance"—resistance that deliberately *encounters*, and then *counters*, the prevailing ideology—that Barth's re-visioning of election in the context of Nazi anti-Semitism can be located. And so we must ask, in what way(s) was *CD* II/2 discursively resistant against the Nazis' war on the Jews?

61. See, e.g., Lindsay, *Reading Auschwitz with Barth*, 90–114.
62. Moltke in Plant, *Taking Stock of Bonhoeffer*, 13.

To answer that question adequately, it is necessary first to recognize the extent to which the Nazis deliberately appropriated Christian language of election. As far back as *Mein Kampf*, Hitler had indicated the need for a reversal of revelatory potential. The Jew, he said, was "an incarnate denial of the beauty of God's image," whereas Aryans were "that highest image of God amongst His creatures."[63] Consistent with a long Romantic tradition of seeing *Gottestum* in *Deutschtum*,[64] this divinization of the German *Volk* stood in dialectical necessity alongside the demonization of the Jews. Thus Reinhold Krause could say, in his infamous Sports Palace speech of November 1933, that on the one hand the "essence of Jesus's teaching . . . is completely identical with the demands of National Socialism," and on the other "the Jews are not the people of God."[65] Both statements stood side-by-side in necessary and logical harmony, indeed the one entailing the other.

But the Jews were not, of course, simply sidelined by the Nazis into covenantal ambiguity; they were determined for destruction, with their final moments resembling a macabre parody of the Last Judgment. In Matthew 25, Jesus places the "sheep" (those who enter the kingdom) on the right hand of the Son of Man while the "goats" (those destined for punishment) are turned to the left. So it was also at the Nazi death camps. Raul Hilberg notes that, when trains arrived at the Auschwitz platform, the SS sent to the left those who were to be taken immediately to the gas chambers. Those who were to be, at least temporarily, spared from execution were sent to the right.[66] Nazi selection procedures thus intentionally reflected biblical imagery and iconography of divine judgment. The difference, though, was that the Jews *as a people* were by definition determined for the "left" (that is, death) because National Socialist ideology had already decreed them to be *Lebensunwertes Leben* (life unworthy of life).

Barth's rhetoric speaks directly to this situation. We are forbidden, he insists, to conceive of election as "bifurcating into a rightward and leftward election." Left and right, insofar as they denote one's determination for life or death, are meaningless in Barth's system except in relation

---

63. Hitler, *Mein Kampf*, 157, 322.
64. Divinity in Germanness.
65. See Mosely, *Nations and Nationalism*, 112–13.
66. Hilberg, *Destruction*, 626. See also Weiss, "Selection at Auschwitz."

to Jesus himself. There is a leftward election, but its object is God and not humankind, neither as a whole nor in any of its individuated parts.[67]

Barth's doctrine also repudiated the arrogation of divinity that Nazism, and SS officers in particular, had taken to themselves. Elie Wiesel writes:

> Substituting himself for God, the SS man sought to recreate the universe in his own image. His endeavor was ontological. . . . One was not allowed to look into the eyes of an SS man, for the SS man was God, and you cannot look into the face of God, just as you cannot look into the face of the Angel of Death.[68]

This image of *potentia absoluta*[69] was precisely what was reflected on the ramp at Auschwitz, and indeed anywhere that guards and soldiers could decide with arbitrary justification whether a particular Jew would in that moment live or die. But Eberhard Busch reminds us that Barth's doctrine of election was predicated, not upon the idea of God as *potentia absoluta* but upon the decision of God that is in its entirety and very foundation utterly *gracious*.[70]

In other words, in his rejection of both bifurcated election and of a subject of electing will who could be correlated to "power in itself," Barth confounded the rhetoric and reality of Nazi ideology. But Barth's counterpoint to the National Socialist dogma of election went further, in particular in its elevation of the Jews' covenantal status.

Precisely what place post-biblical Israel has in Barth's schema has been a matter of intense debate. Katherine Sonderegger is the most articulate exponent of those who view Barth's theology to be ultimately if unwillingly infected by anti-Semitic prejudice.[71] Eberhard Busch and I, on the other hand, represent a smaller number of interpreters who read Barth far more positively than that, with his doctrine of election providing abundant evidence of his theological solidarity with the Jews. While

---

67. *CD* II/2:172.
68. Wiesel, "Some Questions," 11.
69. Absolute power.
70. Busch, *Unter dem Bogen*, 451. Barth had written, "It is not 'the Almighty' who is God. . . . For the 'Almighty' is bad, as 'power in itself' [*potentia*] is bad. The 'Almighty' means Chaos, Evil, the Devil" (Barth, *Dogmatics in Outline*, 48).
71. Sonderegger, *Jesus Christ Was Born a Jew*.

space precludes a thorough treatment of this topic here,[72] the key aspects are readily identified.

*First*, Barth insists that there is a community that is elected in Christ, identifiable with "the reality of both Israel and the Church."[73] While this community offers a twofold witness, yet nonetheless it is manifestly a *single* community, the unity of which is inviolable.

> Just as the electing God is one and the elected man Jesus Christ is one, so too the community as the primary object of the election which has taken place in Jesus Christ is one (*Eine*). Everything that is to be said of it in the light of the divine predestination will necessarily result in an emphasizing of this unity.[74]

In other words, the strict dichotomy drawn by Nazis and the *Deutsche Christen* between Jews and Christians—and even the dichotomy often drawn by the Confessing Church during the *Kirchenkampf* between Christians and Jewish Christians—becomes meaningless in Barth's work. The one indivisible God who elects, elects one indivisible community. There are not two covenants but one—"the bow of the one covenant"[75] of grace arches over both Israel and Church. The reason for this is inherently Christological, for Jesus, who is the very personification of the covenant within which both exist,

> is the promised son of Abraham and David, the Messiah of Israel. And he is simultaneously the head and Lord of the Church. . . . In both these characters he is indissolubly one. And as the One he is ineffaceably both. As Lord of the Church he is the Messiah of Israel, and as the Messiah of Israel he is Lord of the Church.[76]

*Second*, and in consequence, it becomes impossible to identify the Church or Israel as, independently of the other, objects of election or reprobation. On the contrary, "the object of election is neither Israel for itself nor the Church for itself, but both together in their unity."[77] Even in the so-called "Judas Passage" of §35, in which Judas is portrayed as the

---

72. Interested readers can consider the arguments put forward in Busch, *Unter dem Bogen*; Lindsay, *Covenanted Solidarity*, esp. 199–240.

73. *CD* II/2:196.

74. *CD* II/2:197.

75. *CD* II/2:199.

76. *CD* II/2:197–98.

77. *CD* II/2:199.

archetypical figure of rejection and as the one who *prima facie* represents Israel, Barth insists upon a radical continuity between the "elect" and the "rejected." Judas is, says Barth, "undoubtedly a disciple and apostle," standing in the closest proximity to the Church. Indeed, Jesus was betrayed to death, not by Judas acting alone but *"from within the Church."* At this most decisive juncture, "the Church stands and acts in identity with the Israel which rejected its Messiah, together with the heathen world which allied itself with this Israel." At this point, therefore, "the apostles have to share the guilt of Israel and the Gentile world."[78] If *election* accrues to both Israel and Church in indissoluble unity, then so too does the burden of rejection. It is not, and cannot be, borne by just one covenantal partner alone.

*Third*, Barth grounds his doctrine in the freedom of God to act independently of humanity's actions. God is, in this sense, radically *apathetic*, insofar as that means that His eternal determination *pro nobis* is not altered or undercut by human resistance and disobedience. Whereas traditional supersessionism has relegated Israel to judgment and reprobation on account of the Jews' rejection of the gospel, Barth on the other hand steadfastly contends for God's faithfulness. Not by any action of its own can Israel "annul the covenant of mercy . . . [or] alter the fact that the promise is given and applies to itself, than in and with the election of Jesus Christ *it and no other* is God's elected people."[79] Neither biblical nor post-biblical Israel, says Barth, can "create any fact that finally turns the scale against their own election."[80] The uncaused freedom of God to act in this way, for this people, is why, irrespective of their faith or unbelief, "the fundamental blessing, the election, is still confirmed. . . . [The] final word is one of testimony to the divine Yes to Israel."[81]

---

78. *CD* II/2:459-61. As David Demson has rightly said, whenever Barth uses the term "lost and defecting Israel," he "uses it as the middle term between the first term 'lost and defecting apostolate' and the last term 'lost and defecting mankind'" (Demson, *Hans Frei und Karl Barth*, viii). That is, neither Barth's hermeneutic nor his discourse makes it possible to conceive of the idea of a "rejected Israel" in isolation.

79. *CD* II/2:237.

80. *CD* II/2:209.

81. *CD* II/2:15.

## CONCLUSION

It would, of course, be disingenuous to suggest that Barth's theology of Israel was a model of philo-Semitic sympathy. There are places within his doctrine of election in which both his phraseology and his logic are susceptible to profound critique. Indeed, Barth has not escaped censure from some for betraying a latent supersessionary intent. Nonetheless, it is equally evident that his articulation of election—conceived and taught during the first murderous phase of the Holocaust—represented a singularly powerful counterpoint to Nazi ideology. That within both the pages of his *Dogmatics* and, in the first instance, the lecture theatres of his university he would contend for the continuing election of the Jews, their inviolable solidarity with the Church, and their determination by God for *life* and not death, was in remarkable contrast to the anti-Jewish propaganda that had infected European Christianity for centuries.

As we have seen, the theological bases on which Barth was able to affirm this were grounded in: a) God's eternally free decision to be for and not against us—a decision that is not vulnerable to human vicissitudes but that, on the contrary, is secured by God's sovereignty—and b) the unifying bond of the One who is both subject and object of election, Jesus Christ the *Yahweh-Kyrios*, Messiah and Lord.

We have also seen, however, that Barth's doctrine of election evolved over time. The form of its articulation in Göttingen was far more actualistic and far less Christological. One of the consequences of this was a prioritization of the status at any given moment of the *individual*, which meant that *community* of the elect, and Israel in particular, was removed almost entirely from consideration. All this changed, though, when Barth read Pierre Maury's 1936 Geneva paper. From that point on, Barth was no longer able to conceive of election apart from its *locus* in Jesus Christ, and the community that is thus elected in him.

The Göttingen view of election would have been acutely ill-equipped to oppose Nazi ideology. In contrast, the revised form of that doctrine, as Barth taught it between 1939 and 1942, was so thoroughly reconstituted around the eternal Yes of God in Christ Jesus that it was able, as we have seen, to offer "discursive resistance" to both National Socialist anti-Semitism and the Holocaust to which it gave birth. Maury's influence on Barth must therefore rightly be seen to have had not only theological but also political ramifications. If, in a post-Holocaust world, some of the language and logic of *CD* II/2 needs further revision, we should nevertheless not lose sight of how sharply it countered the prevailing prejudices. And for that we have not only Barth, but also Pierre Maury, to thank.

## BIBLIOGRAPHY

Barth, Karl. "Die Kirche und die politische Frage von heute." In *Eine Schweizer Stimme 1938-1945*, by Karl Barth, 69-107. Zurich: TVZ, 1985.
———. *Dogmatics in Outline*. Translated by G. T. Thomson. London: SCM, 1955.
———. "Foreword." In *Reformed Dogmatics: Set Out and Illustrated from the Sources*, by Heinrich Heppe, v-vii. London: Allen & Unwin, 1950.
———. *The Göttingen Dogmatics: Instruction in the Christian Religion*. Vol. 1. Edited by H. Reiffen. Translated by G. W. Bromiley. Grand Rapids: Eerdmans, 1990.
———. *The Knowledge of God and the Service of God*. London: Hodder & Stoughton, 1938.
———. *Letzte Zeugnisse*. Zurich: EVZ, 1969.
———. "Rechtfertigung und Recht." *Theologische Studien* 104 (1989) 5-47.
———. *Revolutionary Theology in the Making: Barth-Thurneysen 1914-1925*. Translated by J. D. Smart. London: Epworth, 1964.
———. *Theologische Existenz heute! (1933)*. In *Vorträge and kleinere Arbeiten 1930-1933*, edited by M. Beintker, et al., 271-363. Vol. 3 of *Karl Barth Gesamtausgabe*. Zurich: TVZ, 2013.
———. *The Theology of John Calvin*. Translated by G. W. Bromiley. Grand Rapids: Eerdmans, 1995.
———. *The Theology of the Reformed Confessions*. Translated by D. J. Guder and J. J. Guder. Louisville: Westminster John Knox, 2000.
Barth, Markus. "Current Discussions on the Political Character of Karl Barth's Theology." In *Footnotes to a Theology: The Karl Barth Colloquium of 1972*, edited by H. M. Rumscheidt, 77-94. Waterloo, ON: Corporation for the Publication of Academic Studies in Religion in Canada, 1974.
Busch, Eberhard. *Karl Barth: His Life from Letters and Autobiographical Texts*. Translated by J. Bowden. Grand Rapids: Eerdmans, 1994.
———. *Karl Barths Lebenslauf: Nach seinen Briefen und autobiographischen Texten*. Munich: Christian Kaiser, 1975.
———. *Unter dem Bogen des Einen Bundes: Karl Barth und die Juden 1933-1945*. Neukirchen-Vluyn: Neukirchener, 1996.
Calvin, Jean. *Institutes of the Christian Religion*. Translated by H. Beveridge. Grand Rapids: Eerdmans, 1995.
Dempsey, Michael T., ed. *Trinity and Election in Contemporary Theology*. Grand Rapids: Eerdmans, 2013.
Demson, D. E. *Hans Frei and Karl Barth: Different Ways of Reading Scripture*. Grand Rapids: Eerdmans, 1997.
Gockel, Matthias. *Barth and Schleiermacher on the Doctrine of Election*. Oxford: Oxford University Press, 2006.

Heppe, Heinrich. *Reformed Dogmatics: Set Out and Illustrated from the Sources.* London: Allen & Unwin, 1950.

Hilberg, R. *The Destruction of the European Jews.* London: W. H. Allen, 1961.

Hitler, Adolf. *Mein Kampf.* Translated by J. Murphy. London: Hurst & Blackett, 1939.

Hunsinger, George. "Election and the Trinity: Twenty-Five Theses on the Theology of Karl Barth." *Modern Theology* 24.2 (2008) 179–98.

———. *How to Read Karl Barth: The Shape of His Theology.* New York: Oxford University Press, 1991.

Jenson, Robert W. *Systematic Theology I: The Triune God.* New York: Oxford University Press, 1997.

Jones, Paul D. "Obedience, Trinity and Election: Thinking With and Beyond the Church Dogmatics." In *Trinity and Election in Contemporary Theology*, edited by Michael T. Dempsey, 138–61. Grand Rapids: Eerdmans, 2013.

Jüngel, Eberhard. *God's Being Is in Becoming: The Trinitarian Being of God in the Theology of Karl Barth.* Translated by John Webster. Edinburgh: T&T Clark, 2001.

Kranzler, D. *The Man Who Stopped the Trains to Auschwitz: George Mantello, El Salvador, and Switzerland's Finest Hour.* New York: Syracuse University Press, 2000.

Lindsay, Mark R. *Barth, Israel, and Jesus: Karl Barth's Theology of Israel.* Aldershot: Ashgate, 2007.

———. *Covenanted Solidarity: Karl Barth's Theological Opposition to Nazi Antisemitism and the Holocaust.* New York: Peter Lang, 2001.

———. *Reading Auschwitz with Barth: The Holocaust as Problem and Promise for Barthian Theology.* Eugene, OR: Wipf & Stock, 2014.

McCormack, Bruce L. "Election and the Trinity: Theses in Response to George Hunsinger." *Scottish Journal of Theology* 63.2 (2010) 203–224.

———. "Grace and Being: The Role of God's Gracious Election in Karl Barth's Theological Ontology." In *The Cambridge Companion to Karl Barth*, edited by John Webster, 92–110. Cambridge: Cambridge University Press, 2000.

———. *Karl Barth's Critically Realistic Dialectical Theology: Its Genesis and Development 1909–1936.* Oxford: Clarendon, 1997.

———. "Let's Speak Plainly: A Response to Paul Molnar." *Theology Today* 67 (2010) 57–65.

———. "Seek God Where He May Be Found: A Response to Edwin Chr. Van Driel." In *Orthodox and Modern: Studies in the Theology of Karl Barth*, edited by Bruce L. McCormack, 261–77. Grand Rapids: Baker Academic, 2008.

McGrath, Alister E. *Christian Theology: An Introduction.* 2nd ed. Oxford: Blackwell, 1997.

———. *Reformation Thought: An Introduction.* 3rd ed. Oxford: Blackwell, 2001.

Molnar, Paul. *Divine Freedom and the Doctrine of the Immanent Trinity: In Dialogue with Karl Barth and Contemporary Theology.* London: T&T Clark, 2002.

Mosely, Carys. *Nations and Nationalism in the Theology of Karl Barth.* Oxford: Oxford University Press, 2013.

Myers, Ben. "Election, Trinity and the History of Jesus: Reading Barth with Rowan Williams." In *Trinitarian Theology After Barth*, edited by Myk Habets and Philip Tolliday, 121–37. Eugene, OR: Pickwick, 2011.

Plant, Stephen J. *Taking Stock of Bonhoeffer: Studies in Biblical Interpretation and Ethics.* Aldershot: Ashgate, 2014.

Schleunes, K. A. *The Twisted Road to Auschwitz: Nazi Policy Toward German Jews 1933–1939*. Urbana: University of Illinois Press, 1970.

Sonderegger, Katherine. *That Jesus Christ Was Born a Jew: Karl Barth's "Doctrine of Israel."* University Park: Penn State University Press, 1992.

Weiss, Martin. "Selection at Auschwitz." *United States Holocaust Memorial Museum*, May 5, 2009. Audio recording and transcript. http://www.ushmm.org/information/museum-programs-and-calendar/first-person-program/first-person-podcast/martin-weiss-selection-at-auschwitz.

Wiesel, E. "Some Questions That Remain Open." In *Comprehending the Holocaust*, edited by A. Cohen, et al., 9–20. New York: Peter Lang, 1988.

"Witness to an Ancient Truth." Interview with K. Barth. *Time*, April 20, 1962.

# 11

## *Harmony without Identity*
## A Comparison of the Theology of Election in Pierre Maury and Karl Barth

MATTHIAS GOCKEL

IN *CHURCH DOGMATICS* II/2 Karl Barth praises Pierre Maury's essay from 1936 ("*Election et Foi*") for having emphasized the Christological basis of the doctrine of election anew, in that Jesus Christ is seen as the one "original and decisive object of the divine election (*and* rejection)."[1]

In fact, Maury's essay in many ways resembles Barth's earlier revision of the doctrine of election in his second Commentary on Romans, which Maury knew, and in his lectures at the University of Göttingen in 1924–25, which remained unpublished at the time.[2] Maury, like Barth, criticizes the traditional view of divine predestination as the separation of two groups, or, in the language of traditional Protestant and Catholic

---

1. *KD* II/2:168; *CD* II/2:154. Barth's further comments are noteworthy. He points out that Maury's essay, delivered as a paper at the International Congress for Calvinist Theology in Geneva, appeared especially instructive in comparison with the other papers, "which were often historically interesting but, in regard to content, moved within the circle of the traditional formulations and were almost hopelessly embarrassed by the difficulties of these formulations" (*KD* II/2:168; *CD* II/2:155).

2. On Barth's earlier views on election, see Gockel, *Barth and Schleiermacher*, 104–156.

teaching, "two separate choirs"[3] of persons destined for either salvation or damnation.[4] Maury also agrees with Barth that it is not helpful to abandon the concept of double predestination in favor of the alternative concept of election as God's foreknowledge of the faith of the believers. Double predestination does not signify a division of two groups of persons, as the strict Augustinian-Calvinist tradition holds,[5] but a twofold content, election and rejection, which concerns *every* person. Moreover, Maury does not take recourse to the idea of a self-contradiction in God, in the sense of "God against God" as did some friendly critics of Barth's emphasis on Jesus Christ as God's unique self-revelation.[6] Finally, despite their shared convictions, Barth acknowledges that Maury "insisted much more energetically on the 'in Christ'"[7] than Barth himself had done in his earlier works.

The present essay takes a closer look at Maury's thinking on election in comparison with Barth's view. We will see that, despite their principal agreement about the need to put the doctrine on a new Christological basis, minor differences remain, especially in regard to the consequences of the new insight for the concept of God. They are also evident in a number of subtle changes of the French text of *"Election et Foi"* in the German translation,[8] which was undertaken by Barth's confidante Charlotte von

---

3. Barth, *Unterricht*, 2:183. The English translation speaks of "two separate groups." See Barth, *Göttingen Dogmatics*, 453.

4. This criticism is already found in Barth's second commentary on Romans (1922). See Gockel, *Barth and Schleiermacher*, 109–110. Barth mentions his interpretation of Romans 9–11 in a letter to Maury on August 21, 1936 (Reymond, *Karl Barth—Pierre Maury*, 100).

5. It should be noted that Calvin does not always speak of double predestination when discussing the topic of election and rejection. His comments during the Bolsec controversy in 1551–52 avoid the concept and emphasize the graciousness of divine election as well as the asymmetry of election and rejection. At the same time, they affirm that God's "immutable counsel" implies the rejection of certain persons by not releasing them from the "universal condemnation" that has befallen the entire human species as a consequence of Adam's sin. See Calvin, "Von der ewigen Erwählung Gottes," 98, 134–36. For an English translation, see Calvin, *Bolsec Controversy*, 695–720. See also Neuser, "Calvin, the Preacher," 60–78.

6. See Vogel, *Praedestinatio gemina*, 222–42.

7. Karl Barth to Pierre Maury, August 21, 1936 (Reymond, *Karl Barth—Pierre Maury*, 100).

8. Maury, *"Election et Foi"* (hereafter EF); "Erwählung und Glaube" (hereafter EG). In the following, citations from the German translation of *"Election et Foi"* might differ from the translation of the French original provided in this volume.

Kirschbaum and concluded in winter 1939/40, at the time when Barth began to lecture on the material that became *Church Dogmatics* II/2.[9] The first section will take a brief look at the most significant translation changes, while the second section offers an outline of the similarities and differences between Maury's essay and Barth's essay from the same year on God's gracious choice.[10] The third section summarizes our findings.

## TRANSLATION AS INTERPRETATION

*In the first section* of Maury's essay, three changes in the German translation of the French original are noteworthy. Maury speaks of predestination as the "divine decree," while the translation speaks of the "divine mystery" and avoids the allusion to the classical Reformed concept of God's decree(s).[11] At the end of the same paragraph, Maury explains that human reason wants to explain election in terms of human righteousness and thereby subjugates God, instead of understanding the true meaning of divine election: "We would make of God and his secret counsel a sophist's enigma."[12] Remarkably, the German translation omits the entire sentence. Perhaps the translator had misgivings about the concept of God's secret counsel, since a secret remains principally unknown, whereas the mystery of election can be known, as it has been revealed in Christ. Finally, the next paragraph offers a subtle change of Maury's expression that his new insight leads to results different from Calvin's view, and precisely in this way "will be truly Calvinist." The German translation here says that "we will be truly Calvin's pupils" and thereby avoids the stronger adjective "Calvinist."[13]

---

9. Barth closely read and commented on von Kirschbaum's translation of "The Great Work of God." See her letter to Maury from June 15, 1941 (Reymond, *Karl Barth—Pierre Maury*, 192). It is likely that he also influenced the translation of "Election and Faith."

10. Barth, *Gottes Gnadenwahl*, 1936.

11. EF 205; EG 6. See pages 43, 45, 57.

12. "Nous ferions de Dieu et son secret une énigme de sophiste" (EF 205). See page 43.

13. EF 205; EG 6. See page 43. On the same day, when Barth wrote to Maury (see note 7 above), he also addressed a letter to his Lutheran friend, Heinrich Vogel, regarding the same topic, and mused: "Whether we must dare to take the thinking of the Reformers into a slightly different direction, if we really want to be their pupils" (unpublished letter from Karl Barth to Heinrich Vogel, August 21, 1936, Karl Barth-Archive, Basel, 9236.0200). My thanks go to the archivist, Dr. Peter Zocher, for

*In the second section*, Maury speaks of the concrete *possibility* where election and faith come together, that is, "the concrete, living *possibility* called Jesus Christ,"[14] which makes it possible that our thinking about election (and faith) becomes concrete and does not remain abstract. Yet the translation speaks of "the concrete, living *reality* called Jesus Christ."[15] It is likely that the change, which is of limited significance in the context of Maury's overall argument, is motivated by Barth's basic conviction of the priority of reality (or actuality) over possibility, especially in the doctrine of God.[16]

*The third section* of the translation includes another omission and one explanatory addition. Maury states that "the cross is unjust, like the election, but this injustice is our righteousness."[17] The words "like the election" are omitted in the German translation, which perhaps wants to avoid the idea that election is a paradox. The explanatory addition follows two sentences later. The translation says that election is always positive election, *election for salvation*, whereas it was *election for damnation* for Christ. Maury uses the opposition between "positive" and "negative" election but not the phrases "election for salvation" and "election for damnation." Similarly, at the end of the third section, the translation explains that "in Christ" there is "no election for damnation" whereas Maury simply says that in Christ there is "no negative election."[18]

*Finally, in the last section* of his essay Maury states that God's election *is* our faith, whereas the translation offers the more cautious wording that God's election *encounters* our faith.[19]

On the whole, there are two related kinds of changes in the German translation: changes emphasizing the difference of Maury's view from the Calvinist tradition and systematic-theological changes. Both kinds of changes support the emphasis that election occurs "in Christ" in contrast

---

granting me access to the material.

14. See page 43.

15. EF 206; EG 7.

16. *KD* II/1; *CD* II/1, especially §28.1, "God's Being-In-Act" (*CD* II/1:257-71). See also *CD* I/2, where the *reality* of revelation is the foundation of its *possibility*. Barth's position in *Church Dogmatics* is clear, but its genesis and development remain contested. See Beintker, *Die Dialektik*, 188-95; McCormack, *Karl Barth's Dialectical Theology*, 434-38.

17. EF 212; EG 13. See page 49.

18. EF 213; EG 14. See page 49.

19. EF 223; EG 24. See page 58.

to the traditional Reformed concept of a *decretum absolutum*, that is, "predestination understood in abstraction from Christ, which only leads to the error of determinism."[20] This brings us to the second section.

## PIERRE MAURY AND KARL BARTH ON DIVINE ELECTION

The similarities in the thinking of the two friends are evident. Maury inspired Barth to locate election and rejection no longer in the encounter between God and the human person, but "in Christ,"[21] particularly in Christ's suffering and death on the cross as the "atoning substitute"[22] to use a phrase from Schleiermacher. Barth himself points out that Maury's "bold proposition" is simply correct: "One can speak of a rejection (*Verwerfung*) predestined by God only in regard to Calvary; but there one *must* speak of it."[23] In fact, election is "nothing else than the eternal and temporal existence of Jesus Christ, our mediator,"[24] and since it is "truth in *Jesus Christ*" the knowledge of election can be "nothing else than a particular form of the knowledge of Jesus Christ."[25]

At the same time, differences become visible when we compare the threefold explanation *of the concept of election "in Christ" by Maury and Barth, respectively.*

*First*, both agree that *God* is the subject of "election in Christ" and that the origin of election does not belong to human reason and experience. Maury emphasizes that God's decision concerning salvation is an eternal decision, independent from time and history. Barth adds that the attribution of the new life "in grace" is a sheer gift given to us by God

---

20. Barth, *Gottes Gnadenwahl*, 44.

21. Barth, *Gottes Gnadenwahl*, 14–15, 19–20.

22. Schleiermacher, *Der christliche Glaube*, 2:146. It can hardly be repeated too often that Schleiermacher does *not* simply reject the idea of Christ's vicarious atonement, as many interpreters claim (for example, see Hunsinger, *Evangelical, Catholic, and Reformed*, 127, 164). In fact, Schleiermacher defends the idea against several misunderstandings and thereby affirms (a) the atoning aspect that Christ "did enough" (it was *genugtuend*) for us and our salvation as well as (b) the vicarious aspect that the suffering of Christ was an act of "substitution" (*Stellvertretung*).

23. Barth, *Gottes Gnadenwahl*, 20. Maury speaks of "perdition," which has slightly different connotations than "rejection" (*Verwerfung*).

24. EF 207; EG 8–9.

25. Barth, *Gottes Gnadenwahl*, 13.

through the work of Jesus Christ, and its foundation is "a decision that is made and executed outside of ourselves."[26]

*Secondly*, the eternal Son made flesh, Jesus Christ, is not only the origin but also the ground of God's eternal election. God chooses because of him, "and only because of him."[27] Barth explains that it is necessary to focus on "the central mystery" of the gospel, that is, the incarnation, which means that "God begins with Himself." By the decision and act of the eternal Son, Jesus was elected to be born and to live a human life as the Son of God, and "in the birth of Jesus Christ everyone who believes in Him is reborn as a child of God" so that they "may believe and receive grace in faith."[28] For Barth, the beginning of the believer's new life in Christ coincides with the beginning of the life of Jesus.[29]

So far, both Maury's and Barth's position complement each other: they explain the concept of election "in Christ" alongside their basic conviction that even the reception of grace is an act of grace and not of preceding human merit whatsoever.[30] The third aspect of the "election in Christ," however, is explained differently. Maury emphasizes that Jesus Christ is not only the ground but also the goal of election and that believers shall "become like Christ." Like Barth, he draws an analogy between Christ and believers, although it is an ontological rather than existential analogy: God's election is "nothing else than the eternal and temporal existence of Jesus Christ, our Mediator."[31]

Barth agrees with Maury's correlation of election with the life and death of Jesus Christ, but he also speaks of *God's self-giving* in the cross and resurrection of Jesus Christ. If we take seriously the idea that God chose the human person Jesus of Nazareth for unity with Himself, Barth argues, then we must conclude that God also took the death of Jesus and the sin of humankind upon Himself, without thereby tearing apart the

---

26. Barth, *Gottes Gnadenwahl*, 14.

27. EF 208; EG 9. See page 45.

28. See Barth, *Gottes Gnadenwahl*, 6.

29. In *CD* II/2, Barth is more cautious and merely speaks of an analogy: "As [Jesus] became Christ, so we become Christians. . . . As he became the object of our faith, so we become believers in him" (*KD* II/2:127; *CD* II/2:118).

30. Barth, *Gottes Gnadenwahl*, 13. The understanding of election—or salvation, justification, etc.—as an act or event of "peculiar, incongruous grace" (Barclay, *Paul*, 242) is by no means self-evident, either among systematic theologians or New Testament scholars.

31. EF 209; EG 9. See page 46.

bond of unity between the Father and the Son.[32] Moreover, Barth explicitly criticizes "the older Reformed theologians" who regarded Jesus Christ as the means but not as the foundation of election and instead assumed that the eternal election occurred in a divine decree "*before* the reality of the cross and the resurrection."[33] In contrast, Barth asserts: "That which happened on Calvary for us and upon us and became manifest on the Easter Day, even while it took place in time, *is* our eternal election"[34] and "our life's predestination."[35]

Further differences become visible when we look at the explanation of the relation between election and reprobation and its soteriological significance. Barth agrees with Maury's linkage between election and the cross: as Christ died "for us and our salvation," God's election occurs "for us and our salvation." Both also agree that the distinction between believers and unbelievers does not simply mirror two separate groups of persons destined for either salvation or damnation. Moreover, Barth now places the teleological relation between *reprobatio* and *electio* in a different context than he did in the *Göttingen Dogmatics*: although *reprobatio* still occurs for the sake of *electio*, it does so no longer in the actual event of faith, when a person comes to believe in God, but in the *death and resurrection of Jesus Christ*.

Without denying the fundamental agreement between Maury and Barth, it is noteworthy that in two respects their thinking leads in different directions.

On the one hand, Maury describes the idea of the election of humankind through the rejection of Christ on the cross as a "paradox."[36] Viewed through human eyes, God's election appears "unjust."[37] It is no surprise that the German translation of Maury's essay omits this claim, since Barth asserts that election is an expression of God's righteousness and thus of "highest justice."[38] For Barth, God's free gracious choice is *not* a paradox. Moreover, Maury says that the election of humankind occurs in the rejection of Jesus Christ, while he does not say that Christ actively

---

32. See Barth, *Gottes Gnadenwahl*, 16.
33. Barth, *Gottes Gnadenwahl*, 17.
34. Barth, *Gottes Gnadenwahl*, 17.
35. Barth, *Gottes Gnadenwahl*, 26.
36. EF 210; EG 11. See page 47.
37. EF 212; EG 13. See page 49.
38. Barth, *Gottes Gnadenwahl*, 22.

chose being elected for rejection. Here, Barth goes further and explains that God "executed [our rejection] in Himself (and not on us)."[39] God remains the subject even in the rejection that accompanies the election of Jesus Christ.[40]

On the other hand, Maury, in accordance with the title of his essay, puts a strong emphasis on the parallel between divine election and the human decision of faith, precisely as the result of his Christological approach. Election is election in Christ, as faith is faith in Christ. Hence, the truth of the election in Christ needs to be actualized in and through faith. Maury explains that the particular meaning of election "for us" is realized, above all, in a human decision: "Such is God's election; such is our choice."[41] At the end of the essay, he says that God's election *is* our faith—in opposition to our unbelief, one could add. This position seems to be closer to Barth's "actualistic" position in the *Göttingen Dogmatics*, and it comes as no surprise, once more, that the German translation changes the wording.

For Maury, the appropriate human response to God's election is to say Yes to our election in Christ and to the implied rejection of sin: "The election of Jesus Christ is not only the election, in which He chooses us, but also the election, in which we choose him and not ourselves anymore," and in which we say No to ourselves "forever."[42] Maury points out that Jesus Christ takes upon himself "our death,"[43] that is, the condemnation of sin. The divine rejection of sin in the death of Christ is mirrored in the believer's rejection of the "old Adam." A person's belief in his or her election always has a double aspect—it means "ruin as much as salvation, rejection as much as adoption"[44]—while it excludes a person's belief in his or her perdition.[45]

Barth, however, puts a greater emphasis on God's Yes as the basis of election. The German translation of Maury's essay expands the quotation of 2 Corinthians 1:20—"there is nothing but 'Yes' in him"[46]—and cites the

39. Barth, *Gottes Gnadenwahl*, 22.

40. In his letter to Heinrich Vogel, Barth speaks about "the *election* precisely of the rejected human being" Jesus of Nazareth.

41. EF 214; EG 15. See page 51.

42. EF 214; EG 15. See page 51.

43. EF 212; EG 13. See page 49.

44. EF 212; EG 13. See page 48.

45. EF 213; EG 13-14. See page 49.

46. EF 212.

preceding verse as well: "For the Son of God, Jesus Christ . . . was not Yes and No, but in him there was only Yes, since in him all the promises of God are Yes" (2 Cor 1:19).[47] Moreover, Barth's own essay avoids the parallel between the rejection of Christ and the self-rejection of the believer. Instead, he points out that Jesus Christ alone is the rejected human being, who "stands in our place"[48] and in whose rejection the election of humankind is grounded, so that all other human beings are freed eternally from the threat of rejection. Jesus Christ chooses to bear our rejection and thereby to cancel (*aufheben*) it once and for all.[49]

Barth thus emphasizes the Christological exclusivity of rejection. Moreover, he asserts that God Himself is affected by the death of Jesus Christ, since God is the subject of election and rejection. Maury avoids such a claim. Barth's elaboration here anticipates the thesis of Jesus Christ as the electing God, who chooses rejection and damnation for himself, in *Church Dogmatics* II/2: "In the election of Jesus Christ, which is the eternal will of God, God has ascribed to the human being election, salvation and life, but to Himself rejection, perdition and death."[50]

While Barth describes the threat of rejection or perdition as a past threat, which is overcome by Jesus Christ, Maury seems to assume that the threat continues to hover over the unbeliever, as long as he or she does *not* choose Jesus Christ,[51] even while adamantly pointing out, against the strict view of limited atonement, that "there is no one that the cross cannot save."[52] Moreover, despite their refusal to assume two separate groups of persons, both Maury and Barth presuppose that the Last Judgment will entail a final decision about every person. While it would be wrong to say that presently there exists a discrimination between those who are elected and those who are reprobated, "we can and must believe"[53] that there *will be* such a discrimination on the Last Day, since it was

---

47. EG 13.

48. Barth, *Gottes Gnadenwahl*, 21. Barth emphasizes that the "Yes" to one's rejection is "primarily and above all" a "Yes" to one's election. See Barth, *Gottes Gnadenwahl*, 29.

49. See Barth, *Gottes Gnadenwahl*, 22.

50. KD II/2:177; CD II/2:163.

51. EF 218; EG 19. See page 54.

52. EF 217; EG 18. See page 53.

53. Barth, *Gottes Gnadenwahl*, 48.

"prophesied to us."⁵⁴ The reservation is not explained further. Probably, it shall dispel the impression of advocating universal salvation.⁵⁵

Finally, Maury and Barth agree that no human being should try to answer the question of who is elected and who is rejected. It is more important to focus on the teleological order of divine acting, that is, on *God's* electing and rejecting (for the purpose of electing).⁵⁶ In *CD* II/2 Barth retains the focus on God's act of electing and rejecting, but the eschatological reservation is given up in favor of the affirmation that a person's insistence on his or her unbelief, as a sign of rejection, is unreal:

> The person who is isolated over against God is rejected by God. But to be this person can only be the godless person's own choice. The witness of the congregation of God to every individual consists in the affirmation that this choice of the godless person is *void*; that he or she belongs *eternally* to Jesus Christ and therefore is not rejected, but elected by God in Jesus Christ; that the rejection which he or she deserves on account of his or her perverse choice is borne and *cancelled* by Jesus Christ; and that he or she is appointed to eternal life with God on the basis of the *righteous, divine* decision.⁵⁷

---

54. EF 217; EG 18. See page 53. Maury probably has NT texts like Matthew 25:31-46 in mind.

55. Barth argues that Romans 11:32 includes a universalism of judgment and grace but leaves "no room for the speculation" about universal salvation (Barth, *Gottes Gnadenwahl*, 27). Maury corroborates this view: "It is God, or rather Jesus Christ, who reserves the right to pass judgment. . . . There *are not* elect and reprobate, there *will be* elect and reprobate. Down here until the Last Day, no one is *elsewhere* than around the cross. . . . And, around the cross, there are no privileged places, that is to say, a place where one would *have less need than the others* of the pardon of the cross. Even more: there is no one that the cross cannot save (hence the universalistic sense of Paul's phrase 'God has shut up all men in disobedience so that he may be merciful to all' Rom 11:32). Around the cross we see everyone because the cross is for everyone, all enemies of God, all loved by God: the godless and the pious believer, the adulterer and the honest person, the lost and the saved, no exceptions" (Maury, *Election and Faith*). See EF 217; EG 18; page 53.

56. According to Barth, the teleological order is implied in Romans 9-11. See Gockel, *Barth and Schleiermacher*, 118.

57. KD II/2:336; CD II/2:306.

## CONCLUSION

Pierre Maury and Karl Barth find themselves in fundamental agreement regarding the need to put the evangelical doctrine of election on a new Christological basis. In doing so, they seek to remain faithful to key insights from the Reformed tradition, without simply repeating them. Barth is clearly aware of the differences. In his letter to Maury, he muses whether Calvin might have regarded their position with the same disdain with which he treated the position of Jerome Bolsec. He adds: "one should not hide the fact that while being good disciples of the Reformation, we are perhaps moving away *further* from their way of thinking than our liberal predecessors, etc., did. There really is no 'Calvinism'!"[58]

Both Maury and Barth emphasize that there shall be no symmetry between election and rejection. Maury speaks of election as "paradox" or "injustice," from a human point of view. Barth insists that the election and rejection of Christ is an expression of divine righteousness. The two claims can be seen in contrast but also in coherence, pointing out different aspects of the doctrine. Furthermore, Maury's focus on election as an event "in Christ" opens up a new perspective for Barth. Still, his emphasis on the human decision and the necessity to choose—or, in the words of Blaise Pascal, "to wager"[59]—is reminiscent of the correlation of election and faith (or rejection and unbelief) in Barth's earlier doctrine, while Barth's elaboration already anticipates, to some extent, his new and comprehensive treatment of the doctrine in *Church Dogmatics* II/2.

Moreover, when we take a closer look at Barth's development, it is noteworthy that his essay from 1936 offers a further building-block towards his mature position, and that he does not simply cast off his earlier ideas but rather refines them. While the second edition of his Romans commentary understands rejection and election (in this order!) primarily as an event "in God," the *Göttingen Dogmatics* focuses on the historical encounter between God and the human person, which leads to unbelief (the likely case) or faith (the unlikely case).[60] The essay from 1936 adds the specific Christological perspective, and all three factors are present in *Church Dogmatics* II/2, which refigures the doctrine on the basis of God's

---

58. Barth to Maury, August 21, 1936 (Reymond, *Karl Barth—Pierre Maury*, 100). In his public writings, Barth was more cautious and emphasized the similarities rather than the differences between his own and the Reformers' views.

59. EF 213; EG 14. See page 50.

60. See Gockel, *Barth and Schleiermacher*, 114, 154–55.

primal decision (*Urentscheidung*) and proclaims Jesus Christ as the electing God. The doctrine of election belongs to the doctrine of God, because in the election of Jesus Christ—by being God "for us"—God determines His own being in all eternity.[61]

Barth's revision of the doctrine of election also impacts the doctrine of the Trinity. It implies that the Father is not only the Father of the Son but the Father of *Jesus Christ*, and the Holy Spirit is "the Spirit of this Father and the Spirit of Jesus Christ."[62] A further discussion of the issue is not necessary here.[63] What is important is that Barth's and Maury's position is rightly called Christocentric, since it sets forth the claim that rejection occurs exclusively *in* Christ and not, as the majority of Christian theologians had thought, *outside of* Christ. In this respect, the year 1936 marks the beginning of an important discovery, as the conventional understanding of the doctrine of God apart from Jesus Christ could no longer be a standard for Barth's own theology.

Finally, let us briefly return to the question of translation. How shall we evaluate the changes in the German translation of Maury's essay? Strictly speaking, they alter the literal meaning of the French text. Are they therefore misrepresentations of his position? Yet, the fact that Maury himself read and evidently approved of the translation[64] suggests a different perspective: the changes are subtle explanations of the mystery of God's gracious choice, and the translator treads on the path laid out by Pierre Maury himself. Certainly, the traditional maxim of any translation—it should be as literal as necessary and as free as possible—also applies to the translation of theological texts.

---

61. *KD* II/2:1; *CD* II/2:3. Unfortunately, the English translation does not fully grasp Barth's position.

62. *KD* II/2:123-24; *CD* II/2:115.

63. It was raised already more than thirty years ago in an essay that is still waiting to be addressed by the so-called "traditionalist" interpreters of Barth. See Goebel, *Trinitätslehre*, 147-66.

64. "I should also have thanked [Charlotte von Kirschbaum] for the remarkable translation of 'Election and Faith.' In reading it, I was pleasantly taken by the fact that this study was better than I thought" (Pierre Maury to Karl Barth, August 10, 1940, in Reymond, *Karl Barth—Pierre Maury*, 184).

## BIBLIOGRAPHY

Barclay, John M. G. "Review of *Paul and the Faithfulness of God*, by N. T. Wright." *Scottish Journal of Theology* 68 (2015) 235–43.
Barth, Karl. *Church Dogmatics*. Edited by G. W. Bromiley and T. F. Torrance. Translated by G. T. Thomson, et al. Edinburgh: T&T Clark, 1936–77.
———. *Die Kirchliche Dogmatik* II/1. Zollikon-Zurich: Evangelischer, 1940.
———. *Die Kirchliche Dogmatik* II/2. Zollikon-Zurich: Evangelischer, 1942.
———. *Gottes Gnadenwahl*. Munich: Chr. Kaiser, 1936.
———. *The Göttingen Dogmatics: Instruction in the Christian Religion*. Translated by Geoffrey W. Bromiley. Grand Rapids: Eerdmans, 1991.
———. *Unterricht in der christlichen Religion*. Vol. 2. Edited by Hannelotte Reiffen. Zurich: Theologischer, 1985.
Beintker, Michael. *Die Dialektik in der "dialektischen Theologie" Karl Barths*. Munich: Chr. Kaiser, 1987.
Calvin, Jean. "Von der ewigen Erwählung Gottes (1551) 1562." In *Reformatorische Klärungen*, edited by Eberhard Busch, et al., 79–149. Vol. 4 of *Calvin-Studienausgabe*. French text with German translation. Neukirchen-Vluyn: Neukirchener, 2002.
———. *Von der ewigen Erwählung Gottes (1551) 1562*. In *The Bolsec Controversy on Predestination from 1551 to 1555*, edited by Philip C. Holtrop, 695–720. Vol. 1.2. English translation. Lewiston, NY: Edwin Mellen, 1993.
Gockel, Matthias. *Barth and Schleiermacher on the Doctrine of Election: A Systematic-Theological Comparison*. Oxford: Oxford University Press, 2007.
Goebel, Hans Theodor. "Trinitätslehre und Erwählungslehre bei Karl Barth: Eine Problemanzeige." In *Wahrheit und Versöhnung: Theologische und philosophische Beiträge zur Gotteslehre*, edited by Dietrich Korsch and Hartmut Ruddies, 147–66. Göttingen: Gerd Mohn, 1989.
Hunsinger, George. *Evangelical, Catholic, and Reformed: Essays on Barth and Related Themes*. Grand Rapids: Eerdmans, 2015.
Maury, Pierre. "*Election et Foi.*" *Foi et Vie* 27 (1936) 203–223. German translation: *Erwählung und Glaube*. Zollikon-Zurich: Theologischer, 1940.
McCormack, Bruce L. *Karl Barth's Critically Realistic Dialectical Theology: Its Genesis and Development 1909–1936*. Oxford: Clarendon, 1995.
Neuser, Wilhelm H. "Calvin, the Preacher: His Explanation of the Doctrine of Predestination in the Sermon of 1552 and in the Institutes of 1559." *HTS Teologiese Studies/Theological Studies* 54 (1998) 60–78.
Reymond, Bernard, ed. *Karl Barth—Pierre Maury: Nous qui pouvons encore parler: Correspondance 1928–1956*. Translated by Bernard Reymond. Paris: Symbolon, L'Age d'Homme, 1985.
Schleiermacher, Friedrich. *Der christliche Glaube nach den Grundsätzen der evangelischen Kirche im Zusammenhange dargestellt (1830/31)*. Edited by Rolf Schäfer. Kritische Gesamtausgabe 1/13. Berlin: de Gruyter, 2003.
Vogel, Heinrich. "Praedestinatio gemina. Die Lehre von der ewigen Gnadenwahl." In *Theologische Aufsätze. Karl Barth zum 50. Geburtstag*, edited by Ernst Wolf, 222–42. Munich: Chr. Kaiser, 1936.

# 12

## *Serious Joy of the Ultimate Decision*

JOHN MARK CAPPER

IT SEEMS, SAID PIERRE Maury, that we are only able to speak of election either to defend or attack it.[1] In many parts of contemporary Christian life it is either ignored or made a touchstone of faith (in one or other of the particular versions in which it manifests). Where it is preached, it is often polemical; where it is taught, it is often analytical or philosophical; and it is rarely visible as a constructive or comforting motif in pastoral texts. We have failed in many places to heed Maury's wisdom: "To determine the true link between election and faith, we need to, above all, avoid speaking abstractly of either of these terms."[2]

For much of Christian history, election has been at the heart of Christian understanding, has fueled the missional and pastoral task of the Church, and has informed human self-understanding in the light of the revealed nature of God. As Mark Lindsay has noted[3] the doctrine of election was inextricably linked with the vocation of preacher for Barth as for Calvin, and similarly for Maury. At a merely instrumental level, the preacher wonders why some hearers respond to the call to repentance, the offer of life and the wonder of hope. Preachers also wonder why some do not. Pastorally it is profoundly vexing that many who hear do not

---

1. Maury, "Election and Faith" [hereafter EF]. See the translation in this volume. EF, p41.

2. EF 44.

3. See page 126.

come to know the saving gift of God (and perhaps that many who claim to know it seem untransformed by it). Pondering election and its polarities in predestination is a means of making sense of this reality, and a step to encouraging steadfastness in the lives of the faithful.

Barth is credited with taking the classical Calvinist conception of election that he had inherited and giving it new depth, through new insights, by focusing on (the act of God in) Jesus Christ, human and divine, electing God and elected Man.[4] The particularity of this move is critical. Out of a theocentric act, election becomes a Christological reality. It becomes part of the life of God. It coheres and resonates with Paul's regular description of the Christian as "in Christ" (and thus in God). The argument, philosophically or pastorally, need not be the either/or regarding whether faith can be lost, but rather the embrace of the reality that God loves and is faithful. God is the one who loves in freedom.[5] God's love is known by its constancy, since God "remains the one He is."[6]

This volume attests to the significance of Pierre Maury in the quantum change in Reformed understanding of election, most commonly attributed to the influence of Karl Barth. This chapter outlines pastoral perspectives on election and points to some connections between the theological and pastoral aspects of both Barth and Maury. Both these theological pastors link election to the living and enjoyment of (Christian) life.

Volume 2 of the *Church Dogmatics* was completed in 1942. The first half-volume, in which Barth addresses the doctrine of God and builds a foundation for his explication of election in the second half-volume, was shaped in the early years of the Second World War and published in 1940. "It is a good thing that the properties of God and predestination and all the rest could be put to paper and printed in the middle of all this [thunder of war]."[7] In that half-volume Barth builds his doctrine of God in constructive and positive terms. Barth eschews the classical presentation of God (immutable, infinite, not-human) as what God is not

---

4. Barth's translators have taken his German "Mensch," a gender neutral term, and have translated it as "man," and in some cases "Man," using the term generically as was typical for the use of English at their time. I will use "Man" where the translators have used it, capitalizing to show its inclusive dimension, though "humanity" will be preferred to refer to all humankind in general.

5. *CD* II/1:257.

6. *CD* II/1:491.

7. Letter to O. Weber, June 20, 1949 (Busch, *Karl Barth*, 301.)

(mutable, finite, human) and uses only positive terms, focused around the view that God Is the One who Loves in Freedom (the five capitalized words are key).[8]

"There is no possibility of knowing the perfect God without knowing his perfections."[9] Barth explicates these in three pairs of perfections of divine loving: grace and holiness; mercy and righteousness; patience and wisdom, and in three pairs of perfections of divine freedom: unity and omnipresence; constancy and omnipotence; and eternity and glory. This exposition ends the first part of the second volume of the *Church Dogmatics*. And critically, it leads into the second part and the exploration of divine election. Using a mixture of metaphors, all linked to show that God's revelation is of God's own glory, Barth continues:

> God's face is more than the radiance of light. And God's glory is the glory of His face, indeed His face itself, God in person, God who bears a name and calls us by name. God is glorious in the fact that He does this, that He reaches us in this way, that He Himself comes to us in this way.[10]

That God's glory is not remote, but is rather present, and that God's glory is seen in God's face, is closely connected with God's reach to us, and God's coming to us. There is a richness of glory described as joyful.

> God's glory is the indwelling *joy* of His divine being which as such shines out from Him, which overflows in its richness, which in its super-abundance is not satisfied with itself but communicates itself. All God's works must be understood also and decisively from this point of view. All together and without exception they take part in the movement of God's self-glorification and the communication of His joy.[11]

Thus it is the human destiny to "offer a true if inadequate response in the temporal sphere to the jubilation with which the Godhead is filled from eternity to eternity."[12] This temporal jubilance will give way to joy in eternity:

---

8. *CD* II/1:257.
9. *CD* II/1:322.
10. *CD* II/1:647.
11. *CD* II/1:647.
12. *CD* II/1:648.

> In the eternity before us the groaning of creation will cease, and Man too will live in his determination to be the reflection and echo of God and therefore the witness to the divine glory that reaches over to him, rejoicing with the Godhead who Himself has eternal joy and Himself is eternal joy.[13]

The "ultimate decision," notes Maury, is problematic in that making a decision that Jesus Christ is the way requires a potential believer to be sure that Jesus Christ really is the way. It is as if to become a believer, one first needs to be a believer. To pray for faith is to have faith to pray. To find if it is true that Jesus is God is to know the truth. Grappling with this conundrum, says Maury, is not a "vain intellectual curiosity" but rather it "represent[s] the mortal torment of suffering souls."[14]

The "ultimate decision" rests on the decisive and ultimate character of Christ's reality. "Marvelous revelation of an unfathomable mystery! When this child is born in a manger, when this man died on the cross and rises again the third day, the eve of the Sabbath, it is our whole life that is swept up in this commitment."[15]

Maury sees the outcome of the "ultimate decision" not as escape from this world, or the removal of fear, pain or suffering. Rather he sees the outcome as a joy:

> So that the mystery of Jesus is not just something that God knows, but also that those who are in Christ, that is to say you and me, will overflow with joy, we need to understand how this unfathomable earthly truth, the life of the Son of Man, is a heavenly secret; in other words, how Jesus Christ is decisive.[16]

The decisiveness, that is, the nature of the "ultimate decision," is that it is God in Jesus Christ who is decisive. The error, implicitly, identified by both Maury and Barth, is to impute the decision to the human agent. To affirm human decisiveness is to take from God that which is God's and give to humankind that which they cannot fully bear. "It bears repeating that for Barth, true humanity is only possible by participation in the redemption of Jesus Christ."[17] Barth's language of encounter is the language

---

13. CD II/1:648–49.

14. Maury, "Ultimate Decision" [hereafter UD]. See the translation in this volume. UD 62.

15. UD 67.

16. UD 67.

17. Durheim, "Human as Encounter," 8n24.

of participation in the divine. (Though Barth does not go as far as the Eastern view of theosis in his four volumes of the *Church Dogmatics*, it is surely a possible trajectory for the unwritten fifth.) Humankind are "being in encounter." It is the encounter that empowers the participation. It might be argued to impute the decisiveness needed for the "ultimate decision."

Encounter, for Barth, between church and society requires a "meeting eye to eye."[18] Durheim notes that this occurs through mutual enrichment, with assistance from church to society characterized by love, with gladness "necessary only on the part of the Church."[19] Durheim notes that "when applied to the Church in relation to society, [this gladness] would likely look more like zeal and patience in suffering" with this drawn "from the agency of God."[20] Indeed, a view of evangelical zeal which considers it to be based in self-knowledge, self-assurance or marketing technique lacks the fundamental veracity to claim to be an expression of God at work. It is, at base and in total, an expression of the zeal and suffering of God. This may be known and experienced in the life of the Christian, but its source and its power are in God, and its result is also in God—not simply in God's providence, as if that could be abstracted from God. The love of God, expressed in human encounter, is the essence of Barth's anthropology. It reflects a view of divine action and decision for humankind by God in Jesus Christ. Gladness, as the response to divine glory in the life of humanity, said Barth, is the crowning of full and free humanness.[21] This parallels his placement of joy in God.[22]

Barth's view of human encounter is summarized as "creaturely being . . . in encounter—between I and Thou . . . a likeness of the being of its Creator and a being in hope in Him."[23] "The humanity of human being is this total determination as being in encounter with the being of the Thou, as being with the fellow-man, as fellow-humanity."[24] Being in encounter "looks the other in the eye,"[25] involves "mutual speech and

---

18. *CD* III/2:250.

19. Durheim, "Human as Encounter," 19.

20. Durheim, "Human as Encounter," 19. Durheim references Mangina, *Karl Barth*, 184–85.

21. *CD* III/2.

22. Capper, *Joy in the Church Dogmatics?*, 98–121.

23. *CD* III/2:203.

24. *CD* III/2:247.

25. *CD* III/2:250.

hearing"[26] in "rendering mutual assistance,"[27] and is "done on both sides with gladness."[28] Being in encounter, the engagement of humans, but particularly of God and humans, is ennobled in election. It is actualized in faith. Eberhard Jüngel describes the joy of faith in being in encounter:

> Faith is that human attitude toward God which is called forth by God himself, in which Man, completely without *coercion* and gladly, relates himself to God. The most original attitude of one ego toward another person, an attitude called forth by that other one, completely uncoerced and realized gladly, is *joy*. For that reason, one can say "joy in God" instead of "faith." . . . The self-definition for which Man is determined in faith can thus be only the immediacy of a defined joy. Joy in God would then be the origin, the source, of the true thought of God, to the extent that joy is that "existential" in which God is thinkable *for the sake of his own self*. For joy is always joy in something for its own sake. . . . To think God without joy in God is a self-contradiction which must lead even the most logical proof of God to absurdity.[29]

Without the gift of human joy, revelation (which is joyfully given) cannot be grasped. It is not simply faith which is imputed. Joy, grace, and truth are also given. Faith in action is joy. Joy in action is faith. To be known and predestined for God is to be conformed to God's image (Rom 8:29), is to be drawn into the joy of God "according to his pleasure and will, to the praise of his glorious grace, which he has freely given us in the One he loves" (Eph 1:5–6). These are key scriptural passages on which Maury builds his theology in "Election and Faith." In "The Ultimate Decision" his scriptural focus is more connected to the narrative of the Gospels. These point to Maury's conclusion to his sermon, where he points to the consummation of human response to God, as 1 John 1:4 puts it, "to make joy complete." Maury notes that Jesus's hearers began to rejoice. Implicitly, for Maury, Jesus is that joy. Maury notes that Calvin and others have sung about "the joy of election" based in the reality that

---

26. *CD* III/2:252.
27. *CD* III/2:260.
28. *CD* III/2:262.
29. Jüngel, *Mystery*, 192.

God is love.³⁰ The Reformers "had understood that *in Christ crucified* there is only cause for the believer to experience a triumphant joy."³¹

> We can truly say that outside of Christ, there is neither election, nor knowledge of election—and I mean the word in its strongest sense, the sense of a sovereign choice, free and with no strings attached on the part of God, having a "double" aspect which has the character of both rejection and welcome. Outside of Christ, we know neither who the God who chooses (elects) is, nor those he elects, nor how he elects them.³²

In the light of this theological motif, it is appropriate to consider the homiletical turn by which the motif is communicated. "The Ultimate Decision" sits between a study affirming revelation in Christ as the only truth and life, and a subsequent study which relates to the human aspect of the choice of life in Christ. Thus it picks up from the question of revelation and the "intellectually scandalous affirmation which leads to "another rebellious movement: dread joined to a sense of the impossible."³³ That impossibility is the affirmation of Jesus as the *only* way, without having explored every other possible way. Without this external reference, the choice of faith in Christ appears to be an enclosed decision in a closed cycle. "This is an eternal vicious circle of faith so rigorously closed that we are confronted with its limits in every thinking moment in our Christian lives."³⁴ To follow, he notes, is to become a disciple. But only a disciple chooses to follow.

Whether this confronting conundrum carries weight in a postmodern world is a worthy question, as is whether it is his modernist world that brings Maury to pose the conundrum as he does. Through this lens, however, Maury draws insight from the gospel narrative. That this is a mystery may be complex to Maury and his hearers. To contemporary hearers, however, the quandary may be overstated at best, and perhaps irrelevant at worst. Yet the light he sheds on the gospel brings insights, surely, to all followers of Christ. They may not be modernist seekers of certainty, but all followers of Christ are called to live with the complexity of mystery, and deal, even if diversely, with uncertainty.

30. EF 49. UD 67, PD 112.
31. EF 49.
32. EF 44.
33. UD 61.
34. UD 61.

Maury identifies two groups for which this uncertainty carries difficulty: "those people who aspire to have faith" and "double-minded Christians, not sure either of their questions or their certitude. . . . Christians for whom spiritual dryness is devastating."[35] For these groups, the questions are not "asked out of some vain intellectual curiosity, but represent the mortal torment of suffering souls."[36] The resolution is to "give up asking these kinds of questions . . . [and] to accept that these are questions which are addressed to *us* and which are resolved *for us* by *Another*, by the God who reveals *Himself*."[37]

"This abandonment, this acceptance, is very precisely the way of Jesus Christ."[38] It is a daily choice and a daily way. It is a commitment of daily and yet of eternal proportions. This is the objectivity which is the claim of Jesus Christ on our behalf. Thus Maury ends his introduction, and sets out the basis for his second section, wherein he addresses the consequences of the "ultimate decision."

Maury, in the second section of "The Ultimate Decision," paints the backdrop of social movements that demand exclusive choice. In Lent 1937 this may be understood as pointing particularly to the scourge building in Europe, as National Socialism demanded absolute allegiance. Today, politics in many places is again benign, but forces emerge demanding absolute commitment—religious cults, and possibly some philatelic society somewhere as well. The Christian decision is not of this kind, since Jesus is not of this world (John 8:23). It is not one totalitarian choice amongst many, but a response to *The Absolute*, the *Unique Son* of God, as Maury places his emphasis. We do not know our choice, but "we need to know by Him *whom* we choose in choosing him."[39]

This short second session leads to a third, with some exposition of the lives of the faithful, from Pascal to Jesus's own hearers. The apprehension that they heard the *living* word of God became the basis for their response. Maury's own comment will probably be echoed yet more strongly today: "I know that this affirmation will always appear to be incomprehensible to those who have not heard the voice of God in Christ."[40] Whether this is because "a faithless generation demands a sign"

35. UD 62.
36. UD 62.
37. UD 62.
38. UD 62.
39. UD 63.
40. UD 65.

or because "faith comes by hearing" will stretch the minds of mission strategists in every age, and vex those who seek simple formulae. Yet it is in the midst of complex factors that witness finds its voice. It is in the midst of mystery that life choices are made.

The fourth section moves to a discussion of "the *decisive* and *ultimate* character of his [Christ's] reality."[41] This is the key topic for this talk. Here, the decisive character relates to Jesus Christ as the decision of God. Humankind are the object of the decision. The ultimate character relates to the finality of the decision. These two aspects are reinforced by appeal to a wide range of scriptures, from John 1:1–3 and Colossians 1:6, both appealing to the completeness of creation in Christ, to the Psalms and the gospel narratives, where the definitive nature of the acts of God in Christ are on display. In this sweep, in the "prodigious audacity" of Jesus, humankind discover that they are not "ephemeral beings, incidental playthings of circumstances or of blind forces, interchangeable links of the missing link of our race." Rather, "we existed, we are known in our most personal reality; for in God's view we have a name!"[42] And in him we are *individualized*.[43] The particularity of Jesus Christ as "a man that we can know because he has been one of us, has lived like us and amongst us human beings" means that "it is with him that we are linked. Such is the sense of our baptism."[44] In our baptism, the human name chosen by our parents is "associated very personally with the name of Jesus Christ."

Maury's turns of phrase are engaging. I was drawn to "prodigious audacity" (above) and find it hard to resist "marvelous revelation of an unfathomable mystery!"[45] In the "Easter event" (to borrow a phrase beloved of Barth) "it is our whole life that is swept up in this commitment."[46] In this simplicity and immensity our life begins and ends. Maury encapsulates this conclusion to the core of his talk in memorable prose:

> Yes! Marvelous revelation! But so that it does not remain an unfathomable divine thought, so that the mystery of Jesus is not just something that God knows, but also that those who are in Christ, that is to say you and me, will overflow with joy, we need

41. UD 66.
42. UD 66.
43. UD 66.
44. UD 67.
45. UD 67.
46. UD 67.

to understand how this humble earthly truth, the life of the Son of man, is a heavenly secret; in other words, how Jesus Christ is decisive.[47]

The theological emphasis emerging is the equating of the act and person of Jesus Christ in salvation. Maury, as Barth, has no truck with a mere forensic engagement of saved humanity with the Act of God in the Easter event. Rather, with Paul (and Barth), he emphasizes the "in Christ-ness" of saved humanity as part of a saved world. This is love which incorporates but does not subsume. It is incorporation which affirms rather than extinguishing uniqueness. This is how salvation in Christ can be ultimate without being totalitarian.

In his fifth section Maury explores the decisiveness of the character of Christ's reality. He does this by referring to the testimony of eyewitnesses to Christ. Implicitly, Maury notes, this testimony accords with the many since who have entered into an understanding that their existence was fulfilled in him. He unpacks this reality in terms of their testimony of Jesus Christ as the one who *comes to them, gives himself to them, and chooses them*. In the day of salvation, as for the paralytic by the pool of Bethesda, healing comes when Jesus comes. Christ's coming reveals intention and direction, and an unwavering will towards others.

In his coming, Christ gives himself. He holds nothing back. For those to whom he offers himself, "it is only ever a matter of receiving, of taking, and of being filled with Him."[48] His choosing "makes plain" his coming and giving. He calls, enlightens, and explains to those who listen. Maury then points to a key moral dimension of election, when he says, "We need to understand this election in its most positive sense, that is to say, as a testimony of his love, and not negatively as a sign of partiality."[49] It is clear from the *Church Dogmatics* that Barth resonated with this sense of election as the divine "Yes!" The human parallel is touching: "A father loves each of his children with a complete and special tenderness, without at the same time setting aside any of them." Yet the realism of this calling is not simply to life, but to endurance through "hostility, persecution, *even* death."[50] In Christ, saving life is losing it, and losing it because of Christ is truly saving it.

---

47. UD 67.
48. UD 69.
49. UD 70.
50. UD 70.

Maury notes that this claim to complete incorporation could be issued by any master in this world. The differentiating mystery is what he does *for* us. He does this because he comes *from above*, in obedience. He "*gives himself* fully, freely, totally" and yet is also given over, and delivered for us by human agents and even *abandoned* by God. His choosing of those who must relinquish their will to him is born of his own relinquishment of his will to God for the sake of others. Jesus Christ asks only for what he has himself done. The ultimacy of this decision thus has a "double sense." It is absolute, as an expression of God's absolute love. It is absolute in that it gives *all things*. Again, Maury cites from the end of Romans 8: God, having given up all things for us, gives us all things, that nothing might separate us from God's love. This is the assurance made possible by the ultimacy of the decisive act of God, the divine ultimate decision, Jesus Christ. Our whole life, hidden with Christ in God, is thus a divine decision. It is good news, and as we have noted, it is a basis for joy.

Maury, in the light of this assurance, notes the power of judgment against us: *Himself*. We can thrill with joy because we know who will be the judge, and what the judgment will be:

> Praise be to God that he has postponed the irrevocable sentence to which we will have to submit, to the ultimate authority. Praise be to God that our judge is the One who has chosen us . . . and who wanted to be chosen by us![51]

The decision we make *for* Christ is the decision we make *in* Christ. This, then, is the basis of our ultimate decision. This is required of us "*with no holding back*." This is not to be based on emotional appeals, rational argument or opinions or doctrines. The choice, the decision, is Jesus Christ. His choice of us becomes our choice of him. It is a "*yes or no*, and never 'perhaps.'"[52] "The intolerable, demanding nature of faith is the mark of *grace* which is ours in faith."[53]

Maury makes an important nuancing, or even a defense, of election when he notes that the ultimacy of the decision "is not the way that Jesus Christ demands our choice."[54] In the light of this, says Maury, we do well to reread the accounts of the encounters with the Lord of those whose lives he turned around is that "they all ran toward Jesus of Nazareth, with

---

51. UD 73.
52. UD 74.
53. UD 74.
54. UD 75.

the same expectancy, with their whole life offered up and reaching out ... [not] ... like a doctor among so many others."⁵⁵ As he brings his talk to a conclusion, and focuses his appeal, Maury recounts the responses of those whom Jesus encountered: throwing themselves on their knees, climbing a tree, and particularly how Jesus recognized them: He recognized them *as his own*.

From their stories, embedded in texts and the past, he poses the "great, formidable question" that remains: "How would we be able *today* to know Jesus Christ ... and how would we be able *today* to choose him without reservation and conditions?"⁵⁶ We do not have the possibility of being with him but, rather, we have a book, and we have a community: the scriptures and the church. Both make Jesus Christ our contemporary; both hear and witness to Jesus Christ; both call us to "decide *for* or *against* Him." Whether slowly or suddenly, the truth presented in the book calls for decision, and the church bears witness to its truth. The call to the ultimate decision is a call in and from a community of witness to a God who is being in encounter, truth, and the ultimate decision. Christ. Life and death. "And the people began to rejoice."

Mystery evoking joy! Jesus Christ, through lives past, by scripture and in the church, calls to human beings, invites encounter, and asks for choice, that the ultimate decision might be made again as it was made once for all. And joy will reign.

For both Maury and Barth, the language of joy and of election intertwine. There is both resonance and coherence between the two. It is evident in Barth's early writing and in his later work. It is evident in Maury's theological writing and in this seminal sermon, "The Ultimate Decision." Joy is the gift of election. God elects in joy and for joy—the completion of God's own joy, and the affirmation of human joy in God. Joy is the hallmark of election: being in encounter. Election is a doctrine of joy, and a call to the joy of being in encounter. Election can and should be a joyful doctrine, a joyful message, and a reason for joy. There are missional and pastoral dimensions of this. And a reading of Barth's sermons shows the same resonance of joy and delight in Jesus Christ.

---

55. UD 75.
56. UD 75.

# BIBLIOGRAPHY

Barth, Karl. *Church Dogmatics*. Edited by G. W. Bromiley and T. F. Torrance. Translated by G. T. Thomson, et al. Edinburgh: T&T Clark, 1936–77.

Busch, Eberhard. *Karl Barth: His Life from Letters and Autobiographical Texts*. Translated by J. Bowden. Philadelphia: Fortress, 1975.

Capper, John Mark. "Joy in the *Church Dogmatics*? A Neglected Theme." In *Karl Barth: A Future for Post-modern Theology?*, edited by Geoff Thompson and Christiaan Mostert, 98–121. Hindmarsh: Australian Theological Forum, 2000.

Durheim, Benjamin. "The Human as Encounter: Karl Barth's Theological Anthropology and a Barthian Vision of the Common Good." *Lumen et Vita* 1.1 (2011) 1–20.

Jüngel, Eberhard. *God as the Mystery of the World: On the Foundation of the Theology of the Crucified One in the Dispute Between Theism and Atheism*. Translated by Darrell L. Guder. Edinburgh: T&T Clark, 1983.

Mangina, Joseph L. *Karl Barth on the Christian Life: The Practical Knowledge of God*. Issues in Systematic Theology 8. New York: Peter Lang, 2001.

Maury, Pierre. "*Election et Foi*." *Foi et Vie* 37 (1936) 203–223.

# 13

## Karl Barth's Influence on Contemporary Christian Universalism

DAMON S. ADAMS

IN 1936 WHEN PIERRE Maury delivered his paper on "Election and Faith" at the Geneva Calvinist Congress, (in celebration of the 400th anniversary of the publication of Calvin's *Institutes*), he unquestionably provided a key concept that was to be the foundation stone to Barth's new take on the classical Reformed doctrine of election.[1] Barth acknowledges Maury's contribution in his *Church Dogmatics*:

> The Christological meaning and basis of the doctrine of election have been brought out afresh in our own time, and with an impressive treatment of Jesus Christ as the original and decisive object of the divine election and rejection. This service has been rendered by Pierre Maury in the fine lecture which he gave on "*Election et Foi*" at the *Congrès internationale de théologie calviniste* in Geneva 1936.[2]

Maury's emphasis on the centrality of Christ as the Elect along with election being "in Christ" provided sufficient impetus to Barth in developing his Christocentric theological system which Matthias Gockel calls "Barth's Christological Revolution."[3] Barth's doctrine of election was

---

1. See also Gockel's detailed mention of Maury's influence on Barth's in the formation of the doctrine of Election (Gockel, *Barth & Schleiermacher*, 159–62).

2. *CD* II/2:154–55.

3. Gockel, *Barth & Schleiermacher*, 158. Gockel has provided a good comparison

inextricably linked to the person of Jesus Christ and thereby became the interpretive point of all other doctrines. However, attached to Barth's newly formulated doctrine of election came explanations that have left many a reader of Barth to conclude that he was effectively teaching a form of Christian Universalism.

Numerous theologians have defended Barth from the charge of Christian Universalism (*apokatastasis*).[4] Some have employed in this defense quotes of Barth's denial.[5] Given that Barth's denial stands, the question needs to be considered in the context of what he wrote and the subsequent consequences of his teaching within both the theological and ecclesial realms. This essay will focus its consideration on the contribution his teaching has made in support of the presently burgeoning Christian Universalism.

Barth's teaching on the doctrine of election, as it appears in his *Church Dogmatics*, is a paradigmatic shift from the classical Reformed doctrine. Barth, in a letter to Maury, acknowledges this when he says: "Only, we should not hide the fact that while being good disciples of the Reformation, we are perhaps moving further than our liberal predecessors, from their way of thinking. There really is no 'Calvinism'!"[6] Although Barth, in writing to Maury, includes himself as moving away from classical Calvinism, it is fair to say that Maury's move is comparatively

---

between Maury and Barth's theology in Gockel, "Harmony without Identity," 129–41.

4. Amongst those who defend Barth from the charge of being a Christian Universalist are Hunsinger, *How to Read Karl Barth*, 128–37; Colwell, "Contemporaneity of the Divine Decision," 139–60; Bettis, "Is Karl Barth A Universalist?," 423–36; O'Neil, "Karl Barth's Doctrine of Election," 318–26.

5. *CD* II/2:417, 422, 477. In these various passages in which Barth rejects *apokatastasis*, he argues on the following grounds: (1) The freedom of the grace of God is not bound by the extent of the circle of grace in having, of necessity, to include all of humanity (*CD* II/2:417). (2) The sovereign control of God also entails His freedom, which means those to be saved "we cannot equate their number with the totality of all men." Likewise, we must affirm "God so loved the world" and "We cannot consider their number as closed, for we can never find any reason for such a limitation in Jesus Christ" (*CD* II/2:422). This is the dialectical dilemma—the closing of the door on the necessity of *apokatastasis* but the anticipation of the opening of the door in hope. (3) The possibility of rejection as a possibility in the freedom of God—as may be the possibility in the case of Judas. "The Church will not then preach an *apokatastasis*, nor will it preach a powerless grace of Jesus Christ or a wickedness of men which is too powerful for it" (*CD* II/2:477). Again, this is the dialectical dilemma—the possibility of rejection by men but the negating of that power by the grace of God in Jesus Christ.

6. Maury, *Election, Barth*, 8.

minor compared with that of Barth's. Maury, in his lecture, "*Election et Foi* [Election and Faith]" (EF), considers the matter of election on the basis of the role of faith. He gives a balanced consideration of the divine and human perspectives on the doctrines of election and predestination, and provides a number of thoughtful correctives to classical Calvinism. He places emphasis on the centrality of Christ in relation to the starting point of the doctrine of election and focuses on the Pauline imperative of "in Christ." His presentation of double predestination, though nudging towards an asymmetrical approach, does not exclude "the mystery, alien to our reason, of *double* predestination," which he maintains "is resolved, in faith."[7] By contrast, Barth has taken some of the key aspects which appear in *Election et Foi* and develops them from a strictly divine perspective which is so strongly Christocentric that some scholars have inappropriately labelled it "Christomonism."[8]

Although Maury had moved away from Calvin on some points on election and predestination, he holds in tension the divine and human elements. This is also clear in his "Predestination" (1956) where he discusses key elements in Barth's more developed Christocentric doctrine of election.[9] He is conscious of the pastoral and human dimension to this majestic doctrine. This is seen when, as he nears his conclusion, he says, "I have never forgotten that election is concerned with living souls."[10] Maury's pastoral instincts appear to take precedence over theological concerns. As far as Reformed orthodoxy's view of Barth's doctrine of election is concerned, Berkhof (1873–1957) described Barth's approach as "*not even distantly related* to that of Augustine and Calvin,"[11] and as recently as 2018, McClymond has questioned Barth's status as a "Reformed" theologian, since, as he states, "Barth sets Calvin on his head."[12]

---

7. EF 52.

8. Editor's note: see page 6 in the introduction.

9. "I ought to point out to you that in these lectures you will often recognize the thought of Karl Barth. We have, in fact, for many years discussed this doctrine together, and he has propounded it in masterly fashion, infusing it with new life, in his *Church Dogmatics* II/2" (Maury, "Predestination") 81.

10. Maury, "Predestination," 117.

11. Berkhof, *Systematic Theology*, 111 (emphasis mine).

12. McClymond, *Devil's Redemption*, 2:792.

## I. BARTH'S UNIVERSALISTIC THEOLOGY

Barth's Christocentric approach to theology led him on a trajectory well beyond the semblance of what has been commonly received as orthodox Reformed theology.[13] His approach to the doctrine of election completely threw out the "system" of classical Calvinism which relies on the logical sequence of the five decrees summed up in the Five Points of Calvinism.[14] Interestingly, Barth claimed his view on Jesus Christ as the Elect makes him a supralapsarian.[15] He took a term that is strictly in the taxonomy of classical Reformed theology and redefined it according to his understanding of the doctrine of election. Macleod points out that Barth saw his explanation of supralapsarianism as a "correction" of the classical Reformed doctrine of predestination and election. Barth called his revision, "Purified Supralapsarianism,"[16] whereas in reality it was far more radical than a mere correction.[17] Therefore, despite his use of a well-known Reformed term connected to the order of the decrees, in substance his re-definition was far and away from "classical" Calvinism.[18] He was well aware that he was breaking from what he deemed was the "metaphysics" of the Reformed tradition in order to establish what he viewed to be a more biblical perspective. So even though his theology leads to numerous questions on many doctrines, it is that of the extent of salvation that has remained the enigmatic question that begs an answer. He would not and could not give a definitive answer to universal salvation.

---

13. Cortez, "What Does It Mean?," 1–17.

14. The five points of Calvinism consist of: (1) Total Depravity (all of Humanity has fallen into sin in Adam and are bound by sin in their thoughts, words and deeds); (2) Unconditional Election (God has in eternity chosen some of fallen humanity by grace to salvation); (3) Limited Atonement (Jesus Christ died on the cross for those specifically elected); (4) Irresistible Grace (the Holy Spirit draws all the elect, in time, to embrace Jesus as their Savior); (5) Perseverance of the Saints (all believers will continue in the faith to the end). Thus, the acronym TULIP.

15. *CD* II/2:127–45.

16. *CD* II/2:142. See Macleod, "Definite Atonement," 413.

17. Macleod, "Definite Atonement," 415.

18. For a clear definition of these two terms, see Schnucker, "Infralapsarianism," 607; Klooster, "Supralapsarianism," 1155.

## Barth's Doctrine of Election

According to Barth, all humanity is elected "in Christ." Jesus Christ is both the accepted and the rejected. He is simultaneously the elect and the reprobate. Thus, in Christ is both "Yes" and "No." "Yes" to acceptance in Christ to all and "No" to rejection of any. Jesus Christ is the substitute for all humans—election is all inclusive—on the basis that Jesus Christ is the Elect, a doctrine of universal election, which results in the first link towards universal salvation.

In *CD* II/1 where Barth discusses the knowability of God and man's readiness and receptivity for grace, Barth is in no doubt that Jesus Christ represented all of humanity in His life and death:

> This participation of ours (all of humanity) in the person and work of Jesus Christ does not have to be added as a second thing. As the one thing which has to be done it is already wholly and utterly accomplished in Him. In that which has taken place in God–in which we are indeed participators on the strength of the nature of the person and of Jesus Christ–it is in itself and from the very outset something which has taken place to and in us.[19]

Thus, Barth's election consists of Jesus Christ as the Elect and in him all humans are elected unto grace. Yet not only are all humans elected but are also "in Christ" and therefore all are *objectively* justified and sanctified:[20] This is made evident by Barth in considering the Glory of the Mediator in Jesus as Victor in *CD* IV/3 where he states:

> Again, the act of God accomplished and expressed in Jesus Christ is the justification and sanctification of man. It is thus the act in which man, whether he realises it or not, is objectively alienated, separated and torn away from this resisting element in him, because he is already set in the liberty of the children of God.[21]

Barth's positive affirmations of the all-pervasive, universalistic objective accomplishments of Jesus Christ, in time, lead Berkouwer (1903–1996) in his seminal work to summarize Barth's theology as "The

---

19. *CD* II/1:157–58.

20. Bloesch, *Jesus is Victor*, 32–42. In this section Bloesch discusses the objective elements of salvation as presented by Barth, including aspects of the *ordo salutis*—justification, sanctification, faith, and conversion.

21. *CD* IV/3:269.

Triumph of Grace."[22] While Barth was appreciative of Berkouwer's comment, he preferred to see his teaching as the declaration of "Jesus as victor!" However, for Olson, "this Christological concentration of Barth's doctrine of election leads ineluctably, inexorably to universalism."[23]

## Barth on Election and Reprobation

Another area of Barth's departure from classical Calvinism is in relation to the doctrine of double predestination. Calvin saw the doctrine of the decree of predestination as double sided—*election* and *reprobation*. Barth did not accept that the double nature of the decree related to a division within humanity. In fact, he saw this teaching of orthodox Reformed theology as odious. According to Barth, all of humanity received their election in the Elect One, Jesus Christ–this generates the YES to humanity. Rejection, the double side of the decree of predestination, according to Barth, exists only in relation to Jesus Christ–He is the rejected one alone, He is the Reprobate One–this generates the NO to Jesus Christ.

It is significant to note that Maury in his lecture *Election et Foi* provided the seminal grounds (the "decisive impetus") for the concept of Jesus Christ as the Rejected One.[24] This is especially seen when Maury says, "it was necessary that the Son of Man be rejected."[25] In addition, Maury introduced the use of the emphatic "NO" and "YES" in response to divine election.[26] This was taken up by Barth and developed strictly from the divine perspective, while Maury hinted at a more *asymmetrical dimension* to double predestination for Jesus experienced the "double' aspect which has the character of both rejection and welcome."[27] Finally, Maury broaches the idea that election is completely Christocentric: "'In Christ' means as well that this eternal election has not only as its origin, but also its ground, the eternal Christ and incarnate Christ as well."[28] Overall, it

---

22. Berkouwer, *Triumph of Grace*.

23. Olson, "Was Karl Barth a Universalist?" Lee, more cautiously than Olson, states: "Barth's doctrine of election fails to distance itself from the doctrine of apokatastasis. Its major claim is God's universal election in Christ" (Lee, "Revelation of the Triune God," 296).

24. EF 46–49.

25. EF 47.

26. EF 49.

27. EF 49.

28. EF 45.

can be claimed that the key difference between Barth and Maury rests in that Maury always includes the divine and human perspectives on the doctrines of election and predestination.

Barth emphasizes that Jesus has dealt with the NO for humanity. God's rejection of Christ was the sum and basis of God's rejection of all human sin and sinners. So this newly reconstructed double predestination of Jesus Christ furnishes a YES to all humanity as elected to life and a NO to all humanity as partaking of any level of rejection. This again underscores Barth's universalism in so far as the only objective position for all humans is acceptance through election without the possibility of rejection[29] In coming to terms with this dilemma, Gockel maintains that "it would be rather simplistic to conclude that he (Barth) has overcome the danger of "a dualistic particularism," only to arrive at a "monistic universalism." Still, it seems that his affirmation of universal election implies some form of universal salvation, despite his own unwillingness to go that far."[30]

## Barth and the Atonement[31]

Along with Barth's revised doctrine of universal election there is also the matter of substitution. McClymond aptly observes that "Barth's logic of election is substitutionary. Despite the debates among modern theologians over the idea of substitutionary suffering, Barth's understanding of election and of the cross of Christ clearly involves substitutionary suffering." This includes the judgment of suffering punishment for our deeds; His election, specifically to suffering; and the taking of the penalty of divine judgment and condemnation for all elected humanity on the cross.[32]

This leads McClymond to conclude:

> It is in fact Barth's substitutionary logic that evokes the question of universalism. Christ's rejection by God was the rejection of

---

29. *CD* II/2:167–68, 346–47.

30. Gockel, *Barth & Schleiermacher*, 189.

31. This essay does not examine Barth's actual teaching of his theory of the Atonement which deviates from the classic evangelical view of Penal Substitution. For Barth's view of the atonement and comparison with Anselm, see Hoon, "Karl Barth's Doctrine," 243–92; Vanhoozer, "Atonement," 194–96; Williams, "Karl Barth and the Doctrine," 232–72.

32. *CD* IV/1:294–95.

all human sinners and sin. Christ's vindication is the vindication of all. God's verdict of "No" against human sin has already been spoken. The rejection of Christ on the cross means that rejection no longer remains–that rejection itself is rejected.[33]

This relationship between the atonement and election in Barth's theology needs to be clearly acknowledged, especially since he attempts to bridge the logical impasse between universal election and universal atonement and eschatological salvific assurance with the ambiguity of the freedom of God, along with the *objective* over against the *subjective* work in redemption. What does it really mean for the atonement to be objectively sufficient and efficient for all with the divide of subjective application? Barth appears to want to keep a chasm between the objective and subjective. This leaves the dialectical impasse of the freedom of God and the subjective rejection of Jesus Christ by some.[34]

There is no question that Barth made statements that were universalistic. He was not bound by the restraint of logic or systems that restricted the freedom and love of God, hence, the all-inclusive intent, extent and efficacy of election, redemption and reconciliation. Declarations of universal salvation abound in Barth. However, God's freedom requires that He not be constrained by a principle. Is universal salvation, *apokatastasis* an absolute given? Barth is clear on this—NO! This leaves many theologians divided—some claiming that Barth was a universalist, while others are equally adamant that he was not. Some call him "a hopeful universalist" and others call him agnostic or ambivalent. There is no simple answer to this question. Barth's copious theological writings are filled with what appear to be contradictory theological statements. The easiest response would be to retreat into the dialectical defence that renders any attempt at systematising a grand imposition. Barth never completed his *Church Dogmatics* with the final planned volume 5 on Eschatology. What there is of Barth's theological "system" is sufficient to justify the conclusion that

---

33. McClymond, *Devil's Redemption*, 768.

34. Barth's use of the freedom of God as one of his major objections to *apokatastasis*, according to Lee, falls short since, regarding Bath's universalism, "it imprisons the freedom of God's just rejection in the freedom of his own merciful election. Barth does not succeed in maintaining the intention to emancipate God from his own freedom. He fails to present God's freedom as a real freedom which he so seriously seeks to defend. For he does not see the possible affirmation of the total freedom of God in election and rejection without making it a doctrine of wrath, condemnation and horror, as Calvin does" (Lee, "Revelation of the Triune God," 296).

his Christocentric orientation provides a reasonable basis for linking him with Christian Universalism, even though he rejected the label outright.

## Karl Barth's Legacy and Christian Universalism

It is indisputable that Barth has had an impact on the theological scene both during and after his life time. His enduring legacy is still very strong today, part of which is his contribution to the resurgence of Christian Universalism. In assessing Barth and the topic of *apokatastasis,* it is all too easy to get caught up in debating whether or not he was a universalist. I venture to propose that there is more to be gained by looking at the influence he has had and still has on the proponents of Christian Universalism. This is pertinent as today his name and works are being touted by many who are advocating various forms of Christian Universalism, which is currently a contentious issue in both academic and popular spheres.

Olson in introducing his article on Barth and Christian Universalism opens by stating: "Looming large over these relatively new movements within Calvinism and evangelicalism is the shadow of Karl Barth. Without doubt, Barth's influence on evangelical theology is stronger, and more controversial, than ever."[35] Van Zyl says of Jonker[36] regarding Barth:

> Jonker is convinced that, although Barth denies the fact that his theology supports a doctrine of unconditional salvation for all of humanity, the thrust of his theology still remains universalistic, and *has contributed to the common universal climate that we find in the world today.* Brunner predicted that Barth's universalism will find widespread approval in the modern mind, since it is in harmony with the spirit of the Enlightenment.[37]

Hilborn and Horrocks in a similar vein to Olson declare: "Possibly the most important conduit of universalistic influence on evangelicals in the past hundred years or so is a scholar who was neither fully aligned with evangelicalism nor finally committed to Talbott's style of dogmatic

---

35. Olson, "Was Karl Barth a Universalist?"
36. South African Dutch Reformed Church Minister and Theologian (1929–2006).
37. Van Zyl, "Karl Barth's 'Modern' and 'Unbiblical' Universalism," 289 (emphasis mine).

universalism[38]—namely, Karl Barth."[39] McClymond points specifically to the centrality of Barth's doctrine of election as the launching pad for the new wave of Christian Universalism, "By placing the doctrine of universal election at the center of his imposing Church Dogmatics, Barth gave legitimacy and prestige to universalist style theology."[40]

Esteban Deak in his later published doctoral thesis, *Apokatastasis: The Problem of Universal Salvation in the Twentieth Century*[41] divides the issue of Christian Universalism in the twentieth-century by using Barth as the point of division—pre-Barthian, Barthian, and post-Barthian.[42] This division is significant in and of itself and supports the claim that Barth's writing had and still has an influence on the question of Christian Universalism. Further, McClymond mentions the Swiss theologian Gotthold Muller "who published an extensive bibliography on Christian universalism, point(ing) to Barth as the one figure who had decisively shifted discussion: 'An entirely new perspective in the history of *Apokatastasis* emerged in the theology of Karl Barth.'"[43]

## Comparison of Barth with Origen and Schleiermacher

In recent years there have been two works that have respectively concentrated on comparing and contrasting Barth with a famous Christian universalist—one with Origen and the other with Schleiermacher. Tom Greggs has compared and contrasted Barth with Origen (the father of *apokatastasis*) in his work, *Barth, Origen, and Universal Salvation: Restoring Particularity*.[44] The other work focusses on Barth and Schleiermacher and is written by Matthias Gockel, *Barth & Schleiermacher on the Doctrine of Election: A Systematic-Theological Comparison*.[45] The fact that these two works concentrate on examining Barth in the light of two

---

38. Thomas Talbott, Professor Emeritus of Philosophy at Willamette University in Salem, Oregon. Talbott advocates a Trinitarian form of Christian Universalism in Talbott, *Inescapable Love of God*.

39. Hilborn and Horrocks, "Universalism and Evangelical Theology," 209.

40. McClymond, *Devil's Redemption*, 2:811.

41. Deak, *Apokatastasis*.

42. McClymond, *Devil's Redemption*, 2:809.

43. McClymond, *Devil's Redemption*, 2:808. McClymond cites Muller, "Idea of an Apokatastasis," 50–51. See also, Muller, *Apokatastasis Panton*.

44. Greggs, *Barth, Origen, and Universal Salvation*.

45. Gockel, *Barth & Schleiermacher*.

renowned universalists shows the continued association of Barth's theology with Christian Universalism. Both Greggs and Gockel effectively conclude that Barth can be seen to traverse a universalist course, if great care is taken not to have him caught between "the Scylla and Charybdis" of all the many restrictions that he had so adamantly rejected. Greggs has additionally produced a strong argument for Barth's universalism in his article, "Jesus is Victor."[46] This is achieved by way of a careful extrication of the feared entanglements that led to Barth's denial of the various established views of Christian Universalism or *apokatastasis*. Greggs concludes:

> What is important for Barth is that the Christian cannot view the non-Christian as anything other than the person for whom God elected, who is elected in Christ and whose rejection is all too well known by the reality of the faith community as well. If we are to charge Barth with universalism, it cannot be that universalism which has been articulated previously. What Barth cannot be charged with is a failure to recognize the monumentally and radically new situation of humanity eternally elected in Christ. Yes, Christ stands at the door and knocks; but in the power of his resurrection, he makes his way into locked rooms.[47]

In his work, Gockel looks at Barth by way of comparison with Schleiermacher, and especially in relation to the topic of Christian Universalism.[48] Both theologians shared some common ground, so much so that as Jonker observed:

> His universalism is perhaps the most convincing testimony to Barth's modernistic tendency. . . . In his universalistic views he remains true to the convictions of the modern era, of Schleiermacher and the nineteenth century. . . . From the very beginning he took a universalistic stand. It is interesting to see how his universalistic idea about the election . . . became the corner stone of his whole dogmatics. . . . What happened later was only the explication of the same conviction in terms of his concept of the Christ-Event in its actual and all-encompassing meaning. It is clear that his universalism affects all other aspects of his dogmatic thinking. His soteriology was affected, but also the doctrine about the church with its preaching and sacraments.

---

46. Greggs, "Jesus is Victor," 196–212.
47. Greggs, "Jesus is Victor," 212.
48. Gockel, *Barth & Schleiermacher*, 198–211; McNicol, "Universal Salvation," 44–48; Goroncy, "That God May Have Mercy," 113–30.

> Moreover, the distinction between the church and the world becomes utterly relative. The church is no more than a sign of the coming salvation of the whole world, and as such it is totally directed towards the world.[49]

Here Jonker saw in Barth far more than just a relationship with Schleiermacher. He believed that Barth was taking his Christocentric theology on a trajectory to *apokatastasis*.

## The Influence of Barth on Advocates of Christian Universalism

In describing Barth's universalistic teachings and their influence on some noteworthy people, a wide spectrum is opened up. Hans Urs von Balthasar, the Roman Catholic theologian (1905–1988), believed that Barth's Christian Universalism was an inevitable result of his Christocentric theology. Throughout von Balthasar's book, *The Theology of Karl Barth*, he challenges Barth on the significance of at least "the hope of universal salvation." At times he questions Barth beyond the "hope" towards *apokatastasis*. In commenting on Barth's work on the Creed he says:

> In his book on the Creed, Barth warns us of eschatological arrogance. He avers that the "positive doctrine of the apokatastasis does not belong to the Creed because it would simple eviscerate it." . . . Nonetheless, despite these demurrals, Barth's doctrine of election does not leave much room open for possibility. There is something inevitable and necessary in his views. What is definite in Barth's thought is grace and blessing, and all reprobation and judgment are merely provisional: . . . This was the cost Barth had to pay to realize his seamless systematization of the economy of salvation. But this is also what gives it its triumphal allure, its unprecedented consistency, its certainty of victory.[50]

Von Balthasar declared himself to be amongst those, like Barth, who held the hope of universal salvation in Christ.[51] Like Barth, he held to the paradox of salvation and judgment. However, he states—"All protestations that he [Barth] does not mean *apokatastasis panton*, 'for a grace that, in the end, would automatically have to include and reach each and

---

49. Jonker, "Some Remarks," 39.
50. Von Balthasar, *Theology of Karl Barth*, 186.
51. Von Balthasar, *Dare We Hope?*

all would certainly be free or a divine grace,' remains, as W. Kreck says, 'ultimately rhetorical.'"[52]

Additionally, Wilhelm Michaelis, the German Theologian[53] (1896–1965) and John A. T. Robinson (1919–1983), the somewhat notorious New Testament scholar, author and Anglican Bishop of Woolwich, followed aspects of Barth's universalistic propositions and became well known for their adherence to Christian Universalism.[54] Robinson declared his stance when he was prompted to write in defence of Barth against Brunner's criticisms of Barth's logical universalism as it appeared in his *Church Dogmatics*.[55] The renowned French Sociologist and Lay Theologian, Jacques Ellul (1912–1994) also advocated Christian Universalism. In his book, *What I Believe*, Ellul unequivocally declared the salvation of all in Christ in the chapter, "Universal Salvation":

> I am taking up here a basic theme that I have dealt with elsewhere . . . the recognition that all people from the beginning of time are saved by God in Jesus Christ, that they have all been recipients of his grace no matter what they have done. . . . This is a scandalous proposition. . . . But I want to stress that I am speaking about belief in universal salvation. . . . After Jesus Christ we know that God is love. This is the central revelation. How can we conceive of him who is love ceasing to love one of his creatures? How can we think that God can cease to love the creation that he has made in his own image? . . . Being love, God cannot send to hell the creation which he so loved that he gave his only Son for it. He cannot reject it because it is his creation. This would be to cut off himself.[56]

According to Neville, "Ellul's theological perspective was shaped largely by his reading of Karl Barth."[57] Echoes of Barth's universalistic teaching can be heard in Ellul's words. The emphasis of the divine attribute of love finds its foundation in Barth's *Church Dogmatics* II/1 in

---

52. Von Balthasar in McClymond, *Devil's Redemption*, 2:801.

53. Editor's note: Gockel points out that "In the main, German-speaking Barth scholars, who have worked extensively on this issue in the last two decades, mostly in the context of eschatology, distinguish between 'universal reconciliation' (*Allversöhnung*) and 'universal redemption' (*Allerlösung*)" (personal communication with the author, 2019).

54. Michaelis, *Versöhnung des Alls*; Robinson, *In the End*.

55. Robinson, "Universalism," 139–55.

56. Ellul, *What I Believe*, 188–90.

57. Neville, "Dialectic as Method," 169–70, 173.

the section titled, "The Being of God as the One Who Loves"[58] which even precedes the section on, "The Being of God in Freedom."[59] Another renowned theologian, also influenced by Barth, Nels Ferré (1908–1971) took Barth's emphasis on the love of God and made it the centre-point of his theology of Christian Universalism.[60] Paul Tournier, the famous Swiss physician (1898–1986) was another whose Christian Universalism was influenced by Barth.[61] "I am not far from Barth's theology," Tournier once remarked; "we agree on many things."[62] In *Guilt and Grace*, he demonstrated his universalism in a statement reminiscent of Barth:

> The order to His disciples to go "into all the world," was simply to proclaim the "good news" (Mark 16:15), to convince all men and to multiply the visible signs of God's grace by mighty works and healings. . . . But this was not the procuring of salvation. Salvation was already there, offered and assured for all men.[63]

The missional and evangelistic thrust of Barth's message of the universal objective liberty in Christ was taken up as the Christian Universalists' justification for the positive necessity of missionary endeavour. The American Lutheran theologian Carl Braaten (b1929) makes particular mention of Barth as providing both theological and motivational impetus to a Christian Universalistic perspective for missions.[64] The major passage presented by Braaten in support of this missional perspective is from Barth's *Church Dogmatics* IV/3:

> There is no good reason why we should forbid ourselves or be forbidden, to the possibility that in the reality of God and man in Jesus Christ there is contained much more than we might expect and therefore the supremely unexpected withdrawal of the final threat, i.e., that in the truth of this reality there might be contained the super-abundant promise of the final deliverance

---

58. *CD* II/1:272–97.

59. *CD* II/1:297–321.

60. Ferré places God's attribute of Love as the dominant and primary attribute of God which effectively subsumes all the other attributes beneath it. See Beougher, "Are All Doomed?," 11–14; Ferre, *Christian Understanding of God*; Hamilton, "Love or Holy Love?"

61. For an analysis of Paul Tournier's theology, see Musick, "Paul Tournier's Universalism."

62. Tournier in Collins, *Christian Psychology*, 80.

63. Tournier, *Guilt and Grace*, 188.

64. Braaten, "Meaning of Evangelism," 16–18.

of all men. To be more explicit, there is no good reason why we should not be open to the possibility. If for a moment we accept the unfinished truth of the reality which even now so forcefully limits the perverted human situation, does it not point plainly in the direction of the work of a truly eternal divine patience and deliverance and therefore of an *apokatastasis* or universal reconciliation?[65]

Braaten asserts that the hope of universal salvation provides the forward motion of the Church's missional mandate. Another theologian who has a strong influence on various sectors of the contemporary Protestant Church is Jürgen Moltmann (b. 1926). While Moltmann was a student at the University of Gottingen he became an avid admirer of Barth and held his *Church Dogmatics* in high regard. Moltmann took up aspects of Barth's "hopeful" Christian Universalism and carried them beyond the strictures of his former theological hero. It would be fair to attribute to Barth some role in setting Moltmann on the course of Ultimate Reconciliation. Moltmann's theology has been well received by many within present day Reformed, Evangelical circles. Various groups from the different branches of current day Christian Universalism look to Moltmann as a kind of "older statesman." Moltmann's book, *The Coming of God*,[66] demonstrates various similarities and differences between his perspective of universalism compared to that of Barth. In the end, like Barth, Moltmann holds to the objective salvation of all in Jesus Christ that needs to be actualised subjectively by the Spirit. However, importantly, unlike Barth, Moltmann is prepared to state that all *will* be saved.

Another scholar who has been a strong voice for Christian Universalism is David W. Congdon, who has put forward a brand of Christian Universalism that has undertones of Barth but is predominately influenced by Bultmann.[67] This interesting blend is presented in his book, *The God Who Saves: A Dogmatic Sketch*.[68] His early move to Christian Universalism came through his study of the works of Karl Barth and is

---

65. *CD* IV/3:477–78.

66. Moltmann, *Coming of God*.

67. Congdon's interest in Barth is further illustrated by articles he has produced around aspects of Barth's theology. See Congdon, "Dialectical Theology," 390–413; "Apokatastasis and Apostolicity," 464–80.

68. Congdon, *God Who Saves*. For an evangelical analysis of Congdon's book, see McClymond, "Apocalypse Now."

evident from early blog entries which quote copious sections of Barth's *Christian Dogmatics*.[69] He defends his position by stating the following:

> Barth is contradictory on universalism. He says that he does not accept the position, because I think he knows it is ecclesial suicide for him to do so in light of the condemnation of universalism as a heresy. But in his actual theology he basically says all the same things, even denying that hell can be a reality for any person.... So does he accept the position? As a label or title, no. But materially, he does, because there is no other position for him to take with any confidence.[70]

## Barth and the Contemporary Resurgence of Christian Universalism

From the publishing of Rob Bell's book, *Love Wins*,[71] in 2011, the doctrine of Ultimate Reconciliation or *apokatastasis* has become a hot topic within the popular Christian sphere.[72] No longer is Christian Universalism limited to the academy. So substantial was the controversy over Bell's implicit Ultimate Reconciliation, Scot McKnight said in an interview with *Christianity Today*, "Rob is tapping into what I think is the biggest issue facing evangelicalism today, and this fury shows that it just might be that big of an issue."[73] Significantly, since the "Rob Bell Debate" of 2011 there has been a proliferation of books, websites and blogs on Christian Universalism.[74] As has been noted above both Barth and Moltmann's thought has added weight to the discussion.

The public profile of Christian Universalism was lifted with the publication of the highly successful Christian novel, *The Shack*.[75] This generated other works such as J. Baxter Kruger's *The Shack Revisited*,[76] which blends some elements of Barth and Moltmann and presents a

---

69. See Congdon, "Why I Call Myself a 'Universalist.'"
70. Congdon, "Why I Call Myself a 'Universalist.'"
71. Bell, *Love Wins*.
72. See Adams, "Reshaping the Gospel?"
73. Bailey, "Rob Bell's Upcoming Book."
74. For an extensive list of books, blogs, and websites, see Adams, "Reshaping the Gospel?"
75. Young, *Shack*.
76. Kruger, *Shack Revisited*.

social Trinitarian 'perichoretic'[77] brand of Ultimate Reconciliation. The extensive spread of Christian Universalism is well demonstrated in an article by John Licitra, (member on the Board of Directors of the Christian Universalist Association), titled, "The Universalist Tulip," which promotes a universalistic form of Calvinism built on Barth's universalism. The traditional TULIP of orthodox Calvinism is remodelled to:

> Total reconciliation
> Unlimited atonement
> Love
> Irresistible grace through the ages
> Perseverance of God[78]

This is illustrative of the extent to which those who adopt a Christian Universalistic stance are prepared to "reshape" their understanding of the Reformed faith as passed down, for example, in the Canons of Dordt and the Westminster Confession. They see themselves as following in the footsteps of Barth, Moltmann and more recently, Jan Bonda.[79]

Added to the contribution of Barthianism to the popular resurgence of Christian Universalism is the revival in the study of Patristics and Origen in particular.[80] The Patristics scholar Ilaria Ramelli has published her monograph, *The Christian Doctrine of Apokatastasis*,[81] which is another tributary to the revival in Christian Universalism. Although Barth did not agree with Origen's form of *apokatastasis*, it can be argued that the two arrived at a similar end point. The supporters of current day Christian Universalism tend to accept a variety of forms as long as they primarily lead to the same conclusion–Ultimate Reconciliation. This does raise serious concerns when a theological luminary such as Karl Barth advances a theology, that, when taken to its logical conclusion, leads unmistakably to *apokatastasis*. The claim of the present supporters

---

77. A Greek term used to describe the triune relationship between each person of the Godhead, a co-indwelling, co-inhering, and mutual interpenetration.

78. Licitra, "Universal Tulip."

79. Jan Bonda, a retired Dutch Reformed minister, has presented his Reformed "flavored" Christian Universalism in which he blends Origen with Karl Barth. See Bonda, *One Purpose of God*. Additionally, another approach is Campana, *Calvinist Universalist*.

80. See Burnfield, *Patristic Universalism*; Harmon, *Every Knee Should Bow*; Ludlow, *Universal Salvation*.

81. Ramelli, *Christian Doctrine of Apokatastasis*.

of Christian Universalism is that it should be seen as "normative" within the Protestant world. Thus, some are arguing that Christian Universalism should come out of the ecclesiastical cold of heresy, pass the periphery of heterodoxy and into the fold of orthodoxy. This call is particularly advocated by Robin Parry (alias Gregory MacDonald),[82] who has labelled this new brand of Christian Universalism, "Evangelical Universalism."[83]

Thus it can be claimed that the spread of Christian Universalism has utilized aspects of Barth's theology which have distinct and clear elements of universalism. Olson has aptly concluded:

> I think that universalism is "in the air" among evangelical theologians because of Barth. Many evangelical theologians have discovered in Barth a conversation partner they have not found in either liberal theology or conservative theology. . . . Of course some evangelicals have come right out and affirmed absolute universalism, not conditional or hopefully or potential universalism. This view can be found expressed and explained in *The Evangelical Universalist* by Robin Parry writing under the pseudonym Gregory MacDonald. I have personally talked with several well-known evangelical theologians who have told me under pain of calling me a liar if I reveal what they said that they have come to embrace absolute universalism—of Jürgen Moltmann's type which is that hell is real but temporal and will eventually be emptied.[84]

This is one of the inescapable aspects of Barth's theological legacy.

## CONCLUSION

One may wonder whether Pierre Maury realised that his revision of the doctrine of election with Christ as the Elect would help set in motion his friend Karl Barth to reformulating his own theology. With clarity Barth developed his theology with a Christocentric focus which included the doctrine of Election informing and reorienting the other doctrines within the gamut of his dogmatics.[85] Barth's "Christological Revolution"

---

82. See MacDonald, "Introduction," 2–10; *Evangelical Universalist*, 4–5.

83. For a discussion on the new universalism under the label of "Evangelical Universalism," see Smith, "Can Hope Be Wrong?"; McDermott, "Will All Be Saved?," 235.

84. Olson, "Universalism Is 'In the Air.'"

85. See Horton, "Stony Jar," 346–81. "Barth remains an important figure to be

led to universalizing all the relational dimensions of God's dealings with humanity. Consequently, his theology followed the logical path to Christian Universalism even though he rejected the conundrum of binding God to the principle of *apokatastasis*. He saw it as contravening his assertion of the freedom of God. Thus, he had to insist on the dialectical dilemma of universalism and the sovereignty of God. One of the substantive legacies of Barth's theology is the provision of a logical conduit to Christian Universalism, *Apokatastasis*, Ultimate Reconciliation. From the outset of the publication of Barth's doctrine of Election in *Church Dogmatics* II/2, voices were raised in warning of Christian Universalism within Barth's theological framework. Since that time, many have grasped hold of Barth's universalism and have found both justification and explication for varying forms of Christian Universalism. As strong as Barth might cry, "No!" to *apokatastasis*, the fruit of his theology has led some to say, "Yes!"

---

reckoned with, neither to be lightly dismissed nor to be uncritically embraced" (Horton, "Stony Jar," 381).

# BIBLIOGRAPHY

Adams, Damon S. "Reshaping the Gospel? The Current Rise of Ultimate Reconciliation." *CRUCIS*, December 13, 2018. http://crucis.ac.edu.au/reshaping-gospel-current-rise-ultimate-reconciliation.

Bailey, Sarah Pullman. "Rob Bell's Upcoming Book on Heaven & Hell Stirs Blog, Twitter Backlash on Universalism." *Christianity Today*, February 26, 2011. https://www.christianitytoday.com/news/2011/february/rob-bells-upcoming-book-on-heaven-hell-stirs-blog-twitter.html.

Barth, Karl. *Church Dogmatics*. Edited by G. W. Bromiley and T. F. Torrance. Translated by G. T. Thomson, et al. Edinburgh: T&T Clark, 1936–77.

———. *The Humanity of God*. Louisville: John Knox, 1960.

Bell, Rob. *Love Wins: A Book About Heaven, Hell, and the Fate of Every Person Who Ever Lived*. New York: HarperOne, 2011.

Bender, Kimlyn J. *Karl Barth's Christological Ecclesiology*. Eugene, OR: Cascade, 2013.

Beougher, Timothy K. "Are All Doomed to Be Saved? The Rise of Modern Universalism." *The Southern Baptist Journal of Theology* 2.2 (1998) 6–24.

Berkhof, Louis. *Systematic Theology*. Edinburgh: Banner of Truth, 2003.

Berkouwer, G. C. *The Triumph of Grace in the Theology of Karl Barth*. Translated by Harry R. Boer. Grand Rapids: Eerdmans, 1956.

Bettis, Joseph D. "Is Karl Barth A Universalist?" *Scottish Journal of Theology* 20 (1967) 423–36.

Bloesch, Donald. *Jesus is Victor! Karl Barth's Doctrine of Salvation*. Eugene, OR: Wipf & Stock, 2001.

Bonda, Jan. *The One Purpose of God: An Answer to the Doctrine of Eternal Punishment*. Translated by Reinder Bruinsma. Grand Rapids: Eerdmans, 1998.

Braaten, Carl E. "The Meaning of Evangelism in the Context of God's Universal Grace." *The Academy for Evangelism in Theological Education* 3 (1988) 9–19.

Burnfield, David. *Patristic Universalism: An Alternative to the Traditional View of Divine Judgment*. Boca Raton, FL: Universal, 2013.

Burton, Bryan. "Universalism." In *The Westminster Handbook to Karl Barth*, edited by Richard Burnett, 217–18. Louisville: Westminster John Knox, 2013.

Campana, Stephen. *The Calvinist Universalist: Is Evil a Distortion of Truth? or Truth Itself?* Eugene, OR: Wipf & Stock, 2014.

Chung, Sung Wook, ed. *Karl Barth and Evangelical Theology: Convergences and Divergences*. Grand Rapids: Baker Academic, 2006.

Congdon, David W. "*Apokatastasis* and apostolicity: a response to Oliver Crisp on the question of Barth's universalism." *Scottish Journal of Theology* 67.4 (2014) 464–80.

———. "Dialectical Theology as Theology of Mission: Investigating the Origins of Karl Barth's Break with Liberalism." *International Journal of Systematic Theology* 16.4 (2014) 390–413.

———. *The God Who Saves: A Dogmatic Sketch*. Eugene, OR: Cascade, 2006.

———. "Why I Call Myself 'Universalist,' or, Why 'Reverent Agnosticism' is Not a Position." *The Fire and the Rose* (blog). June 26, 2006. https://fireandrose.blogspot.com/2006/06/why-i-call-myself-universalist-or-why.html.

Collins, Gary R. *The Christian Psychology of Paul Tournier*. Grand Rapids: Baker, 1973.

Colwell, J. "The Contemporaneity of the Divine Decision: Reflections on Barth's Denial of "Universalism." In *Universalism and the Doctrine of Hell*, edited by N. M. de S. Cameron, 139–60. Grand Rapids: Baker, 1992.

Cortez, Marc. "What Does It Mean to Call Karl Barth a 'Christocentric' Theologian?" *Scottish Journal of Theology* 60.2 (2007) 1–17.

Crisp, Oliver D. *Deviant Calvinism: Broadening Reformed Theology*. Minneapolis: Fortress, 2014.

———. "The Letter and the Spirit of Barth's Doctrine of Election: A Response to Michael O'Neil." *Evangelical Quarterly* 79.1 (2005) 53–67.

———. "On Barth's Denial of Universalism." *Themelios* 29.1 (2003) 18–29.

Deak, Esteban. *Apokatastasis: The Problem of Universal Salvation in the Twentieth Century*. Toronto: Selbstervlag, 1979.

Ellul, Jacques. *What I Believe*. Translated by Geoffrey W. Bromiley. Grand Rapids: Zondervan, 1989.

Ferré, Nels F. S. *The Christian Understanding of God*. London: SCM, 1952.

Gibson, David, and Daniel Strange, eds. *Engaging with Barth: Contemporary Evangelical Critiques*. Nottingham: Apollos, 2008.

Gockel, Matthias. *Barth & Schleiermacher on the Doctrine of Election: A Systematic Theological Comparison*. Oxford: Oxford University Press, 2007.

———. "Harmony without Identity: A Comparison of the Theology of Election in Pierre Maury and Karl Barth." In *Election, Barth, and the French Connection*, edited by Simon Hattrell, 129–41. Eugene, OR: Pickwick, 2016.

Goroncy, Jason A. "'That God May Have Mercy Upon All': A Review-Essay of Matthias Gockel's Barth and Schleiermacher on the Doctrine of Election." *Journal of Reformed Theology* 2 (2008) 113–30.

Greggs, Tom. *Barth, Origen, and Universal Salvation: Restoring Particularity*. Oxford: Oxford University Press: 2009.

———. "'Jesus is Victor': Passing the Impasse of Barth on Universalism." *Sottish Theological Journal* 60.2 (2007) 196–212.

Gunton, Colin. "Karl Barth's Doctrine of Election as Part of His Doctrine of God." *The Journal of Theological Studies* 25.2 (1974) 381–92.

Hamilton, Kenneth. "Love or Holy Love? Nels Ferre versus P.T. Forsyth." *Canadian Journal of Theology* 8.4 (1962) 229–236.

Hanson, John Wesley. *Universalism: The Prevailing Doctrine of the Church During Its First Five Hundred Years*. Pickerington, OH: Beloved, 2015.

Harmon, Steven. *Every Knee Should Bow: Biblical Rationales for Universal Salvation in Early Christian Thought*. Lanham, MD: University Press of America, 2003.

Hilborn, David, and Daniel Horrocks. "Universalism and Evangelical Theology: An Historical Theological Perspective." *Evangelical Review of Theology* 30.3 (2006) 196–218.

Hoon, Woo B. "Karl Barth's Doctrine of the Atonement and Universalism." *Korea Reformed Journal* 32 (2014) 243–91.

Horton, Michael S. "A Stony Jar: The Legacy of Karl Barth for Evangelical Theology." In *Engaging with Barth: Contemporary Evangelical Critiques*, edited by David Gibson and Daniel Strange, 346–81. Nottingham: Apollos, 2008.

Jonker, W. D. "Some Remarks on the Interpretation of Karl Barth." *Ned. Geref, Teologiese Tydskrif* deel xxix 40 (1988) 29–40.

Klooster, Fred. *The Significance of Barth's Theology: An Appraisal with Special Reference to Election and Reconciliation*. Grand Rapids: Baker, 1961.

———. "Supralapsarianism." In *Evangelical Dictionary of Theology*, edited by Walter A. Elwell, 1155–56. 2nd ed. Grand Rapids: Baker Academic, 2003.

Koonz, M. "The Old Question of Barth's Universalism: An Examination with Reference to Tom Greggs and T. F. Torrance." *Theology in Scotland* 18.2 (2011) 33–46.

Kronen, John, and Eric Reitan. *God's Final Victory: A Comparative Philosophical Case for Universalism*. New York: Bloomsbury Academic, 2013.

Kruger, J. Baxter. *The Shack Revisited: There Is More Going On Here than You Ever Dared to Dream*. New York: FaithWords, 2012.

Lee, Sang Hwan. "The Revelation of the Triune God in the Theologies of John Calvin and Karl Barth." PhD diss., Durham University, 1995.

Licitra, John. "The Universal Tulip." *Christian Universalist Association*. https://christianuniversalist.org/resources/articles/universalist-tulip.

Ludlow, Morwenna. *Universal Salvation: Eschatology in the Thought of Gregory of Nyssa and Karl Rahner: Eschatology in the Thought of Gregory of Nyssa and Karl Rahner*. Oxford: Clarendon, 2007.

MacDonald, Gregory. *The Evangelical Universalist*. Eugene, OR: Wipf & Stock, 2012.

———. "Introduction: Between Heresy and Dogma." In *"All Shall Be Well": Explorations in Universal Salvation and Christian Theology from Origen to Moltmann*, edited by Gregory MacDonald, 1–25. Cambridge: James Clarke, 2011.

Macleod, Donald. "Definite Atonement and the Divine Decree." In *From Heaven He Came and Sought Her*, edited by David Gibson and Jonathan Gibson, 401–435. Wheaton: Crossways, 2013.

Maury, Pierre. "*Election et Foi*." In *Election, Barth, and the French Connection*, edited by Simon Hattrell, 41–59. Eugene, OR: Pickwick, 2016.

———. "Predestination." In *Election, Barth, and the French Connection*, edited by Simon Hattrell, 80–119. Eugene, OR: Pickwick, 2016.

McClymond, Michael J. "Apocalypse Now: The Neo-Bultmannian Universalism of David Congdon's—*The God Who Saves*." *Themelios* 43.2 (2018) 220–34.

———. *The Devil's Redemption: A New History and Interpretation of Christian Universalism*. 2 vols. Grand Rapids: Baker Academic, 2018.

———. "How Universalism, 'The Opiate of the Theologians,' Went Mainstream." *Christianity Today*, March 11, 2019. https://www.christianitytoday.com/ct/2019/march-web-only/michael-mcclymonddevils-redemption-universalism.html.

McDermott, Gerald R. "Will All Be Saved?" *Themelios* 38.2 (2013) 232–43.

McNicol, Allan J. "Universal Salvation and the Christian Story." *Christian Studies* 22 (2008) 44–48.

Michaelis, Wilhelm. *Versöhnung des Alls: die frohe Botschaft von der Gnade Gottes* [*Reconciliation of the Universe: The Good News of the Grace of God*]. Verlag: Siloah, 1950.

Moltmann, Jürgen. *A Broad Place: An Autobiography*. London: SCM, 2007.

———. *The Coming of God: Christian Eschatology*. Minneapolis: Fortress, 2004.

Muller, Gotthold. *Apokatastasis Panton: A Biography*. Basel: Basler Missionsbuch-Handlung, 1969.

———. "The Idea of an *Apokatastasis ton Panton* (Universal Salvation) in European Theology from Schleiermacher to Barth." *Journal of the Universalist Historical Society* 6 (1966) 47–64.

Musick, Daniel D. "Paul Tournier's Universalism." MA thesis, Wheaton College, 1978. http://www.paultournier.org/autre/UNIVERSALISM.html.

Neville, David J. "Dialectic as Method in Public Theology: Recalling Jacques Ellul." *International Journal of Public Theology* 2 (2008) 163–81.

O'Neil, Michael. "Karl Barth's Doctrine of Election." *Evangelical Quarterly* 76.4 (2004) 311–26.

Olson, Roger E. "Universalism Is 'In the Air' (Much Discussed) Among Even Evangelicals: What About It?" *Patheos*, January 14, 2015. https://www.patheos.com/blogs/rogereolson/2015/01/2627.

———. "Was Karl Barth a Universalist? Another Look at an Old Question." *Patheos*, March 10, 2013. https://www.patheos.com/blogs/rogereolson/2013/03/was-karl-barth-a-universalist-a-new-look-at-an-old-question.

Ramelli, Ilaria. *The Christian Doctrine of Apokatastasis: A Critical Assessment from the New Testament to Eriugena.* Brill, 2013.

Robinson, John A. T. *In the End . . . God: A Study of the Christian Doctrine of the Last Things.* London: James Clarke, 1960.

———. "Universalism—Is it Heretical?" *Journal of Scottish Theology* 2.2 (1949) 139–55.

Schnucker, R. V. "Infralapsarianism." In *Evangelical Dictionary of Theology*, edited by Walter A. Elwell, 607. 2nd ed. Grand Rapids: Baker Academic, 2003.

Talbott, Thomas. *The Inescapable Love of God.* Eugene, OR: Cascade, 2014.

Thompson, Geoffrey. "Not Quite Unconfined? Rahner and Barth Halt at Apokatastasis." In *Immense, Unfathomable, Unconfined: The Grace of God in Creation—Essays in Honour of Norman Young*, edited by Sean Winter, 109–122. Eugene, OR: Wipf & Stock, 2013.

Tournier, Paul. *Guilt and Grace: A Psychological Study.* New York: Harper & Rowe, 1962.

Van Til, Cornelius. "Has Karl Barth Become Orthodox." *Westminster Theological Journal* 16 (1954) 135–81.

Van Zyl, M. S. "Karl Barth's 'Modern' and 'Unbiblical' Universalism according to Willie Jonker: Valid Critiques? Or the Way Forward in a Pluralistic Society?" *Ned. Geref, Teologiese Tydskrif* 48.1–2 (2007) 284–95.

Von Balthasar, Hans Urs. *Dare We Hope That All Men Be Saved? With a Short Discourse on Hell.* Translated by David Kipp and Lothar Krauth. San Francisco: Ignatius, 2014.

———. *The Theology of Karl Barth: Exposition and Interpretation.* Translated by Edward T. Oakes. San Francisco: Communio, 1992.

Williams, Garry J. "Karl Barth and the Doctrine of the Atonement." In *Engaging with Barth: Contemporary Evangelical Critiques*, edited by David Gibson and Daniel Strange, 232–72. Nottingham: Apollos, 2008.

Young, William Paul. *The Shack.* Newbury Park: Windblown Media, 2011.

Yu, Anthony C. "Karl Barth's Doctrine of Election: A Critical Study." *Foundations* 13 (1970) 241–68.

# 14

## The Human Election of God

### Leo Stossich

IN HIS AUTOBIOGRAPHICAL CONTRIBUTION to *The Christian Century* published in 1939, *How I Changed My Mind*, Karl Barth described the previous decade as one of a theological "deepening." His study of Anselm of Canterbury had been pivotal in allowing him to fully abandon theological liberalism and shape a theology which consented to Credo and proceeded from faith to understanding—*fides quaerens intellectum*.[1] This new trajectory shaped his general approach to the *Church Dogmatics*, the first two volumes appearing in 1932 and 1938.

A further key factor in this development was the Calvin Conference[2] held in Geneva in June 1936, where Barth heard a lecture by Pierre Maury on the subject of election. In Karl Barth's original foreword to *Predestination and Other Papers*[3] he says,

> Most of those present at the Calvinist Congress were neither prepared, nor apt to receive in their hearts, nor just simply to register with their brains, what Pierre Maury was saying to them then. There were but few who had any idea of the implications of his thesis in the course of the years that followed, when

---

1. Faith seeking understanding.
2. In celebration of the 400th anniversary of the publication of Calvin's *Institutes*.
3. Maury, *Predestination and Other Papers*, 15, 16.

preoccupations of a political nature loomed so large that they scarcely left time or energy for theological reflection of this sort. But I remember one person who read the text of that address with the greatest attention—myself! . . . It was he who contributed decisively to giving my thoughts on this point their fundamental orientation. Before I read his study, I had met no one who had dealt with the question so freshly and boldly.[4]

The central theme of Maury's paper, *Election and Faith*, was that *the concrete reality* of election and predestination which is made known in Jesus Christ cannot be separated from *the doctrine* of election. He boldly stated "outside of Christ, there is neither election, nor knowledge of election."[5] Maury placed Christ as the object of God's predestinating activity making for "a truly Christological grounding of predestination."[6] McCormack maintains that while "this did not hand Barth's later doctrine to him on a platter . . . complete in all of its details,"[7] it did provide the stimulus for revision toward the fully developed doctrine of *CD* II/2. Barth said:

> I had to learn that Christian doctrine, if it is to merit its name and if it is to build up the Christian church in the world as she must needs be built up, has to be exclusively and conclusively the doctrine of Jesus Christ—of Jesus Christ as the living Word of God spoken to us men.[8]

Christ became the point of departure for Barth's theological reflection. He referred to this as his "Christological concentration."[9]

Barth later acknowledges the significance of this conference to his own development in his *Church Dogmatics*.[10] Likewise, Maury acknowledges the thinking of Barth in his own lectures. He indicates that, "We have . . . for many years discussed this doctrine together, and he has

---

4. Maury, "Predestination" [hereafter PD]. See the translation in this volume.

5. Maury, "Election and Faith" [hereafter EF]. See the translation in this volume. EF 44.

6. McCormack, *Karl Barth's Dialectical Theology*, 457.

7. McCormack, *Studies*, 213.

8. Barth, *How I Changed My Mind*, 45.

9. Barth, *How I Changed My Mind*, 44.

10. *CD* II/2:188–94

propounded it in masterly fashion, infusing it with new life, in his *Church Dogmatics* II/2."[11]

The following statements by Maury and Barth provide *three foci* in looking at Barth's thinking about election. Maury said: "The election of Jesus Christ is not only the means by which he has chosen us, it is also the way in which we choose him, and *no longer ourselves*."[12] He likewise said: "He chooses to love, in order to be loved himself in return, voluntarily and freely, by his creature."[13] Barth stated that "The purpose and meaning of the eternal divine election of grace consists in the fact that the one who is elected from all eternity can and does elect God in return."[14]

These three foci are: *the election of grace, the Holy Spirit, and human freedom*.

The truth that humanity is elect in Christ cannot be dissolved and so a contradiction remains between objective and subjective reality.[15] God bestows on humanity the gift of freedom in Jesus Christ through the Spirit, making himself available, so humanity might respond to him. Nonetheless, human freedom involves "a genuine decision and act in the right direction."[16]

## THE ELECTION OF GRACE

Barth's mature development of the doctrine had shifted focus to pivot around the election of Jesus Christ as both the electing God and the elected man.[17] The inclusion of the doctrine of election within the volume on the doctrine of God gave election precedence over subsequent doctrines. Maury said "it qualifies them all."[18] Greggs maintains, for Barth, "Election logically is the prior step that allows God's self-revelation to take place, and it is God's decision in election that leads to His self-revelation to the world in the person of Jesus Christ."[19] God could only be known in

11. PD 81.
12. EF 50.
13. PD 91.
14. *CD* II/2:178.
15. *CD* IV/3:474.
16. Barth, *Humanity of God*, 76.
17. *CD* II/2:103.
18. PD 82.
19. Greggs, *Barth, Origen, and Universal Salvation*, 19.

His self-disclosure—"Jesus Christ is the ground, the center and the focus of all human speech about God."[20]

Barth understood election to be primarily about God. God is the very God we encounter in Jesus Christ. He argues from revelation to ontology. He maintained "There is no such thing as a will of God apart from the will of Jesus Christ."[21] Barth believed that Calvin had separated God from Jesus Christ.[22] Hence, for Barth and also Maury, Jesus Christ, the electing God, replaces the idea of a *decretum absolutum*,[23] together with the abstract division of humanity into those chosen for heaven and those chosen for hell.

For Barth the doctrine of election had a pastoral function. The election of grace is,

> the sum of the Gospel.... Its function is to bear basic testimony to the eternal, free and unchanging grace as the beginning of all the ways and works of God.... It is itself evangel: glad tidings, news which uplifts and comforts and sustains... a proclamation of joy... not a mixed message of joy and terror, salvation and damnation.[24]

God, as such, loves in freedom before the world exists but elects "fellowship with man for himself" and "fellowship with Himself for man."[25] Barth maintains that "in the act of love which determines His whole being God elects.... God is none other than the One who in His Son or Word elects Himself, and in and with Himself elects His people."[26] As O'Neil puts it,

> As elect person, Jesus Christ is not simply one of the elect, nor only the means of the election of all other elect persons, but he is himself *the* elect of God *in* whom all humanity are likewise elected.[27]

---

20. O'Neill, "Karl Barth's Doctrine of Election," 312.
21. *CD* II/2:115.
22. *CD* II/2:110–11.
23. *CD* II/2:104.
24. *CD* II/2:3, 12–13.
25. *CD* II/2:168.
26. *CD* II/2:76.
27. O'Neil, "Karl Barth's Doctrine of Election," 315.

For Barth, the goal of this election is "the wonderful exaltation and endowment of man to existence in covenant with Himself."[28] Greggs maintains that "Barth does not want to confront humanity with a God who might as well condemn people as save them."[29] For Barth,

> Man is not rejected ... from all eternity God has determined upon man's acquittal at His own cost. ... God has ordained that in the place of the one acquitted He Himself should be perishing and abandoned and rejected—the Lamb slain from the foundation of the world.[30]

Maury says, "here at the center of God's revelation, we find the chosen one who ceases to be chosen, or rather who is the non-elect, the rejected one, the beloved Son who is abandoned."[31] For Barth, predestination is "the non-rejection of man."[32] Jesus Christ was elected to take the rejection of the human race upon himself. McCormack says "The goal of His rejection is the election of the human race."[33] Maury, to whom Barth attributes the insight into the reprobation of Christ in the cross for us, says, "The cross where Christ is condemned does not condemn *us*, it makes us children of God ... the Son has made our death his ... as Paul says 'There is only yes in him.'"[34]

For Barth, the recognition of Jesus Christ as the elector means humanity is now elected actually "in Him" and not just passively "for Him."[35] As McCormack puts it, "Our election is a reality in Him, not just a possibility."[36] Election is a "passive and objective reality" for humankind, but becomes an "active and subjective reality" for believers.[37] Barth states that "The purpose and meaning of eternal divine election of grace consists in the fact that the one who is elected from all eternity can and does elect God in return."[38] Maury expresses the same sentiment: "Praise

---

28. *CD* II/2:168.
29. Greggs, *Barth, Origen, and Universal Salvation*, 24.
30. *CD* II/2:167.
31. PD 104.
32. *CD* II/2:167.
33. McCormack, *Karl Barth's Dialectical Theology*, 459.
34. EF 49.
35. *CD* II/2:112.
36. McCormack, *Karl Barth's Dialectical Theology*, 459.
37. Greggs, *Barth, Origen, and Universal Salvation*, 32.
38. *CD* II/2:178.

be to God that our judge is the one who has chosen us ... and who wanted to be chosen by us."[39] Grebe says:

> This picture of God in election nullifies any concept people might have of God as a tyrant and points the believer towards Jesus Christ as the only way of understanding who God is—love. In light of this it becomes clear why for Barth the doctrine of election is not a doctrine of discomfort but of comfort, indeed, the very essence of the good news.[40]

While universal salvation has been achieved in Jesus Christ, O'Neil maintains "It is crucial to recognize that for Barth, election has two 'moments.'"[41] Election is both the pre-temporal determination under God to elect humanity in Jesus Christ, and the active and subjective election of a community in time. Barth speaks of an "inner circle," which is "a fellowship elected by God in Jesus Christ and determined from all eternity for a peculiar service," and an "outer circle of the election," which includes the rest of humanity.[42] Holmes maintains that this "helps us begin to see the extent to which Barth's doctrine of election is a doctrine that is formative of a peculiar people."[43] The inner circle "is not so closed or predetermined that it cannot expand ... and enlargement of the circle of election occurs as the Church faithfully pursues it calling of witness and proclamation in the world."[44] Barth says,

> It has been chosen out of the world for the very purpose of performing for the world the service which it most needs and which consists simply in giving it the testimony of Jesus Christ and summoning it to faith in Him.[45]

On the frontier between "the inner circle"—"the environment of the man Jesus"[46] and "the outer one of the rest of men," the Gospel is to be preached—"glad tidings for all who are defrauded and deprived of

---

39. Maury, "Ultimate Decision." [hereafter UD]. See the translation in this volume. UD 73.
40. Grebe, *Election, Atonement*, 43.
41. O'Neil, "Karl Barth's Doctrine of Election," 317n30.
42. *CD* II/2:196–97.
43. Holmes in Dempsey, *Trinity and Election*, 183.
44. O'Neil, "Karl Barth's Doctrine of Election," 317.
45. *CD* II/2:196.
46. *CD* II/2:265.

their rights, for all captives and sick persons, for all who are astray and in distress."[47]

For Barth, it is God's concern that "there should be these frontier crossings ... how and when they should take place ... [and] what is to be the final extent of the circle."[48] The "hidden" but "real" crossing of frontiers occurs in Jesus's giving himself to be known—He "wills to go out into the world."[49] He gives himself to be known by the Spirit. The event of revelation is the work of the Holy Spirit.

## THE HOLY SPIRIT

In *Karl Barth's Table Talk*, Barth states that due to the theological situation in 1932, he wanted to strongly emphasize the objective side of revelation in order to redress the over-subjectivizing of election.[50] Barth viewed Schleiermacher and the theologians of immanence as attempting an essentially pneumatocentric approach to theology. Schleiermacher appealed to "a general and innate human God consciousness as both the basis and the object of theological reflection."[51] While the exposition of the subjective side of revelation resonated with Barth, he saw that the effects were the relativizing of Christ and dissolution of the Word; and hence, concluded that the theme of Schleiermacher's theology "is not the Holy Spirit, but, as Schleiermacher claims, merely man's religious consciousness."[52] Macchia states that,

> Barth came to combat this "anthropocentric" (or, more accurately, "believer-centric") point of departure for theology not only with a Christological center for defining revelation but increasingly from the vantage point of the implications in God's self-giving as Spirit.[53]

According to Hunsinger, two points are prerequisite to understanding Barth in relation the Holy Spirit. Firstly, there is an ontological divide and distinction between the Creator and creature. In 1930, in his essay

47. *CD* II/2:266.
48. *CD* II/2:417.
49. *CD* II/2.
50. Barth in Godsey, *Karl Barth's Table Talk*, 27.
51. Hart, *Regarding Karl Barth*, 8.
52. Barth, *Protestant Theology*, 472.
53. Macchia, "Spirit of God," 152–53.

"The Holy Spirit and the Christian Life," Barth rejects any *analogia entis* (analogy of being) between the creature in the fallen world and God. There is no analogy between the human being and the divine being by the sharing of a commonality in "being." In the *Church Dogmatics* "From the beginning of the series to the end, his rejection of the *analogia entis* did not waver."[54] There is no inherent human openness to and capability of knowing God. Any continuity between God and the creature by which God can be revealed to people must only belong to the Creator. Likewise Maury says God "reveals *himself*—and if he himself doesn't reveal himself, he remains hidden, inexorably."[55] Further Maury says, "without God we do not know God; if we were not chosen by God, we would never have the idea of choosing him, if we were not drawn by the Father, we would never come to Jesus Christ."[56]

Barth maintains that

> continuity between God and me in my creatureliness is not (as Przywara asserts) my "tranquil, assured" quality. It is not something that "has been given," but it consists in God's continual "giving." . . . It is purely and simply the office of the Holy Spirit to be continually opening our ears to enable us to receive the Creator's word. . . . The hearing of the Word of God the Creator, which makes human life to become Christian life, is not man's work but God's: the Holy Spirit's work.[57]

Secondly, Jesus perfectly accomplished salvation for all humanity. Hunsinger says, for Barth,

> salvation needs nothing to complete it. Subsequent events can only receive it, attest it, share in it, and eagerly await its consummation (or fail to do so)—and these events of human reception, attestation, participation, adoration, and expectation are precisely the work of the Spirit as the mediator of communion.[58]

The work of the Holy Spirit is to subsequently mediate the union and communion of believers with Christ, the Trinity and one another.[59]

---

54. Hunsinger, *Disruptive Grace*, 7.
55. UD 62.
56. EF 47.
57. Barth, *Holy Spirit and the Christian Life*, 8, 10.
58. Hunsinger, *Disruptive Grace*, 10.
59. Hunsinger, *Disruptive Grace*, 10, 150. See also Maury PD 97.

Barth understands that the Holy Spirit's temporal and eternal roles concur. There is an *analogia operationis* (analogy of operation) in the work of the Spirit in eternity and the work of the Spirit in time.[60] He brings about communion among human beings just as He is the communion of the Father and the Son. It is because the triune God is also God the Holy Spirit, God in the third mode of His being, that He brings us into the same eternal union He has with the Father and the Son, so that God can be said to be *our* God. The Holy Spirit is "the subjective side in the event of revelation,"[61] God personally manifest to and in people. Barth says,

> The fact that God gives His *pneuma* to man or that man receives this *pneuma* implies that God comes to man, that He discloses Himself to man and man to Himself, that He gives Himself to be experienced by man, that He awakens man to faith. . . . He becomes theirs and makes them His.[62]

The unveiling of the hidden, inconceivable Father, made objectively manifest in the Son, is now manifested subjectively in human beings. This subjective side of the event of revelation is God the Holy Spirit coming to people, imparting salvation, binding them to Him and claiming them for Himself.[63] When this deep union and knowledge is experienced by people, it can only be described as the work of God—

> It is God's reality in that God Himself becomes present to man not just externally, not just from above, but also from within, from below, subjectively. It is thus reality in that He does not merely come to man but encounters Himself from man. God's freedom to be present in this way to man, and therefore to bring about this encounter, is the Spirit of God, the Holy Spirit in God's revelation.[64]

The Holy Spirit's role in revelation is rooted in the triune decision to unite human beings with God—

> In the beginning it was the choice of the Father Himself to establish this covenant with man by giving up His Son for Him. . . . In the beginning it was the choice of the Son to be obedient

60. Nimmo in Dempsey, *Trinity and Election*, 170.
61. *CD* I/1:450.
62. *CD* I/1:450.
63. *CD* I/1:450.
64. *CD* I/1:451.

> to grace, and therefore to offer Himself, and to become man. . . . In the beginning it was the resolve of the Holy Spirit that the unity of the God, of Father and Son should not be disturbed or rent by this covenant with man, but that it should be made the more glorious, the deity of God, the divinity of His love and freedom, being confirmed and demonstrated by this offering of the Father and this self-offering of the Son. This choice was in the beginning.[65]

The Holy Spirit thus executes in history the divine resolution in the election of Jesus Christ, and then makes actual in the life of the believer what is already true in the eternal plan of God for all people, their predestination in Him.

For Barth,

> the event of revelation has clarity and reality on its subjective side because the Holy Spirit, the subjective element in this event, is the essence of God Himself. What He is in revelation He is antecedently in Himself.[66]

He is "'antecedently in Himself' the act of communion, the act of impartation, love, gift."[67] What the Holy Spirit is antecedently in himself, he is also in his revelation.[68] The prior essential role of the Holy Spirit in the intra-divine relationship enables a genuine subjective side to the event of revelation in Christian experience. The Holy Spirit effects in human beings "the very relation to the Father and the Son which He causes to exist in the Godhead."[69]

The Spirit, in making the divine calling of humanity into the believer's personal experience of being called, works in people, enlightening them to know what is already true of them in Christ. The Holy Spirit is the primary agent in the vocation of the believer. To be called is to know what is already true of one's destiny because of Christ. Not to be called is to remain ignorant and unable either to proclaim to themselves their election as it took place in Jesus Christ, or to determine themselves to believe in this proclamation—

---

65. *CD* II/2:101–2.
66. *CD* I/1:466, 470–71.
67. *CD* I/1:470–71.
68. *CD* I/1:466, 470–71.
69. Rosato, *Spirit as Lord*, 61.

> Without the Holy Spirit, and therefore without their calling, they would necessarily be the same as others in all respects in which they are distinguished from them. Apart from their calling they, too, would be godless. . . . There is no called man who was not once uncalled; there is no hearer of the proclamation for whom it was not once strange and unknown; and there is no believer who was not once an unbeliever. . . . And so there is none who has any reason at any time to see anything other than the expiating grace of Jesus Christ even in his calling and in the gift of the Holy Spirit.[70]

By the awakening power of the Holy Spirit, people choose "that for which . . . [they are] already chosen by the divine decision, and beside which . . . [they have] no other choice, that is to say, faith."[71] They are now opened up to say *Yes* to God's grace and as such enter new life and freedom—"freedom as joyful and active consent to the mystery of divine grace."[72]

## HUMAN FREEDOM

Implicit in the election of grace, wherein "God pledges and commits Himself to be the God of man," is his further activity which "begins the history, encounter and decision between Himself and man."[73] By the Spirit, "God awakens man to existence before Him and summons him to His service."[74] But God does not practice "a blind, brute power working causally and mechanically," and he does not "force or suppress or disable in the exercise of it."[75] Barth says, "for his part man can and actually does elect God."[76] Similarly, Maury says:

> The reality of Jesus Christ is a decision of God, therefore without any recourse, as far as we are concerned, a decision of one other than ourselves and of which we are the object. . . . In the second

---

70. Rosato, *Spirit as Lord*, 348.
71. CD IV/1:748
72. Webster, *Barth's Moral Theology*, 99.
73. CD II/2:177.
74. CD II/2:177.
75. CD IV/3:328.
76. CD II/2:177.

place ... Jesus Christ calls for a decision on our part, a final [or permanent] decision."[77]

God's command "applies to us all."[78] All human beings are responsible agents before God, knowingly or unknowingly. There is "a simple but comprehensive autonomy of the creature which is constituted originally by the act of eternal divine election and which has in this act its ultimate reality."[79] Human autonomy is not "the law of our being grounded in ourselves" but is rather grounded "in the grace of God"—"given by God and remains only so long as God continues to be its support."[80] Gunton says, "According to Barth, creation is a giving of space for autonomous human reality.... In reconciliation ... we are determined to be children of God, but not ... compelled."[81]

God's command applies to us all, but is received as "our personal question ... addressed to us personally."[82] When through the Spirit one is summoned by the risen Lord to "believe, obey and confess," that person "unites himself with Christ, giving himself to the One who first gave Himself to him."[83] God wants that person to respond to his summons with their own will in freedom. While human freedom is "God-given," it is nonetheless "genuine choice ... genuine decision and act in the right direction."[84] Oh says, "In obedience to God's command, man listens and follows His command out of his own choice and willingness."[85] The question is "whether we are prepared to allow our own will and its aims to be controlled by the will of God as we meet it in His command."[86]

The question of "man's self-determination ... responsibility ... decision ... obedience and action"[87] arises under the divine imperative opened up by the Spirit. It is only and always the Spirit who draws human beings to participate in the reconciliation accomplished through Jesus Christ.

---

77. UD 66.
78. CD II/2:176.
79. CD II/2:176.
80. Gunton, "Barth, the Trinity," 324.
81. Gunton, "Barth, the Trinity," 325.
82. CD II/2:654–55.
83. CD IV/3:544.
84. Barth, *Humanity of God*, 76.
85. Oh, *Karl Barth's Trinitarian Theology*, 157.
86. CD II/2:654.
87. CD II/2:511.

While "the activity of His grace" is an "irresistible activity," nonetheless "He respects . . . the creature to whom He is gracious."[88] Torrance says:

> God's grace is irresistible because it precedes the tide of human activity. God encounters that person before she can cover her eyes; God speaks to her before she can cover her ears; God humbles her before she can embrace her pride; and God animates her before she can turn to sloth. God acts towards her in this way because he chose her in Christ before the foundation of the world to be holy and blameless towards him in love (Eph 1:4), and because God has knitted her together in our mothers' wombs to be his covenant partner in Christ. . . . However, the precedence of God's grace does not mean that God's grace is necessarily effectual.[89]

A distinction is to be made between the gift of God's grace and the appropriation of that grace. Barth, according to Torrance, does not understand grace to be "an impersonal gift that God passes on to the elect with the effect of bestowing new properties on to them."[90] Torrance points to Barth's rejection of an understanding of grace as "a third element mediatorial between God and His creatures."[91] God's grace rather "is [his] personal, beneficent disposition and action . . . the way that . . . [he] lovingly relates to persons . . . persons who possess the capacity to follow the will of God."[92] Hence for Barth, "the enactment of grace is not attached to the diverse range of effects [we see] . . . on particular sinful human beings." There is no foreseeable impact that the grace of God might have on a person. While "the activity of His grace" is an "irresistible activity," nonetheless "He respects . . . the creature to whom He is gracious."[93] While grace leaves only one option for the exercise of human freedom, a person may remain inactive in deciding and as such remain in bondage and darkness.

True freedom, for Barth, is not freedom as independence nor the freedom to choose between options. Freedom is not being able to say yes or no to God. Barth says:

---

88. *CD* III/3:149.
89. Torrance, "Karl Barth," 115.
90. Torrance, "Karl Barth," 106.
91. *CD* II/1:353.
92. *CD* III/3:149.
93. *CD* III/3:149.

> The decisive point is whether freedom in the Christian sense is identical with the freedom of Hercules: choice between two ways at a crossroads. This is a heathen notion of freedom. Is it freedom to decide for the devil? The only freedom that means something is the freedom to be myself as I am created by God. God did not create a neutral creature, but His creature.[94]

He maintains, "Trying to escape from being in accord with God's own freedom is not human freedom. Rather, it is a compulsion wrought by powers of darkness or by man's own helplessness."[95] Such a person is in "contradiction" rather than "correspondence" to their true nature. Maury likewise says it is a mistake "to define the choice that we make concerning him as one of multiple human possibilities which are offered to us . . . the Christian decision . . . is not of this kind! . . . [rather] the *unique* Son of God . . . demands the obedience of faith."[96]

For Barth true freedom is liberation—"the work of the Spirit consists in the liberation of man for his own act"[97]; human action that is free from the bondage to self-will, self-determination and self-rule, and free for the will of God. True freedom is the freedom to obey the divine will—to say *Yes* to God's grace. True freedom is "a being in activity in line with God's own goodness."[98] Grebe qualifies and illustrates Barth's notion of freedom in this way:

> Humanity does not stand free on the road to make a choice between left and right. Instead, she is trapped in a ditch or chained in a prison cell from which she cannot free herself. What God offers . . . is the free gift of a rope out of the ditch or, better, freedom from the chains of captivity.[99]

Where the Holy Spirit is present there is freedom, but election and freedom are to a definite end. Couenhoven says, "It is not freedom to choose evil, and grace does not make us free by giving us more choices, or a greater power of choice, but rather makes us a 'slave of Christ.'"[100] Human beings are freed by God for God. Jenson says, "God has eternally

---

94. Barth in Godsey, *Table Talk*, 37.
95. Barth, *Humanity of God*, 77.
96. UD 63.
97. *CD* IV/2:785.
98. Couenhoven, *Commanding Grace*, 248.
99. Grebe, *Election, Atonement*, 241.
100. Couenhoven, *Commanding Grace*, 247.

decided to create us. He has eternally decided to transcend that creation and make us sons led by His Son."[101]

Jesus was uniquely filled and governed by the presence and power of the Holy Spirit without measure, and consequentially totally and lastingly free, and necessarily raised from death—"In His wholehearted obedience, in His electing of God alone, He is wholly free."[102] The early apostles discovered in Jesus "the new man," that is, "rediscovered the true nature of man."[103]

> They discovered the man upon whom the Spirit . . . rests, who does not merely live from the Spirit but in the Spirit. They discovered the spirit of man in which life dwells with the fullness with which it is addressed by God to the creature. In other words, they discovered the man who lives in sovereignty, who has power of Himself to live in likeness to God.[104]

Jesus as the true man is free "to be in His humiliation as the Son of God the truly exalted and royal Son of Man."[105]

True humanity begins with recreation and with the One True Man, the resurrected Jesus Christ, the royal Son of Man, who is the destiny of humankind, and the potential destiny of every human being. The Holy Spirit provides the link between "Christ's royal humanity and free human action."[106] He "unmasks and rejects man's lack of freedom, but also discloses and magnifies his freedom."[107] Maury says, "When God speaks to us in Christ it is not in order to display a truth, but to reveal to us our situation before him, and the attitude that he adopts before us."[108] He places a person "at a very definite point of departure, in a very definite freedom," resulting in a "free and spontaneous and active doing or non-doing."[109] Barth maintains that this "will always be our doing or non-doing from this point and in this freedom."[110] The Christian life, then, is the recogni-

---

101. Jenson, *Alpha and Omega*, 158.
102. CD II/2:179.
103. CD III/2:334.
104. CD III/2:334.
105. CD IV/2:311.
106. Gunton, "Barth, the Trinity," 321.
107. CD IV/2:374.
108. UD 65.
109. CD IV/2:363.
110. CD IV/2:363.

tion that the Holy Spirit is drawing us on to become what we already are, children of God and loving covenant partners of God. Barth says:

> Man is actively and passively introduced as a partner in the covenant of grace . . . installed in his position as God's partner . . . given the Spirit by God . . . [and becoming] another man—a man of God, the kind of man whom God uses, and who as he is used by God begins to live a new life.[111]

Through this gift of true freedom, unfree humanity is set free in thankfulness, joy and hope.

## CONCLUSION

Barth radically transformed the doctrine of election into a positive message of salvation for all humanity. For Barth, God, in his freedom, wants to be with and for humankind despite human sinfulness. It is his eternal will that he be our God and we be his people. He graciously bestows on human persons the gift of freedom in Jesus Christ through the Spirit. God's determination for humanity is "blessedness, thanksgiving and witness," available through Christ, realized through the work of the Spirit and appropriated by human choice. In making himself available for humanity in this way, he frees people to respond to him in thankfulness, to one another in love, to unbelievers as virtual Christians, and have the joy and hope of being his children in covenant partnership now and forever. The election of grace and all that entails is the sum of the Gospel and as such our Gospel is re-enlivened as good news.

---

111. *CD* III/2:357.

# BIBLIOGRAPHY

Barth, Karl. *Church Dogmatics*. Edited by G. W. Bromiley and T. F. Torrance. Translated by G. T. Thomson, et al. Edinburgh: T&T Clark, 1936–77.
———. *The Humanity of God*. Richmond, VA: John Knox, 1960.
———. *The Holy Spirit and the Christian Life: The Library of Theological Ethics*. Louisville: John Knox, 1993.
———. *Karl Barth's Table Talk*. Richmond, VA: John Knox, 1963.
———. *Protestant Theology in the Nineteenth Century: Its Background and History*. Grand Rapids: Eerdmans, 2001.
Couenhoven, Jesse. "Karl Barth's Conception(s) of Human and Divine Freedom(s)." In *Commanding Grace: Studies in Karl Barth's Ethics*, edited by Daniel L. Migliore, 239–55. Grand Rapids: Eerdmans, 2010.
Grebe, Matthias. *Election, Atonement, and the Holy Spirit: Through and Beyond Barth's Theological Interpretation of Scripture*. Cambridge: James Clarke and Co., 2015.
Greggs, Tom. *Barth, Origen, and Universal Salvation: Restoring Particularity*. Oxford: Oxford University Press, 2009.
Gunton, Colin E. "Barth, the Trinity, and Human Freedom." *Theology Today* 43.3 (1986) 316–30.
Hart, Trevor A. *Regarding Karl Barth: Toward a Reading of His Theology*. Eugene, OR: Wipf & Stock, 2005.
Holmes, Christopher R. J. "'A Specific Form of Relationship': On the Dogmatic Implications of Barth's Account of Election and Commandment for His Theological Ethics." In *Trinity and Election in Contemporary Theology*, edited by Michael T. Dempsey, 182–200. Grand Rapids: Eerdmans, 2011.
Hunsinger, George. *Disruptive Grace: Studies in the Theology of Karl Barth*. Grand Rapids: Eerdmans, 2000.
Jenson, Robert W. *Alpha and Omega: A Study in the Theology of Karl Barth*. New York: Nelson, 1963.
Macchia, Frank D. "The Spirit of God and the Spirit of Life: An Evangelical Response to Karl Barth's Pneumatology." In *Karl Barth and Evangelical Theology: Convergences and Divergences*, edited by Sung Wook Chung, 149–71. Grand Rapids: Baker Academic, 2006.
Maury, Pierre. "*Election et Foi.*" In *Election, Barth, and the French Connection*, edited by Simon Hattrell, 33–49. Eugene, OR: Pickwick, 2016.
———. *Predestination and Other Papers*. Richmond, VA: John Knox, 1960.
———. "The Ultimate Decision." In *Election, Barth, and the French Connection*, edited by Simon Hattrell, 50–68. Eugene, OR: Pickwick, 2016.
McCormack, Bruce L. *Karl Barth's Critically Realistic Dialectical Theology: Its Genesis and Development 1909–1936*. Oxford: Clarendon, 1997.
———. *Orthodox and Modern: Studies in the Theology of Karl Barth*. Grand Rapids: Baker Academic, 2008.
Nimmo, Paul T. "Barth and the Election-Trinity Debate: A Pneumatological View." In *Trinity and Election in Contemporary Theology*, edited by Michael T. Dempsey, 162–81. Grand Rapids: Eerdmans, 2011.
Oh, Peter S. *Karl Barth's Trinitarian Theology: A Study in Karl Barth's Analogical Use of the Trinitarian Relation*. London: T&T Clark, 2006.

O'Neil, Michael. "Karl Barth, 'The Gift of Freedom' Pt. 1." *Theology and Church* (blog), April 15, 2015. http://www.theologyandchurch.com/2015/04/15/karl-barth-the-gift-of-freedom-pt-1.

———. "Karl Barth, 'The Gift of Freedom' Pt. 2." *Theology and Church* (blog), April 21, 2015. http://www.theologyandchurch.com/2015/04/21/karl-barth-the-gift-of-freedom-pt-2.

———. "Karl Barth's Doctrine of Election." *The Evangelical Quarterly* 76.4 (2004) 311–26.

Rosato, Philip J. *The Spirit as Lord: The Pneumatology of Karl Barth*. Edinburgh: T&T Clark, 1981.

Torrance, Andrew B. "Karl Barth on the Irresistible Nature of Grace." *Journal of Reformed Theology* 10.2 (2016) 103–128.

Webster, J. B. *Barth's Moral Theology: Human Action in Barth's Thought*. Grand Rapids: Eerdmans, 1998.

# 15

## *The Light of the Gospel*
Election and Proclamation

### Michael D. O'Neil

Something immediately apparent from the testimonials in this volume is the sense that Pierre Maury was above all else, a pastoral theologian and a *preacher*. Our editor has dedicated the volume to "the great company of French preachers of the Reformed family both past and present, of which Pierre Maury was an illustrious example."[1] Suzanne McDonald calls Maury a "pastor-theologian" whose pastoral and homiletical treatment of the doctrine of election reminds us that exploration of this doctrine is not simply for those in the academy, but for those who priorities are "preaching and teaching in the churches."[2] Jacques Maury refers to his father as an *evangelist* who was nonetheless, a "theologian in all his activities," but one whose theological activity "always bore the stamp of the primacy of preaching."[3] "He wanted to be first of all, and has been, a 'preacher of the Gospel.'"[4] Robert Mackie shares anecdotes of having experienced the uplifting spiritual power of Maury's theology by

1. Hattrell, *Election, Barth*, xii.
2. Hattrell, *Election, Barth*, xiv.
3. Hattrell, *Election, Barth*, 23–24.
4. Hattrell, *Election, Barth*, 24.

means of his proclamation: "Pierre Maury communicated faith."[5] And finally, Karl Barth also notes that "Pierre Maury's great gift ... was his ability to ally the keenest and most objective theological curiosity with an undeniable feeling for the human and the 'personal,' and his constant concern to use this double insight in preaching the Gospel to the parish, in both the narrowest and the widest sense of the word."[6]

Similarly, something less immediately apparent to many of Karl Barth's readers is the pastoral nature and homiletical orientation of his theology, not least in his reconstruction of the doctrine of election. Barth, too, was concerned with the communication of the faith, that the "walls which separate the [twentieth] century from the first become transparent! Paul speaks, and the man of the [twentieth] century hears."[7] Dogmatics, for Barth, occupies the midpoint between biblical exegesis and Christian proclamation, responsible to the former and oriented to the latter.[8] Yet, even this abbreviated statement does not quite capture the complex relation between dogmatics and proclamation. "Dogmatics," says Barth, "is the self-examination of the Christian Church in respect of the content of its distinctive talk about God."[9] The criterion of this self-examination is the Word of God himself: "Does Christian utterance derive from Him?

---

5. Hattrell, *Election, Barth*, 32.

6. Hattrell, *Election, Barth*, 36.

7. Barth, *Epistle to the Romans*, 7. Mark Lindsay's essay in this volume notes this aspect of Barth's ministry, noting that Barth, like Calvin, "was a preacher at heart" (see Hattrell, *Election, Barth*, 126).

8. This simplified way of expressing the matter finds support in Barth, *Evangelical Theology*, 175–83. However, as I go on to suggest, Barth's formal treatment of the topic is more nuanced, and he insists that "the fact from which dogmatics starts and to which it returns is the human word of Church proclamation" (*CD* I/2:798). Nevertheless, in its task of serving proclamation dogmatics summons the teaching church to listen again to Jesus Christ as he is attested in Holy Scripture: "The dogmatic norm, i.e., the norm of which dogmatics must remind Church proclamation, and therefore itself first of all, as the objective possibility of pure doctrine, can be no other than the revelation attested in Holy Scripture as God's Word" (*CD* I/2:812, 815). Nor is dogmatics reducible to exegesis, but exegesis is the "decisive presupposition and source of dogmatics" (*CD* I/2:821). Barth has already suggested as much in the first part of volume 1: "Dogmatics as such does not ask what the apostles and prophets said but what we must say on the basis of the apostles and prophets" (Barth, *CD* I/1:16). Dogmatics calls the teaching church *back* to the continually renewed *hearing* of the Word of God so that it may then call it *forward* to be once again and simultaneously, the *teaching* church (*CD* I/2:844).

9. *CD* I/1:12.

Does it lead to Him? Is it conformable to Him?"[10] In this sense, dogmatics arises as a response to the proclamation of the church and exists in service of its ongoing proclamation.[11] The relationship of these two discrete spheres of Christian service help us understand what Barth was attempting in his doctrine of election, and highlights the resonance that developed in the respective theologies of Pierre Maury and Karl Barth.

This essay explores the relation between election and proclamation in Barth's doctrine, in hope of highlighting more explicitly Barth's pastoral and homiletical orientation. Before commencing that task, however, it will be helpful to note the relation as it is set forth in the three pieces by Maury included in this volume.

Pierre Maury insists that his approach to the doctrine of election is practical and pastoral rather than "scholastic," biblical rather than "philosophical"; his aim is to help his hearers in their ministry.[12] To treat the doctrine philosophically reduces it to dilemmas and logical impasses which introduce a form of paralysis with respect to the believer's confession of their faith.

The most explicit reference to the relation between election and proclamation in Maury occurs toward the end of his lecture on Predestination:

> We must not preach predestination; that would be the worst error, and also the worst betrayal, I believe, of the Gospel. We must preach Jesus Christ. . . . We must preach salvation and not damnation, the forgiveness of sin rather than sin, and call our flocks unceasingly to the renewal which daily manifests our new birth, which is a "birth of God" (John 1:13). We must learn to proclaim the Man of Sorrows, abandoned, rejected *for us*, "who was delivered up for our offences, and was raised again for our justification" (Rom 4:25). And we must dare to do what in spite of his love—because of his love—he so often dared to do: I mean, to speak of the holy wrath of God who is "of purer eyes than to behold evil" (Hab 1:13), and who "is not mocked" (Gal 6:7), for "it is a fearful thing to fall into the hands of the living God" (Heb 10:31). As we dare to do all this, which does not mean preaching hell, let us remember that, as Jesus did, we cannot but proclaim deliverance from the forces of hell by the victorious Christ.[13]

10. *CD* I/1:4.
11. *CD* I/1:76, 82–83.
12. EF 41–44, PD 81–83.
13. PD 118.

Two things may be said about the initial prohibition in this citation. First, is to note a distinction between the two ministries of teaching and preaching. In this very lecture Maury is *teaching*, explicating the doctrine, highlighting its biblical basis and contours, and unfolding its biblical logic. He cannot mean that there is no place for *teaching* the doctrine, even in the congregational context, so that the people of God might have a deeper apprehension of the gospel that they believe, trust in, and proclaim. Certainly ministers of the gospel must be instructed, as Maury, here, instructs them. Second, Maury correctly notes that the content of the church's proclamation is Jesus Christ, both his person and his work, but especially, his saving work on the cross where, as the Man of Sorrows, he takes upon himself the divine wrath and rejection which humanity otherwise must suffer. The announcement of the gospel includes also what this saving death accomplished for humanity: the forgiveness of sins, deliverance from death and hell, reconciliation and justification, and new birth as a child of God. The proclamation of the gospel, then, has a dual focus; *negatively*, it portrays the self-offering of the Son, his rejection and abandonment in our place; *positively*, it elaborates the accomplishment of his life and work on *our* behalf and *for us*. As such, the proclamation is *not* predestination, but it has nevertheless been decisively shaped by the theological reflection on the person and work of Christ that is the substance of the doctrine. Or to state the matter differently, the Christ we preach is the eternal Son made known to us in the work of God accomplished in his earthly existence but which is grounded not merely in that existence in itself, but in the eternal self-determination of God to *be* Jesus Christ and to suffer thus for us that we might be saved.

There is, then, for Maury, a genuine proclamation of what might be called "double predestination," although it is known only in what Paul called "the word of the cross" (1 Cor 1:18). Maury refers to this dual focus, this negative and positive aspect of proclamation, in the 1936 lecture at Geneva that so moved Barth. Here he insists that one cannot speak of perdition or ruin with respect to the divine intention except by reference to Calvary, although there we must speak of it.[14] There at the cross Christ was punished that peace might be extended to humanity. He was struck that humanity might be welcomed. If there is a "negative' election"— and Maury avers that there is—then it is here, and here alone, but here truly, where Christ is condemned on the cross that does not condemn

---

14. PD 101.

humankind but reveals the divine love in all its depths and richness.[15] At the cross we see both ourselves and the love of God; ourselves as deserving the fate that fell upon him who stood in for us, and the love of God in the One who for us would do this in order to free us from this fate that the positive grace of welcome might truly belong to us. But to know this truth *as* "double predestination" is something only for the church, and not for the proclamation addressed to the world.

> Predestination is therefore very much *double*, not as if there were two categories of people that it would separate by "sorting," but double because of having two *terms: election* and *rejection, grace* and *condemnation*. So we can apply this [double decree] to ourselves, because we deserve the negative verdict in it as much as we welcome the positive grace in it. In other words, double predestination is a truth which only the church knows and never philosophy, but also a truth which concerns the *church* and which the church is only able to preach to her members.[16]

In the proclamation addressed to the world we simply but truly preach *Christ* with a message that is overwhelmingly *positive*, concerning the grace of God directed toward us in him and on account of his suffering on our behalf.[17] One can, of course, address the negative aspect of the divine judgment but only with reference to Jesus's suffering on the cross, or with respect to the final judgment which lies still in the future.[18] What one can never do is suggest that God deals with humanity on the basis of two classes of people, one elect and the other rejected.

As Maury ponders why the great teachers of predestination in the history of the church exalted the mystery of the "absolute decree" he suggests that they were moved by their worship of the divine majesty. Nonetheless, this move had the result of turning the question of election into "a mystery as impenetrable as night, the secret of an opaque God." He argues that although election is indeed a mystery, it is a mystery of light and that we must know and preach the mystery as nothing other than the peace that passes understanding, grounded in the unfathomable love of

15. EF 49.
16. EF 52–53.
17. EF 52.
18. UD 72–73. EF 53–54. Note, however, that when Maury raises the question of the final judgment in his sermon, "The Ultimate Decision," he does so *positively*, asserting that in the final judgment the Judge we face is the One who has come to us and given himself for us that we might be his. See Hattrell, *Election, Barth*, 62–63.

God. "It is not in the darkness of an eternal obscurity that God lives and makes his decision, but in light 'unapproachable,' yes, but light!"[19]

## THE LIGHT OF THE GOSPEL IN BARTH'S DOCTRINE

As we turn to consider the relation of election and proclamation in Barth's theology, we find at the very beginning of his work a concern for the proclamation of the church. His initial discussion of election concerns the orientation of the doctrine, and Barth insists that the election of grace is the "sum of the Gospel," and even more strongly, "the whole of the Gospel, the Gospel *in nuce* ... the very essence of all good news."[20] In the light of this election the whole of the Gospel is light. As such its proclamation is one of joy, and not a mixed message of joy and terror, or salvation and damnation. It is true that the doctrine casts a shadow, but if the shadow is allowed to dominate—as it has in much of the tradition—"then it is quite certain that we can never again receive or proclaim as such the Gospel previously declared."[21]

In his preface to *Church Dogmatics* II/2 Barth refers to the anxiety he experienced with reference to his work on the doctrine of election:

> I would have preferred to follow Calvin's doctrine of predestination much more closely, instead of departing from it so radically. ... But I could not and cannot do so. As I let the Bible itself speak to me on these matters, as I meditated upon what I seemed to hear, I was driven irresistibly to reconstruction.[22]

The reason for Barth's departure from Calvin and the tradition is not difficult to ascertain. His correction of the tradition is an attempt to maintain the freedom of God's election as *grace*, as *gospel*. Barth suggests that the traditional formulations of the doctrine erred by separating the election from Jesus Christ who is the criterion and measure of all God's works, and importantly, of our knowledge of God. In so doing they constructed a doctrine in which the bad news overshadows the good, in which the essence of *gospel* is swallowed up in the indeterminate decision of the *decretum absolutum*. "How can the doctrine of predestination be anything but 'dark' and obscure if in its very first tenet, the tenet which

19. PD 93.
20. *CD* II/2:13–14.
21. *CD* II/2:13–14.
22. *CD* II/2:x.

determines all the rest, it can speak only of a *decretum absolutum*? ... We abandon this tradition, but we hold fast by John 1:1-2."[23]

Thus, Barth rejects the *decretum absolutum* on methodological grounds and because of the darkness it casts over the doctrine of election.[24] He notes that the Reformers spoke of Christ as the light or the mirror of election, seeing in him the first of the elect according to his human nature, and as the elected means by which human salvation would be accomplished. This understanding of the election had a pastoral function: believers are to cleave to Jesus Christ as their hope of eternal life. It is not possible to penetrate beyond him to the eternal and terrible decree that lies at the foundation of all reality, that lies in the depths of God's inscrutability, the absolute decree that divides humanity into both elect and reprobate. Barth insists that this formulation of the doctrine in fact robs the believer of assurance by obscuring the source of election:

> How can even the Word of God give us assurance on this point if Jesus Christ is ... only an elected means whereby the electing God—electing elsewhere and in some other way—executes that which He has decreed concerning those whom He has—elsewhere and in some other way—elected. The fact that Calvin in particular not only did not answer but did not even perceive this question is the decisive objection which we have to bring against his whole doctrine of predestination. The electing God of Calvin is a *Deus nudus absconditus*.[25] ... All the dubious features

---

23. *CD* II/2:104. Barth provides a definition of the *decretum absolutum* in his discussion of supra- and infralapsarianism: "It is an act of the divine freedom whose basis and meaning are completely hidden, and in their hiddenness must be regarded and reverenced as holy.... Behind (this) view there stands the picture of the absolute God in Himself who is neither conditioned nor self-conditioning, and not the picture of the Son of God who is self-conditioned and therefore conditioned in His union with the Son of David; not the picture of God in Jesus Christ" (*CD* II/2:134). His complaint is that, "if the distinctive and ultimate feature in God is absolute freedom of choice, or an absolutely free choice, then it will be hard to distinguish His freedom from caprice or His mystery from the blindness of such caprice. It will be no less hard to maintain His righteousness in any form except that of mere assertion. It will then be difficult to make it clear that God is not merely a tyrant living by His whims, that He is not merely blind fate, that He is something other than the essential inscrutability of all being" (*CD* II/2:25). We see here that Barth is not only seeking to retain the characteristic of gospel as the fundamental characteristic of the doctrine, but he is also deeply concerned with the ontology presupposed in the traditional formulation.

24. *CD* II/2:146.

25. A "bare" hidden God, One who in his remoteness seems to ignore human suffering.

of Calvin's doctrine result from the basic failing that in the last analysis he separates God and Jesus Christ.[26]

Barth is strident, "There is no such thing as a *decretum absolutum*. There is no such thing as a will of God apart from the will of Jesus Christ. . . . He is the Lamb slain, and the Lamb slain from the foundation of the world. For this reason, the *crucified* Jesus is the 'image of the invisible God.'"[27]

Like Maury from whom he learnt it, Barth insists on a christological rendering of the doctrine; God's eternal election is known only in Jesus Christ, and supremely, at the cross. Simply put, his doctrine consists "in the assertion that the divine predestination is the election of Jesus Christ."[28] This simple phrase, however, is pregnant with significance. *First*, it signifies that before election has a human referent it refers to God's eternal and unconditional act of self-determination, in which God ordained himself to be God-for-humanity in the person and under the name of Jesus Christ. Election is firstly and primarily about God. *Second*, Barth intends that the genitive in this phrase be understood as both subjective and objective: that is, Jesus Christ is both the Subject and the Object of election, both Elector and Elected, the electing God and the elected person.

In accord with the Reformed tradition Barth posits a double predestination, albeit one which has been radically reconfigured. As noted, he rejects the absolute decree which divides humanity into those elect and those rejected. Rather, he insists that in the primal decree God elected himself for rejection, and in Jesus Christ, bore that rejection in time, so that humanity could be elect in him.[29] Thus Barth is adamant:

> Man is not rejected. In God's eternal purpose it is God Himself who is rejected in His Son. . . . He is rejected in order that we might not be rejected. Predestination means that from all eternity God has determined upon man's acquittal at His own cost. . . . We shall never find . . . the decreed rejection whether of ourselves or of any other men. This is not because we did not

---

26. *CD* II/2:110–11.
27. *CD* II/2:115, 123.
28. *CD* II/2:103.
29. *CD* II/2:162–65.

deserve rejection, but because God did not will it, because God willed the rejection of His Son in our stead.[30]

The pastoral and homiletical orientation of Barth's doctrine is explicit in the opening sections and sub-sections of his exposition. His reconstruction of the Reformed doctrine serves to clarify the identity and nature of the electing God and in so doing to purge the doctrine not only of its distorted vision of an arbitrary and even tyrannical God, but to proclaim ever more clearly the gracious initiative of this God who has chosen and claimed us as his own and at great cost to himself. By these moves Barth sought to reclaim and protect the proclamation of the gospel precisely as *gospel*, as "the very essence of all good news."

## THE TWO "MOMENTS" OF ELECTION

A second feature of Barth's doctrine that illuminates the relation between election and proclamation, and that also addresses a persistent difficulty in the interpretation of his doctrine, has to do with his actualistic approach to election which was prominent in his early treatments of the doctrine prior to 1936, but which continued in an attenuated fashion even after its christological reworking. In his early theology, Barth's doctrine had no real emphasis on election "in Christ," but was, rather, grounded in the decision of God that occurred in the concrete moment of revelation. In revelation the person is confronted with a dual possibility which is grounded in the nature of revelation itself. In his revealing God remains veiled, and the possibility of whether one "sees" beyond the veil or otherwise does not "does not lie in our hands but in God's."[31] In this regard Barth's doctrine is theocentric rather than christocentric, and it was only after Maury's 1936 lecture that Barth would speak of election solely in terms of Jesus Christ, and the eternal will of God which was revealed in him.[32]

---

30. *CD* II/2:167-68. "The rejection which all men incurred, the wrath of God under which all men lie, the death which all men must die, God in His love for men transfers from all eternity to Him in whom He loves and elects them, and whom He elects at their head and in their place. God from all eternity ordains this obedient One in order that He might bear the suffering which the disobedient have deserved and which for the sake of God's righteousness must necessarily be borne" (*CD* II/2:123).

31. Barth, *Göttingen Dogmatics*, 451.

32. McCormack, *Karl Barth's Dialectical Theology*, 373, 457. See also Mark Lindsay's essay in this volume (Hattrell, *Election, Barth*, 123-45). For additional discussion

It is already apparent that Barth, in his early discussion of election, is seeking a way beyond the classical expression of the doctrine he inherited from his Reformed tradition. In his mature exposition Barth notes that in the traditional formulations of the doctrine the focus "has always begun with this problem, and has made no essential progress beyond it . . . the question of the eternal (positively or negatively determined) order of the private relationship which exists between God and all individual human beings."[33] He seeks to correct this by positing, in accordance with the Scripture, a "mediate and mediating" election of the community, between the election of Jesus Christ and that of the individual.[34] Barth employs the image of the circle to present this understanding of election. Those called and gathered around Jesus Christ, the one community in the two-fold form of Israel and the Church, constitute an "inner" circle of the election which has taken place in and with the election of Jesus Christ. Beyond this there exists a wider circle which includes the rest of humanity, and which is labeled by Barth as "the outer circle of the election which has taken place (and takes place) in Jesus Christ."[35]

It is important to note Barth's parenthetical comment in this sentence which indicates that he considers election an event which occurs in time, as well as in pre-temporal eternity. It is crucial to recognize that election for Barth has two "moments" and that those in the outer circle are in one sense elect, and in another, yet to be elected, or better, to have their election actualized and made a concrete reality.

Barth devotes over a hundred pages to the dialectic relation between Israel and the Church in the election of God. The two forms of the one community are gathered around Jesus Christ who is both the crucified Messiah of Israel and the risen Lord of the Church. This double identification of Jesus in relation to each of the forms of the one community functions in an important way for Barth. Both groups are elect and serve as witnesses to Jesus Christ, each in their own particular manner, reflecting the double predestination of Christ. Israel witnesses to the judgment which has come upon humanity for their disobedience, and to that form of life from which humanity are delivered in Christ. The Church witnesses to the blessedness and grace that is given to humanity as the elect

---

of Barth's doctrine of election in his early career, see O'Neil, *Church as Moral Community*, 159–60, 170–74, 197–99; McDonald, "Barth's 'Other' Doctrine of Election."

33. *CD* II/2:306.
34. *CD* II/2:195–96.
35. *CD* II/2:196–97.

of God. Barth insists that this relation is not absolute but relative: the Church finds itself prefigured in the faith of the few in Israel who do hear and believe God's promise, and through them, "Israel participates with the Church in the perfect form of the community, in the body of Christ ... Israel's election is also confirmed positively."[36] According to Barth,

> The one community is *mediate* in that it is the middle point between the election of Jesus Christ and (included in this) the election of those who have believed, and do and will believe, in Him. It is *mediating* in so far as ... all the election that has taken place and takes place in Jesus Christ is mediated, conditioned and bounded by the election of the community ... *Extra ecclesiam nulla salus*.[37] This proposition has its place already in the doctrine of predestination, in the doctrine of God.[38]

When Barth speaks of the elect individual he asserts that they are elect only in and with the community, "elect through its mediacy and elect to its membership ... an election to participation in the ministry of the community."[39] This is the inner circle of proclamation and faith, and those outside of it live lives that are "lost," bearing the rejection of those who are apart from Jesus Christ.[40] Barth continues:

> Election means faith. And since those who believe are the Church, election means to be in the Church. We have here a closed circle which cannot be penetrated. There is no election to anything else or to any other situation. There is no election of an individual man on the basis of which he is not led by the Word into faith, and therefore into the fellowship of believers, and therefore into the Church ... Election and the Church are coinciding circles.[41]

Yet this circle is not so closed or predetermined that it cannot expand:

> The election of each individual involves, and his calling completes, an opening up and enlargement of the (in itself) closed

---

36. *CD* II/2:266.

37. Outside the Church there is no salvation.

38. *CD* II/2:196-97. See also *CD* II/2:239. Note again, in this citation, that election "has taken place" *and* "takes place."

39. *CD* II/2:410.

40. *CD* II/2:415.

41. *CD* II/2:427-28.

circle of the election of Jesus Christ and His community in relation to the world—or (from the standpoint of the world) an invasion of the dark kingdom of the lies which rule in the world. . . . The existence of each elect means a hidden but real crossing of frontiers, to the gain of the Kingdom of God.[42]

An enlargement of the circle of election occurs as the church faithfully pursues its calling of witness and proclamation in the world. It cannot regard the world as rejected for they are those to whom God has graciously turned in the election of Jesus Christ. The elect are called to proclaim the message of the triumphant grace of God, and to summon the world to faith in him. By so doing "Jesus Christ stands in the midst of His own, and proclaimed by the service of His own wills to go out into the world. This is what has to happen continually and at every point between the inner circle of the community and the outer one of the rest of men. The gospel is to be preached on this frontier."[43]

We thus see clearly that Barth envisages "two moments" of election: The primal election of Jesus Christ with all humanity included in him, and the "election" of each individual—the actualization of their election in time—which occurs in the moment of revelation through the proclamation of the elect community. To say that the community *mediates* the election through its proclamation would be, I think, too strong, and to over-interpret Barth's statement that the community is "*mediating*." It is better to affirm his own expression that *Jesus Christ* goes out into the world by means of the proclamation of his own. In this way Jesus Christ remains the Electing God not merely in terms of the primal decision but also in the event of revelation in which "the real crossing of the frontier" occurs.

Nevertheless, the crucial role of the church's proclamation is evident in Barth's exposition of election. As the mediate and mediating community, it is elect for the purpose of vocation, giving to the world the testimony of Jesus Christ and summoning it to faith in him. Should the community cease this service it has "forgotten and forfeited" its election.[44] The community, having its being in the election of Jesus Christ,

---

42. *CD* II/2:417. See also *CD* II/2:419.

43. *CD* II/2:195. See also *CD* II/2:266.

44. *CD* II/2:196–97. For an extended discussion of election understood in terms of "vocation" see O'Neil, "Communities of Witness." See also McDonald, *Re-Imaging Election*, which develops this sense of vocation in terms of representation. For example: "The church is called to represent God to the world" (McDonald, *Re-Imaging*

exists for his service and his witness, as "'a light of the Gentiles,' the hope, the promise, the invitation and the summoning of all peoples and at the same time, of course, the question, the demand and the judgment set over the whole of humanity and every individual man."[45]

What is true for the elect community is true also of the elect individual. Barth deplores the privatizing of election that occurred in the history of theology.[46] He argues that, "inwardly and inseparably bound up with that which God is for him, is that which he may be for God; with his deliverance, his employment; with his faith in the promise of God, his responsibility for its further proclamation; with his blessedness, his obedience in his service and commission as a witness of the divine election of grace."[47] The elect person is indeed elected to eternal salvation, but

> whereas the Church's doctrine of predestination ends and halts with this definition as in a *cul-de-sac*, and whereas its last word is to the effect that the elect finally "go to heaven" as distinct from the rejected, the biblical view—in a deeper understanding of what is meant by the clothing of men with God's eternal glory—opens at this point another door. For as those who expect and finally receive eternal life, as the heirs in faith of eternal glory, the elect are accepted for this employment and placed in this service. They are made witnesses.[48]

Barth's exposition of the two moments of election, together with a recognition of the central role of proclamation helps us address one of the key criticisms made of his doctrine: that it is ineluctably universalist.[49] Those who criticize Barth for this perceived weakness typically fail to give sufficient weight to one or more significant factors. First, of course, Barth repeatedly rejects *apokatastasis* as a doctrinal position which can be maintained by the church, although not as a hope that the

---

*Election*, 91).

45. *CD* II/2:53.
46. *CD* II/2:423.
47. *CD* II/2:414. See also *CD* II/2:343, 345.
48. *CD* II/2:414. See also *CD* II/2:449.
49. Numerous interpreters have insisted that Barth's doctrine is universalist. For a brief sample, see Brunner, *Christian Doctrine of God*, 1:314; Berkouwer, *Triumph of Grace*, 116; Crisp, "Letter and the Spirit"; "I Teach It." It should be noted, of course, that not all interpreters are concerned with the idea of universal salvation. See also Damon Adam's essay in this volume. It will be evident that my approach to the question differs significantly from his own approach.

church might hold and for which it might pray.⁵⁰ Second, the interpreters do not always give sufficient weight to those instances where Barth insists that election must be received, activated, and made concrete; that the proclamation of the church must be met with genuine faith, decision and obedience.⁵¹ Third, they also minimize those passages where Barth warns of the real threat of eternal rejection awaiting those who fail to obey their election.⁵² Finally, and perhaps decisively, Barth's critics appear to lift Barth's universalistic statements from the context in which they are grounded: that is, the witness and proclamation of the believing community to the world at large. The rubric under which Barth discusses these matters, that is, the *Leitsatz* (guiding principle or maxim) of section 35, "The Election of the Individual," reads as follows:

> The man who is isolated over against God is as such rejected by God. But to be this man can only be by the godless man's own choice. The witness of the community of God to every individual man consists in this: that this choice of the godless man is void; that he belongs eternally to Jesus Christ and therefore is not rejected, but elected by God in Jesus Christ; that the rejection which he deserves on account of his perverse choice is borne and cancelled by Jesus Christ; and that he is appointed to eternal life with God on the basis of the righteous, divine decision.⁵³

Barth insists that the content of the proclamation is the objectivity of Christ's atonement, with specific application being pressed upon the individual hearer, thus encountering them with the divine claim upon

---

50. For a discussion of this matter in the context of his doctrine of election, see *CD* II/2:417–19, 484–87, 496–97. For his "final word" on the topic, see *CD* IV/3.1:477–78. "Barth's point is to emphasize the distinction between what may be a valid theological proposition and what may be a real possibility for God. Barth consistently rejects universalism as a doctrine, but he leaves open the possibility that within God's freedom all men may indeed be saved" (Bettis, "Is Karl Barth a Universalist?," 427). Bruce McCormack comes to a similar conclusion in McCormack, "So That He May Be Merciful."

51. I discuss this theme in the next section of the essay.

52. For example: "To the man who persistently tries to change the truth into untruth, God does not owe eternal patience and therefore deliverance any more than He does those provisional manifestations. We should be denying or disarming that evil attempt and our own participation in it if, in relation to ourselves or others or all men, we were to permit ourselves to postulate a withdrawal of that threat and in this sense to expect or maintain an *apokatastasis* or universal reconciliation as the goal and end of all things. No such postulate can be made even though we appeal to the cross and resurrection of Jesus Christ" (*CD* IV/3.1:477).

53. *CD* II/2:306.

their lives and calling for a positive response from them in the light of the message proclaimed.[54] On the grounds of the election of grace in Jesus Christ none are to be considered rejected and the summons to faith is to be issued to all with undiluted strength.

## THE DECISION OF FAITH

In "The Ultimate Decision" Pierre Maury correctly notes that the human decision for Jesus Christ is *sui generis*,[55] not analogous to other human decisions between a range of options, or even the self-commitment of one to an imagined absolute or cause.[56] Nor is rational argument concerning the legitimacy of Christian claims the way to commitment to Christ. Rather, says Maury, the way to this commitment occurs as one is engaged directly in a relational encounter with Jesus the Word, a dialogue in which the person is addressed and in which they respond.[57]

For Maury, the ultimate decision is not the human decision of faith, but the divine decision concerning humanity in which all and each are the object of God's eternal love in Jesus Christ. This decision has a dual aspect: first, Jesus Christ is himself the eternal decision of God, and in him "eternally and in eternity," "even our short, poor lives, are linked to that life even by the will which created them. It is from all eternity, in eternity, that between Jesus Christ and us a relationship is established."[58] Jesus Christ is decisive also in the second sense that he has come, given

---

54. Thus, see also *CD* II/2:322, 324, 423. One of the few interpreters to make the connection between Barth's universalistic statements and proclamation is John Colwell who insists that "we must recognize that it is not Barth's intention in these passages to speculate concerning the ultimate destiny of each individual but rather to emphasize and define the inclusive nature of the church's witness to each individual" (Colwell, "Contemporaneity of the Divine Decision," 147). The careful reader will note the different interpretation I give this passage compared to that given by Matthias Gockel in his excellent essay in this volume. Whereas I view the passage as identifying the *witness of the community* toward the godless, Gockel views it as saying the godless person's decision is "unreal." To my mind this does not do sufficient justice either to Barth's other statements in this section, nor to his portrayal of human agency generally. It seems to depend upon an understanding of Barth's election in which only the "eternal moment" is of consequence. No doubt this discussion must continue.

55. Of its own kind/genus.

56. UD 63, 74.

57. UD 64, 65.

58. UD 66, 67.

himself and chosen us—as an act of *God*, and as such enacting that decision made in eternity.[59] The divine decision is ultimate because it deals with ultimate things—the final judgment, although even here the Judge awaiting us is Jesus Christ who has come for us, given himself for us, and chosen us! Finally, the decision is ultimate because it demands *our* decision, an ultimate decision in which we give ourselves wholly and without reserve to him.[60]

Barth too, as we mentioned above, also discusses the necessity of the human decision in the "second moment" of election. For example, "For his part man can and actually does elect God, thus attesting and activating himself as elected man."[61] Or again,

> He may refuse to listen or believe . . . on the other hand, he may listen and believe. . . . But this is something which is not decided in the word of promise. It is decided in the adoption of the attitude which this subject adopts to the address made to him, and in which he shows whether he is instructed or uninstructed by the promise, that is, whether he is converted or unconverted.[62]

These two samples are representative of many instances in which Barth insists on the necessity of human response and human decision. Election is not something that occurs, as it were, "over our heads" and without the requirement of this response. Importantly, Barth patterns his understanding of human response on that of Jesus Christ.[63] The basis of the election of Jesus Christ as the elect person lies in the primal obedience of the Son of God in which, as the electing God together with the Father and the Spirit, he willed to be obedient to the determination willed for him by the Father. His election as the elect person occurred in the event of his obedience to that which was determined for him:

59. UD 68–71.
60. UD 71–73.
61. *CD* II/2:177.
62. *CD* II/2:323–24.
63. This way of expressing the matter is important if we are to be faithful to Barth's intent. Human decision is crucial, though not as a means of adding to or supplementing the work of divine grace; Barth does not advocate synergism. Nor is human decision independent with respect to God, but enabled and made possible precisely by divine grace. The human decision of faith toward God *corresponds* to the divine decision of the faithfulness of God toward humanity which occurred in Jesus Christ. This correspondence is an appropriate response *conformed* to God and to the covenantal relation that exists between God and the creature. See *CD* I/1:237–44; Neder, *Participation in Christ*, 9–11; Guretzki, *Explorer's Guide to Karl Barth*, 58–60.

> The obedience which He renders as the Son of God is, as genuine obedience, His own decision and electing . . . the fact that He is elected corresponds as closely as possible to His own electing. In the harmony of the triune God He is no less the original Subject of this electing than He is the original object. And only in this harmony can He really be its object, i.e., completely fulfil not his own will but the will of the Father, and thus confirm and to some extent repeat as elected man the election of God.[64]

According to Jüngel, the eternal Son *chooses* his being chosen by the Father, affirming the determination willed for him by the Father.[65] Further, as the elect human he repeats and confirms his election. So, too, those who hear the gospel are summoned to respond in faith, choosing the God who has chosen them, and so "activating" themselves as among the elect.

In his 1939 lecture on "The Sovereignty of God's Word and the Decision of Faith" Barth argues that human agency is genuine and necessary, but also always responsive to and dependent upon the prior work of divine grace.

> The Word of God is sovereign in that it is spoken and reaches us in divine freedom. . . . This is the freedom which gives freedom to others, which gives us and allows us our freedom, which asks of us that we place ourselves at its disposal in freedom—not forced, not pushed, not overpowered, but in adoration. But that is to assert the priority and superiority of the divine freedom over this freedom of ours! . . . We may and ought to choose, but it is His decision, the decision of the Word of God, just when and where our choice is the choice of truth in adoration.[66]

In the decision of faith the human agent "participates in the completion" of the divine act which from the outset is directed toward them as its object. This participation takes the only form it can, given it is a creaturely participation in a divine work, that is, as a recipient of a gift.[67] Barth insists that "faith always means choice, crisis, transition. . . . Faith is always decision."[68] For Barth, faith is an entire surrender to the Word

64. *CD* II/2:105.//
65. Jüngel in Thompson, "Humanity of God," 253.
66. See Barth, *God Here and Now*, 22–23. Eberhard Busch notes the date of the lecture in Busch, *Karl Barth*, 292.
67. Barth, *God Here and Now*, 24.
68. Barth, *God Here and Now*, 26–27.

of God, a conscious and deliberate decision as a work of the Holy Spirit within us.[69] There can be no "persistence in neutrality" at this point: it is *the person* who must believe, who must trust instead of denying, who must entrust themselves to the One, who must surrender rather than assert themselves, who in turning toward Jesus Christ must also in and by this turning, turn away from all else.[70]

> In faith we acknowledge that we deserve wrath and rejection, the wrath and rejection which Jesus Christ has taken upon Himself in our place, in order to place us, whose life is glorified in Him, in the light of divine grace. We can only choose as men who have already been chosen![71]

From the days of his pastoral work in Safenwil until the final volume of *Church Dogmatics* Barth consistently brought the question of human agency in the light of divine sovereignty into his discussion of salvation and ethics. And although there is undoubtedly development in his thought over the course of his career, and in the manner in which he expressed the relation between divine and human agency, Barth unswervingly insisted upon the reality of genuine human agency as a responsive and empowered agency dependent upon the prior gracious and liberating work of God which freed the human agent for such response, faith and obedience. It should come as no surprise that this pattern of divine-human interaction is found also in his doctrine of election.[72]

---

69. See the essay in this volume by Leo Stossich ("The Human Election of God"), particularly the section on the Holy Spirit (201–5).

70. Barth, *God Here and Now*, 27. See also Barth's beautiful and lyrical meditation on the meaning of faith in Barth, *God Here and Now*, 26.

71. Barth, *God Here and Now*, 28.

72. I cannot, in this essay, discuss this point at length. I provide detailed examination of this theme in Barth's career from 1915–22 in O'Neil, *Church as Moral Community*, and especially in the chapters on the two *Römerbrief* commentaries. An example from Barth's mature theology is clearly evident in his discussion of sanctification. The accomplished sanctification of all humanity *de iure* in the exaltation of the Son of Man is realized in the lives of specific persons in the event of revelation by the power of the Holy Spirit in which the person is addressed by the very specific word of direction which comes to them disturbing their sinful slumber and inactivity and calling them to awaken and arise, to lift themselves up, and to look unto him who sets them free for a new obedience. In this event of revelation not only is their sinful nature disturbed and limited, but in the Holy Spirit a new creation emerges—a new orientation, a new subjectivity, a new revelation and fellowship, a new direction, such that they are now saints, even while still sinners. Their lives are now set in a movement from the old to the new, a movement of grateful response to the reception of divine grace. See *CD* IV/2

## PROCLAIMING THE FREE GRACE OF GOD

In May 1934 the sixth thesis of the Barmen Declaration stated, in part, that "the church's commission upon which its freedom is founded, consists in delivering the message of the free grace of God to all people in Christ's stead."[73] Karl Barth riffed on this thesis in the title of a 1947 lecture entitled "The Proclamation of God's Free Grace."[74] Written after the publication of his doctrine of election, Barth insists that "the Church exists by living for this commission. Thus, it does not exist as an end in itself. It has no line of retreat into a churchly subjectivity. . . . It exists alone for the message of God's free grace."[75] God's free grace is nothing else than God himself in "his own most inner and essential nature,"[76] God himself as he "turns" toward humanity in the election of Jesus Christ, in infinite condescension seeking and creating fellowship between God and humanity in him, and reconciling humanity by triumphing over all their unworthiness, opposition, and sin. In his grace God makes *himself* the gift, offering *himself* in fellowship to the other and thereby showing that he is the God who loves.[77] It is for this reason that "in this Gospel the love of God is the first word."[78] Further, it is the message and witness of the church to *all*, for in the election of Jesus Christ there are none who are *not* chosen, none that is, who are rejected. There are none for whom Christ did *not* die, and none whose sins have not been taken away. And if we should worry that such proclamation is too generous, too one-sided; and if we should worry that such proclamation might lead us toward a doctrine of *apokatastasis*, Barth will only reply,

> Strange Christianity, whose most pressing anxiety seems to be that God's grace might prove to be all too free on this side, that hell, instead of being populated with so many people, might someday prove to be empty! But if the freedom of grace is preserved on both these sides, something else has to be said: that

---

§66 (*CD* IV/2:499–613). Barth's discussion of the relation between Spirit-baptism and water baptism in the final volume of the *Dogmatics* provides another example.

73. For the full text of the sixth thesis together with a commentary discussing its meaning, see Busch, *Barmen Theses*, 87–101.

74. See Barth, *God Here and Now*, 34–54.

75. Barth, *God Here and Now*, 50.

76. Barth, *God Here and Now*, 37.

77. *CD* II/1:353–54.

78. *CD* II/1:351.

> whoever and wherever he may be, man is not only reached and blessed by grace, but in one way or another he is taken by grace into its service. Grace calls us into the decision of faith. Grace allows us no idleness, no neutrality, no standing aside.[79]

Although Pierre Maury insisted that the church's proclamation is not predestination per se but Jesus Christ, nevertheless his own exposition shows that his proclamation of Jesus Christ is decisively shaped by his doctrine of election. In this respect Karl Barth and Pierre Maury stand on common ground. Barth, too, developed his doctrine of election with proclamation in view, seeking a form of the doctrine in which the gospel proclaimed is light rather than darkness. Proclamation also plays a pivotal role in the existential realization of election, for Jesus Christ himself goes forth into the world in and through the proclamation of his people, and by this means calls individuals across the frontier from the kingdom of darkness into the kingdom of God. The proclamation constitutes a genuine event in which the divine—human encounter occurs and in response to which a genuine human decision of faith is required. That this decision is forthcoming is, of course in Barth's theology, the work of the Holy Spirit—something for which we can and may and must fervently pray!

We have also seen that Barth intended his doctrine to guide the substance of proclamation, for the content of the message is nothing else than Jesus Christ who is in his person and work the very Word and grace and reconciliation of God given and accomplished "for us and for our salvation." Faithful Christian proclamation will hold forth the word of this reconciliation with great confidence, as Paul has shown in his marvelous discussion in 2 Corinthians 5:14–21. It will not be a message of Yes or No or Maybe. It will not vacillate as though God's will is inscrutable and hidden. It will instead press each hearer with actuality of Jesus Christ and his work on their behalf and call forthrightly for a decision of faith, a positive response to a positive declaration of the abundance of divine grace given to each and to all in Jesus Christ.

What might such proclamation look like in practice? Allow me to conclude this essay with a representative sample of how Karl Barth's exposition of election has shaped my own proclamation of the gospel:

> God was in Christ reconciling the world—reconciling *you!* Yes, especially and precisely *You!*—to himself, *not* imputing their

---

79. Barth, *God Here and Now*, 42.

trespasses against them! God is *not* imputing *your* trespasses against you. No! God has forgiven *your* sins and *mine*, our sins and all sins. Already you have been forgiven, utterly, completely and forever. Already God has loved you in Christ and given you everything. Already he has reconciled you, and me and all to himself forever. "Behold the Lamb of God *who has taken away the sins of the world.*" Including yours; including mine. God does not want to be God without you! He has come for you and come to you and comes to you again this very moment. God is calling you right here, right now: *be reconciled to God!* From all eternity he has chosen *you* to be his child, a member of his family and a citizen of his kingdom. From all eternity God has determined that *your* sins will not separate you from him. Rather he has borne them himself: "*God was in Christ reconciling the world to himself!*" Christ has died on your behalf that you "should no longer live for yourself but for him who died for you and rose again." And today he calls you; Jesus Christ is calling *you*: how will you respond? I urge you in Christ's stead, *be reconciled to God!* As he has given himself to you and for you, so he calls you to give yourself to him and for him. Say Yes to the God who has from all eternity said Yes to you. Choose the God who has already and from all eternity chosen you.

# BIBLIOGRAPHY

Barth, Karl. *Church Dogmatics*. Edited by G. W. Bromiley and T. F. Torrance. Translated by G. T. Thomson, et al. Edinburgh: T&T Clark, 1936–77.
———. *The Epistle to the Romans*. Translated by E. C. Hoskyns. 6th ed. Oxford: Oxford University Press, 1933.
———. *Evangelical Theology: An Introduction*. Translated by G. Foley. Grand Rapids: Eerdmans, 1963.
———. *God Here and Now*. Translated by Paul M. van Buren. London: Routledge, 1964.
———. *The Göttingen Dogmatics: Instruction in the Christian Religion*. Translated by G. W. Bromiley. Vol. 1. Grand Raids: Eerdmans, 1991.
Berkouwer, G. C. *The Triumph of Grace in the Theology of Karl Barth*. Translated by H. R. Boer. Grand Rapids: Eerdmans, 1956.
Bettis, Joseph D. "Is Karl Barth a Universalist?" *Scottish Journal of Theology* 20.4 (1967) 423–36.
Brunner, Emil. *The Christian Doctrine of God*. Vol. 1. of *Dogmatics*. Translated by O. Wyon. London: Lutterworth, 1949.
Busch, Eberhard. *The Barmen Theses Then and Now*. Translated by Darrell Guder and Judith Guder. Grand Rapids: Eerdmans, 2010.
———. *Karl Barth: His Life from Letters and Autobiographical Texts*. Translated by J. Bowden. Philadelphia: Fortress, 1976.
Colwell, John. "The Contemporaneity of the Divine Decision: Reflections on Barth's Denial of 'Universalism.'" In *Universalism and the Doctrine of Hell*, edited by N. M. de S. Cameron, 139–60. Carlisle: Paternoster, 1992.
Crisp, Oliver D. "'I Teach It, but I Also Do Not Teach It': Karl Barth (1886–1968) on Universalism." In *All Will Be Well: Explorations in Universalism and Christian Theology*, edited by Gregory MacDonald, 305–324. Eugene, OR: Cascade, 2010.
———. "The Letter and the Spirit of Barth's Doctrine of Election: A Response to Michael O'Neil." *Evangelical Quarterly* 79.1 (2007) 53–67.
Hattrell, Simon, ed. *Election, Barth, and the French Connection: How Pierre Maury Gave a "Decisive Impetus" to Karl Barth's Doctrine of Election*. Translated by Simon Hattrell. Eugene, OR: Pickwick, 2016.
McCormack, Bruce L. *Karl Barth's Critically Realistic Dialectical Theology: Its Genesis and Development 1909–1936*. Oxford: Oxford University Press, 1995.
———. "So That He May Be Merciful to All: Karl Barth and the Problem of Universalism." In *Karl Barth and American Evangelicalism*, edited by Bruce L. McCormack, et al., 227–49. Grand Rapids: Eerdmans, 2011.
McDonald, Suzanne. "Barth's 'Other' Doctrine of Election in the Church Dogmatics." *International Journal of Systematic Theology* 9.2 (2007) 134–47.
———. *Re-imaging Election, Divine Election as Representing God to Others and Others to God*. Grand Rapids: Eerdmans, 2010.
Neder, Adam. *Participation in Christ: An Entry into Karl Barth's Church Dogmatics*. Louisville: Westminster John Knox, 2009.
O'Neil, Michael D. *Church as Moral Community: Karl Barth's Vision of Christian Life, 1915–1922*. Milton Keynes: Paternoster, 2013.
———. "Communities of Witness: The Concept of Election in the Old Testament and in the Theology of Karl Barth." In *Text and Task: Scripture and Mission*, edited by Michael Parsons, 172–86. Carlisle: Paternoster, 2005.
Thompson, John. "The Humanity of God in the Theology of Karl Barth." *Scottish Journal of Theology* 29.3 (1976) 249–69.

# 16

## *Afterword*

Being and Becoming in Gratuity: Barth After Maury

JOHN C. MCDOWELL

IN HIS AUTOBIOGRAPHICAL STUDY, Eberhard Busch relates that in April of 1934, at the behest of the Protestant Theological Faculty in Paris, Karl Barth delivered a trio of lectures.[1] In the third, simply entitled "Theology," he gave a beautiful but demanding statement of the nature of theology's task: "Of all disciplines theology is the fairest, the one that moves the head and heart most fully, the one that comes closest to human reality, the one that gives clearest perspective on the truth which every disciple seeks. It is a landscape like those of Umbria and Tuscany with views which are distant and yet clear, a work of art which is as well planned and as bizarre as the cathedrals of Cologne or Milan." A little later Barth expressed a cautionary note: "Of all disciplines theology is also the most difficult and the most dangerous, the one in which a man is most likely to end in despair, or—and this is almost worse—in arrogance.

---

1. Busch, *Karl Barth*, 244. This visit to Paris was very much the initiative of Pierre Maury, as Charlotte von Kirschbaum relates in her account. See Reymond, *Karl Barth—Pierre Maury*, 283–91.

Theology can float off into thin air or turn to stone, and worst of all it can become a caricature of itself."[2]

Two years later again the by then close friend of Barth, French Reformed pastor Pierre Maury, in his conference paper "*Election et Foi*," focused the nature of the difficulty somewhat, and of what it is that can become a caricature of a well-ordered theology: "It is always difficult and it is also always a formidable task to speak of *election*, or predestination, or double predestination. It seems that we can only do it in order to defend it or attack it."[3] What makes the theological task difficult at this point? One might expect the response to be "because it is about God," and his paper does later make a reference to the "sovereign freedom, the incomprehensible mystery of God." But that reference appears after a leading and suggestive comment about the problem introduced by "human logic." So he announced, "Around it we see theological disputes, objections, indignations, and mockeries, or knowledgeable constructions of a far too humanly based logic."[4] Maury may here have been alluding to the distinction, common since Blaise Pascal, between the God of the Philosophers, and the God of Hebrew Patriarchs.[5] The notion was not developed by Maury further at this point, but even if there was a certain coyness at this stage, it was certainly absent from his *La Predestination*. There he indicated that a crucial difficulty in the reflection on, and the hesitance in the acceptance of, the mystery of predestination is that "everyone speaks about it, more or less, as philosophers."[6] Of course, there is often a generalizing shorthand way of proponents of any position dealing genealogically with their opponents. For theologians to classify "philosophy" as the problem is just such a shorthand and should therefore be read with some care. And yet, the generalization focuses the critical theological imagination on attention to the streams that contribute to its form and shape, recognizing that "human logic" is frequently malformed and requiring of appropriate mortification and vivification in the light of its subject matter. Maury's work on election, in other words, positioned itself to be a theologically therapeutic one for a doctrine that is deemed as frequently misdirecting its witness or, as he put it in *La Predestination*,

---

2. Busch, *Karl Barth*, 244.
3. See page 41.
4. See page 41.
5. See Maury, *Trois Histoires Spirituelles*, 155–99.
6. See pages 82–83.

as preventing us "from professing our faith" on the matter of "God's absolute sovereignty."[7] The notion of "prevention" from true witness is a serious theological matter, and not one of simple academic pedantry. Vladimir Lossky puts it well when he speaks of "two monotheisms."[8] This critical claim then comes to take several forms, one of which is worth noting here: that "the God of Descartes is a mathematician's God," the distorted product of human calculation, and the expression of *De deo uno*.[9] Lossky's judgment is damning: "The point of departure and the point of arrival . . . remain human," and by "human" Lossky means the faithless or unreconfigured human.[10]

For his part, Maury identified three areas of concern with the doctrine: the conception of time and eternity, the relation of mystery and revelation, and the issue of justice in what he calls divine favoritism. Each of these is driven by a falsifying rendering of the term "predestination" as used "in accordance with philosophic categories of thought."[11]

⁓

In his 1995 study Bruce McCormack acknowledges the importance of the doctrine of election for shaping and theologically grounding Karl Barth's burgeoning "christocentrism."[12] After all, Barth himself famously comes to announce with some gusto that "the doctrine of election is the sum of the Gospel because of all words that can be said or heard it is the best."[13] More historically interesting is McCormack's recognition of the impact on Barth of Maury's lecture in June 1936 at the conference devoted to the 400th anniversary of the Reformation in Geneva. "More than any other influence in Barth's life, it was Maury who deserves the credit for opening the way to that form of 'christocentrism' which became synonymous with the name of Karl Barth."[14] Exactly what Maury provides

7. See pages 82–83.
8. Lossky, *Orthodox Theology*, 21, 27.
9. Lossky, *Orthodox Theology*, 19.
10. Lossky, *Orthodox Theology*, 20.
11. See page 84.
12. McCormack, *Karl Barth's Dialectical Theology*, 453–63.
13. *CD* II/2:3.
14. McCormack, *Karl Barth's Dialectical Theology*, 455. While Eberhard Busch does not expand much on the relationship between the two men in his account, he explains that "Maury particularly attracted" Barth (Busch, *Karl Barth*, 249).

Barth with is actually not altogether clear, however. As McCormack has more recently admitted, Barth's redevelopment of election occurred over a six-year period, and only subtle hints of that shifting treatment can be detected in, for instance, the Gifford Lectures delivered in Aberdeen in 1937 and 1938.[15] This would suggest that considerable work of engaging a number of sources would have been part of Barth's study over the period. Secondly, and more theologically significantly, what emerges in *Church Dogmatics* II/2 diverges in several substantive ways from Maury's reflections—especially once Maury's paper has been altered in Charlotte von Kirschbaum's German translation[16]—suggesting that perhaps what Barth materially takes from Maury might even have been relatively minimal. Thirdly, and this is an even more complicated matter, the influence of Barth on the Parisian pastor should equally not be underestimated, and this suggests that what Barth may have taken from Maury has been a particular sharpening of his own theological trajectory. Can we say more, however?

It had been over a decade since Barth's lectures on election at Göttingen, and the fact that *CD* II/2 comes to play such a significant role in sharpening the theological direction his work on Revelation had been taking, and articulates what he perceives to be "the sum of the Gospel," points to a noteworthy development that occurs not long after enjoying Maury's lecture. As Barth later admits, the Genevan conference "dealt exclusively with the problem of predestination," but was theologically hampered by its movement "entirely within the circle of traditional formulations" and by being almost "hopelessly embarrassed by their difficulties."[17] Maury's lecture stood out and has had enough of an impact upon Barth for the Swiss theologian to very soon begin to spend time reflecting on the theology of election to such an extent that it becomes, as "sum," arguably the regulative moment for all his theological work that follows. As "the sum" of the doctrine of election it is not possible to set the doctrine in any neat way alongside other elements of Barth's theology, as only "one of the

---

15. McCormack, *Orthodox and Modern*, 263; cf. McCormack, "Election and the Trinity," 126.

16. See Matthias Gockel, 147–50.

17. *CD* II/2:155.

most crucial chapters in the *Church Dogmatics*."[18] So Maury acknowledges explicitly in *La Predestination*, election "is bound up with all the other truths of the Christian faith. In fact, it qualifies them all, they and it being unintelligible in isolation."[19] Of course, one needs to carefully spell out how this regulation works in order not to succumb to the kind of systematizing of Barth that he often was allergic to in others,[20] but I will not spend time theologically reflecting on this here.

∽

Beyond that impact, what impressed Barth about Maury's "instructive contribution" was not only its vigor and freshness in an otherwise theologically stale setting, but the hermeneutic expressly regulating it. From Barth's account of the matter, he reveled specifically in the lecture's drawing out "the Christological meaning and basis of the doctrine of election."[21] In particular, he relates as notably impressive the "treatment of Jesus Christ as the original and decisive object of the divine election and rejection." Later, in his foreword to the posthumous publication of Maury's 1954 lectures on *Predestination*, Barth again announces the bold "Christological basis" of the doctrine in the French pastor's work that so impressed him as to admit that "One can certainly say that it was he who contributed decisively to giving my thoughts on this point their fundamental orientation." Just how radical a shift this was for Barth's thinking at the time, however, is tricky to pinpoint precisely. His work had been more and more moving in the direction of focusing its attention on the regulating significance of Christology for talk of both God and creature. Barth himself speaks of this in 1939, not terribly helpfully though, as "a Christological concentration."[22]

18. Webster, *Karl Barth*, 88.

19. See page 82.

20. In a lecture in 1949, Barth distinguishes *systems* from the Good News of God's life-giving presence: "The gospel . . . is neither a principle, nor a system, nor a point of view, nor a moral philosophy. It is spirit and life, a good message of God's presence and work in Jesus Christ" (Barth, *God Here and Now*, 124).

21. *CD* II/2:154.

22. Karl Barth on September 20, 1939: "In working at this task—I should like to call it a Christological concentration—I have been led to a *critical* (in a better sense of the word) discussion of church tradition, and as well of the Reformers, and especially of Calvin" (Barth, "How My Mind Has Changed," 684). The reason for the unhelpfulness

This is an emphasis in election that Barth repeats in his Gifford Lectures, albeit this time without explicit reference to Maury. In the seventh lecture Barth opens by acknowledging that while "the heading of Article 8 [of the Scots Confession] is 'of Election'" its "contents . . . seem at first sight to be of a purely Christological character."[23] The "at first sight" is an indication that Barth detects something different going on, but not too different, since what he commends about the Confession is that "By this arrangement its authors have made it known unambiguously that they wish the whole body of material which is called the *doctrine of Predestination* to be explained through *Christology* and conversely *Christology* to be explained through the *doctrine of Predestination*."[24]

It is precisely this way of construing God and creature "in Christ" that Maury and Barth found to be troublingly lacking in much of the Reformed understanding of the doctrine of election. They were distinctly allergic to the logic of predestination that necessitates a *deus absconditus*.[25] "There is a danger," Barth claims, in any theology that is ordered by a "concept of God as omnipotent Will, governing and irresistibly directing each and every creature according to His own law."[26] Commenting on this passage, John Webster explains that "What is being objected to here is not so much the underlying notion of divine sovereignty, but the indeterminateness of such a concept of deity. The error which Barth feels it so necessary to censure is that of "supposing that God is irresistibly efficacious *in abstracto*,[27] naked freedom and sovereignty"[28] And within the error lies that against which the entire *Church Dogmatics* is directed: "God in general [*CD* II/2:49], uncorrected and undisciplined by the name of Jesus, and therefore an open field for the exercise of the speculative arts."[29] In contrast, Barth insists, "To know Jesus Christ is to know

---

in the phrase is that it is insufficiently concrete and particular: there are numerous ways of developing quite different types of Christological concentration, as McCormack usefully argues with relation to the equally imprecise terms "christomonism" or "christocentrism" (McCormack, *Karl Barth's Dialectical Theology*, 453–54).

23. Barth, *Knowledge of God*, 69.
24. Barth, *Knowledge of God*, 69–70.
25. A hidden God or God who, in his remoteness, seems to ignore human suffering.
26. *CD* II/2:44.
27. In or from an abstract point of view.
28. Webster, *Karl Barth*, 89.
29. Webster, *Karl Barth*, 89.

God, the one and only God," and to prevent a schism between God *in se*[30] and God "in His *decision* in favor of man."[31]

Barth's concern, then, is with theological abstraction, self-projection even, and this is especially evident in his perception of what constitutes the grounds of the problem expressed in National Socialism. So in 1939, complaining of the Hitler regime, he proclaims that "the abstract, transcendent God, who does not take care of the real man ('God is all, man is nothing!'), the abstract eschatological awaiting, without significance for the present, and the just as abstracted church, occupied only with this transcendent God and separated from state and society by an abyss" is not something that he teaches, although he had been accused of doing so by numerous critics.[32] Rather, to return to the Gifford Lectures, "to know Jesus Christ means not only to know God but also to know the *election* of man, which takes place as God *executes* His decision, and thus to know Jesus Christ means to know a new man, the elect *man*."[33]

It is important to notice here that attempts to claim that Barth was turning either Calvin or even the quite different claims of theological liberalism on their heads are quite problematic. It is with Calvin that Barth simply refuses to separate the knowledge of God and of human being. Human beings, *qua* creatures, are irreducibly bound to a theo-ontology, and that means that Barth is not displacing an anthropocentric starting-point for a theocentric one as if one can contest naïve methodological moves "from below" with assertive theological ones "from above." Barth's "christomorphic" dialectic cannot allow for such a monodirectional approach (it is at one and the same time anthropocentric, since what we mean by "human being" is Christ, and theocentric since what we mean

---

30. In Himself.

31. Barth, *Knowledge of God*, 71.

32. Barth, "How My Mind Has Changed," 686. One must be careful when speaking of Barth's theology as being driven by biblical and dogmatic concerns, even if one recognizes that it has particularly pronounced political implications—including requiring a theological hesitancy over the claims about its political virtues of the so-called "free world" order and capitalism. Leaving aside the hermeneutical understanding that no biblical or dogmatic interpretation is politically innocent, it remains the case that many of the tactical decisions Barth made in his *CD* and the language used there often directly nodded towards political questions and issues. When Barth refused to allow political circumstances to direct his theology he tended to have in mind the need for resisting a theo-political version of the *analogia entis*. That is, theology is deformed when it allows positions committed to political and cultural hegemonies to position and transfigure it.

33. Barth, *Knowledge of God*, 74.

by God is concretely bound to Christological claims about the incarnation of the Word of God). What this means for human beings, among other things, is that they cannot be other than what they are under the conditions of the purposefulness of divine creativity (for Barth, of course, that purposefulness is what the doctrine of election grounds). To be human is not to be engaged in an enterprise of self-construction, or in the natural realization of the gusts of *Geist*.[34] Rather, it is to find oneself having been grounded in, and formed by, the gift of God's election of Jesus Christ as "*the* elect One."[35] In other words, it is to know oneself as determined in *God's* electing choice. (This set of claims also has the effect of displaying how far off the mark readings of Barth's account as being "christo*monistic*" actually are. Humanity is *grounded* in and constituted by, but not *swallowed up* without ontological integrity by, God in Christ. After all, he argues, "the existence of this human individual is does not therefore exhaust itself in its individuality.")[36]

That is why the earlier language of God as *totaliter aliter*[37] comes then to take a different shape so as not to suggest that God's being God is set over against the creatureliness of the creature in a competitive frame, one that would separate God and creature through an essentializing distinction between the *logos asarkos*[38] and *logos incarnandus*.[39] As Barth would so clearly articulate later in his lectures on Romans 5, this covenantal framing of talk of God as the God for us in Christ is the reason why the sinfulness of Adam is not theologically determinative, but is rather the disrupting intrusion of Adam's genuine reality that is formed in and through the humanity of God in Christ, a humanizing of God that Adam remains bound up in and within God's redemptive faithfulness to God's Self-determination (*Selbstbestimmung*) to be for the creature in Jesus. Maury in "*Election et Foi*" argues that election is "therefore not a question here of *our* choice . . . but the choice of which we are the object,

---

34. Editor's note: Geist is a German word which has a particular importance in German. When translated into English it can mean: ghost, spirit, mind, etc., and is particularly associated with the philosopher Hegel and his view of the march of human history (often Prussian). It is quite common today, i.e., when we speak of the Zeitgeist, the "spirit of the age."

35. Barth, *Knowledge of God*, 75 (emphasis mine).

36. Barth, *Christ and Adam*, 33.

37. Totally different.

38. Unincarnate Word.

39. Word that will be incarnated.

that which is made . . . of us."⁴⁰ It is certainly not incidental, therefore, that Barth develops the language of the *Führer* in *CD* II/2. As Tim Gorringe observes, "The leader concept Barth understood as a secular imitation of the concept of the election of Jesus Christ. It is the utter reversal and caricature of that election. In it we have the apotheosis of Western individualism. . . . Christ is the reverse of this because what he has, he has for others."⁴¹

Consequently, Maury and Barth force the Reformed tradition to ask substantively what is meant by claiming that "*God* was in Christ" if Revelation is separated from the very Word of God eternally articulated, and God's being (as will) is hidden behind Christ so that the gracefulness of God expressed in Christ is particularized in the *decretum absolutum*⁴² and is therefore not essential to what is meant by God. Can this two-stage deity make sense of the development of Christian Trinitarianism and therefore the Christological doctrine of the *homoousion*?⁴³ Reasoning strongly that it cannot, Maury and Barth locate here the regulation of a philosophical abstraction in much of the tradition.⁴⁴ Criticizing both the Calvinist and Lutheran versions of the doctrine of predestination, Barth detects in them "traces of a natural theology . . . traces, that is, of a

---

40. EF 42.

41. Gorringe, *Karl Barth*, 148, referring to *CD* II/2:311.

42. Absolute decree.

43. *Homoousion*: same in being, substance or essence. Thomas F. Torrance provides the following exposition of the *homoousion* which one suspects has as much to do with his opposition to a dimension in the Reformed tradition as it does to the various forms of fourth-century Arianism: "God is inherently and antecedently in himself, and will be to all eternity, what he has revealed himself to be in Jesus Christ. God is not one thing in Christ and another thing in himself. He has not shown us one face in Jesus Christ but kept his real face hidden from us behind the inscrutability of his ultimate unknowableness. He has not sent Jesus Christ to be a mere messenger whose words and deeds of love he does not back up with the pledge of his own Being and Reality and Love. On the contrary, God has wholly and unconditionally committed *himself* to us in the incarnation of his Son in Jesus Christ, so that all that he eternally is and will be as God Almighty is pledged in Jesus Christ for us and our salvation. Jesus Christ and God are so utterly one in Being and Action that God does not, cannot, go back on Jesus Christ and his Cross, for that is who *God* is, he who came in Jesus Christ, and that is what *God* does, what Jesus Christ does" (Torrance, *Incarnation*, xvii).

44. In "*Election et Foi*" Maury announces that "arguably one can suspect him [Calvin] of having ceded to the necessities of a very human reasoning, going beyond the limits laid down by biblical revelation. That is why we must not allow ourselves to be held back by the fear of a divergence from the conclusions of the *Institutes of the Christian Religion*." EF 54.

general view of the freedom of God, based on one philosophical system or another."[45] The appeal to "natural theology" and "one philosophical system or another" is rather imprecise, but the import of the shorthand criticism is nonetheless clear enough. The Gospel has to do with what Barth suggestively delineates in his seventh Gifford Lecture through the phrase "the Revelation of God, the *God* who deals with *man*."[46] This he would articulate as the irreducible "concreteness, the contingency, the historical singularity of the eternal, absolute, divine Word" of God (and, of course, as *CD* III/2 impresses, of humanity as well).[47] Accordingly, Maury appeals in "*Election et Foi*" to election as being "about God."[48]

It is clear, then, that there is much at stake, dogmatically speaking. The reparative effort exerted on the doctrine of election was not to provide an overblown rhetorical flourish or biblical turn that would fail to theo-*logically* support the weight the rhetoric was placing upon it, as if theo-*logic* does not require the kind of sophisticated rigor claimed by more philosophical forms of reasoning.

∽

What is clear is that by 1942 Barth had not only developed and deepened in his own work that which he appreciated about Maury's "*Election et Foi*," but that he had pressed this material in all kinds of quite distinctive and theologically rich directions. In particular, as Barth's ontological reflections on the Who of the One who Self-identifies as being "in the beginning," Christology now comes not merely to provide the particularizing reference to the *object* of election (as in Maury) or the *mediator* of election (as in the Reformed tradition as Barth understood it).[49] Cru-

45. Barth, *Knowledge of God*, 79.
46. Barth, *Knowledge of God*, 70.
47. Barth, *Witness to the Word*, 86.
48. EF 42.
49. It is unfortunate that Barth occasionally sounds as if he regards the doctrine of election as always having been *unchristologically* developed rather than as christologically worked out in an *inappropriate* fashion. So he claims that "The word "predestination" is unfortunate in so far as by it something has been understood other than what has taken place in Jesus Christ. The treatment and proclamation of the doctrine of Predestination has all along suffered from the defect that its exponents have to a greater or less degree detached it from this connection from God's revelation in Jesus Christ.... Calvin's doctrine of Predestination suffers from this error of distinguishing God's decree and the existence of Jesus Christ" (Barth, *Knowledge of God*, 77). Barth is

cially, in addition, it demands attention to the very active electing *subject*, and this in terms of the *Logos incarnandus* (the Logos in anticipation of being *incarnatus*) as the form that the hominization of God's Self takes. Among other things, this means that the Athanasian formula that "there was no time in which the Logos was not" is actually saying considerably more than "that the Logos was before all time."[50] It now also has the sense in which there is no time, no times, free from the Logos. Such a move crystallizes and intensifies Barth's earlier claim that "So great is the Revealer that in him we see not merely a later, ad hoc fellowship between God and the world, set up merely for the purpose of redemption, but a fellowship that is original."[51] Nonetheless, it is here that the issues for scholars have recently become distinctly thorny and seemingly irresolvable, particularly those sparked by McCormack's contribution to *The Cambridge Companion to Karl Barth*.[52]

It is certainly not insightful or novel to claim that this paper recognizes that the doctrine of election, in the first and pre-eminent place, belongs in a doctrine of God. It has been long recognized that for the Barth of *CD* II/2 election is not *part* of the life of God as if there are other parts of the divine life alongside, or behind, it. What is new, however, is how that commonplace in Barth-studies has been theologically unpacked. It makes little sense to rehearse the main lines of the dispute since they have been articulated elsewhere.[53] What is useful in this context, however, is a brief observation of questions relevant to the way in which McCormack and those who critique his work handle the key themes mentioned earlier, and it will be interesting to watch the subsequent qualifications and clarifications that occur in these Barth-reading positions over the coming years: the gracious giving of God (against Pelagianisms); that *God* is in Christ (against the *deus absconditus*); and the sheer graciousness of God to all things (against divine preferentialism). This demands a more

---

here stumbling towards arguing that traditional Reformed accounts are insufficiently shaped by confessions of God's *being* in Jesus Christ as the just graciousness of the election of all things. The concept of Jesus Christ as the *subject* as well as the *object* of election will come to help him make his point more carefully. In *La Predestination* Maury argues that 1 John 1 presents Jesus as choosing as well as chosen, electing as well as elected. PD 102–3.

50. Barth, *Witness to the Word*, 21.
51. Barth, *Witness to the Word*, 31.
52. See McCormack, "Grace and Being," 92–110.
53. See, for instance, Dempsey, *Trinity and Election*, 1–28.

appropriate theological engagement than could be provided by any series of citations from Barth's work, even from his work of 1942 onwards. It also demands more rigorous *theological* work to be done in conversation with Barth than with simply appealing to a hermeneutic of charity. What is clear from McCormack's proposals is that the specific *logic* of Barth's redeveloped account of election requires the use of Barth against Barth, given that the Princeton-based commentator laments that the Swiss theologian refused to consistently apply his radical insights. Of course, this raises questions in its own right. Barth was not renowned for shrinking away from making difficult decisions in the context of the traditions he moved in and of offering unpopular theological reconfigurations. His correspondence with Maury over the implications of criticizing Calvin's doctrine of predestination is a noteworthy example of his lack of timidity. His unceremonious confrontation with Emil Brunner in print in 1934 is another even more infamous example. Consequently, it needs to be asked what prevented him from effecting a consistent revision of his doctrine of God.[54] Further, assuming that an inconsistency can in fact be conclusively demonstrated, what is there to prevent the logical consistency coming from the other side of the pole? The key is to identify what is theologically at stake for the various disputants, and to appreciate what problems they are trying to solve.

With regard to the first issue mentioned above, in his Gifford Lectures Barth professes that "God could exist without us. He is under no debt to give Himself to us. For neither in His Divine nature does He need us, nor can any such obligation rest on Him as Creator of the world and man."[55] A serious concern, however, has been raised as to whether McCormack's reparative actualistic reading of Barth's account of Jesus Christ as the subject of election, which means that God's being is eternally determined as being-for-this-event, has made the creature necessary to God's being, and has thereby limited the freedom of God that is conceptually necessary for the gratuity of grace. How would the integrity of God's being God be protected from being evacuated into the structures or consciousness of the creature and its history without it? In response, McCormack draws attention to the ways in which Barth differs from Hegel: election has to

---

54. More is required at this point than the claim that "to acknowledge the question and its importance might well have forced upon him the necessity of "beginning again at the beginning" in a quite literal sense—which by this point in time (early 1940s) was utterly unthinkable" (McCormack, "Grace and Being," 103).

55. Barth, *Knowledge of God*, 71.

be a free act of God (election is a *Self*-determination by God, an eternal decision of *God's Self*), and God's coming to Self-realization is an eternal act and the product of an eschatological process that occurs historically through humanity's consciousness of God. Theologically speaking, McCormack's Barth does not make *God's* existence dependent upon the existence of the creature. Instead, it demands that God not be understood as acting independently of *human* action, or spoken of apart from God's "inhominisation." Accordingly, it is a mistake to speak of God making God's Self available to humanity as if there can be a God unavailable, or lying behind God's being as the being-for us. But, as being constituted *pro nobis*,[56] is it arguable that God's being triune, and therefore the identifiable grounding of the very origin of Son and Spirit in the divine life, is being pinned to the divine economy?[57]

With regard to the second matter, McCormack worries that Paul Molnar and George Hunsinger have themselves introduced two acts into the eternity of God in such a way that God lies behind God's Self-electing determination in "a mode of existence in God above and prior to God's gracious election."[58] This, McCormack suggests, is "the very thing he accused Calvin of having done." For a start, there is an epistemic issue: how can God be known to be Triune *a se* other than in God's revelation *pro nobis*? God can only be known as God's own Self in the action of God's revelatory appearing to us in and as Jesus Christ. Such a theological account of the independent aseity of God and of a *Logos asarkos*, without the qualification the protological approach to the *Logos asarkos/ensarkos* provides, can only, McCormack asserts, be regarded as "free-floating . . . [and, therefore] as a mythological abstraction."[59] It is "a concept of ontological independence" that reflects that which McCormack singularistically defines as the classical concept: that "which is controlled by the thought of "pure being," an abstract, wholly timeless mode of existence"

---

56. For us.

57. "Hence [for McCormack] God could not be triune without electing to create time and to relate with us in time. In reality, therefore, God would have no triune existence in himself without his relationship with us" (Molnar, "Can the Electing God?," 87).

58. McCormack, "Grace and Being," 102; "Election and the Trinity," 121. McCormack claims that Edwin van Driel seems to do the same (McCormack, *Orthodox and Modern*, 274).

59. McCormack, "Grace and Being," 103.

onto which "the doctrine of the Trinity was simply added."[60] According to McCormack, Barth's understanding of God's essence is that "it is not an independent 'something' that stands behind all of God's acts and relations. God's being, for Barth, is a being-in-act."[61] This means that there can be no God other than the electing God who is free for the creature. Therefore, McCormack argues—and this has been the most controversial aspect of his proposals—"the incarnation of the 'Son' (and, we should add, the outpouring of the Holy Spirit) are *constitutive* of the being of God in eternity."[62]

What is required in Molnar's and Hunsinger's reading is an indication that the distinction within Triune-being-in-act does not permit a separation within the one God, since it is the same *subject* who is spoken of in modes. In other words, with a doctrine of simplicity in tow—what Barth refers to as the "consistency" of God[63]—one could claim that the God referred to as logically requiring a Triune mode of being-in-act *a se* is the *same* God *without reserve* who reveals God's *Self*.

This criticism can, however, be potentially turned around. If God has God's being in God's act, and that primal act is God's Self-election to be the Triune God of Jesus Christ and through him of all creatures, then there is a logical ordering of priority and successiveness that makes the Triunity of God's being a willed act of God's Self-election for the creature, an assigning to God's Self the Triune shape of the "being he will have for all eternity."[64] This is not the same as applying temporality and thereby claiming with the Arians that "there was when he [the Logos] was not": "if election is an eternal decision then it has never not taken place."[65] So arguing with temporal categories in mind significantly distorts the dispute, and exaggerates what is at stake. As McCormack argues, according to Barth, God's "eternal decision . . . has never not taken

---

60. McCormack, *Orthodox and Modern*, 273. In responding to Hunsinger, McCormack argues that "talk of an 'ontological priority' must mean that *being precedes act*" (McCormack, "Election and the Trinity," 117). Is it arguable, following this logic, that, if the election is *constitutive* of the Trinity, that act precedes being? Either way, God is no longer *being-in-act*.

61. McCormack, "Grace and Being," 99.

62. McCormack, "Grace and Being," 99.

63. *CD* II/2:187.

64. McCormack, "Grace and Being," 98.

65. McCormack, "Grace and Being," 101.

place."⁶⁶ Nevertheless, it remains important to ask just how equating the immanent and economic Trinities as the constitutive outcome of God's decision does not introduce something of an ontological logic of a two-stage Logos and Pneuma similar to the pre-Nicene "orthodoxy," so that Logos and Spirit become conceived of as functionally related to God or as "merely instrumental to the Father's relationship to the world."⁶⁷ "God," McCormack announces, "is triune *for the sake of* his revelation."⁶⁸ Asserting the simultaneity of God's Triune being and God's Self-electing does not aid matters, since the issue is an ontological and not a temporal one. The question remains, what does it mean to assert that *God* freely elects *God's Self*? It is suggestive, then, that a clarification comes in the form of insisting that "we would be speaking more accurately if we were to speak of the 'Father' as the subject who gives himself his own being in the act of election."⁶⁹ Does this imply that logically speaking there is Father and *then* Son and Spirit, and therefore two stages or even events?⁷⁰

The third issue has to do with the nature of the Good News. The worry has been voiced that Molnar's perspective is being hampered by an abstract understanding of divine freedom, especially with regard to the notion of God's freedom *from* the creature.⁷¹ What is needed, at least, is a clear explanation of how to conceive God's freedom *from* and *for* to be not two separable moments that result in any way of God being conceived of *behind* the event of revelation (because, given that God is the electing God, there is no God other than the electing God), or of the gracious electing of God as an arbitrary act (because election is not an act that is abstractable from the gratuity of the loving relations that God is).

As "sum of the *Gospel*" the doctrine is Good News, and accordingly both Maury and Barth are disturbed by accounts of predestination that spell

66. McCormack, "Grace and Being," 101.
67. Hunsinger, "Election and the Trinity," 109.
68. McCormack, "Grace and Being," 101.
69. McCormack, *Orthodox and Modern*, 266; cf. 272.
70. Molnar writes: "It is problematic to say that God gives himself his own being as Father, Son, and Holy Spirit. This statement suggests to me that God was in fact 'indeterminate' as God and only then became triune by giving himself his being as triune as a result of an act of will" (Molnar, "Can the Electing God?," 81).
71. This is a point made by Hector, "God's Triunity and Self-Determination," 41.

mercy for some and rejection for others, what the Frenchman in *La Pre-destination* calls the injustice of divine favoritism.[72] Barth's worry here is that such accounts miss the crucial point of claiming that God was in Christ, and that is that "the divine freedom is not the whim of a tyrant, able to incline equally well in one direction or in another."[73] Pressing this point harder, he maintains that "God does not become unfaithful to Himself when He shows us His incomprehensible faithfulness." Instead, this is a divine Self-articulation of God's own being-in-act, of a "God [who] is not only merciful," but "is *just* when He is merciful." He is careful to root this divine graciousness in God who is God's own eternal decision in order to offset any "monstrous" potential "for us to make our human capacities and merits the ground for demanding that God must have fellowship with man."[74]

Douglas Horton in 1928 claimed that "Karl Barth, in a word, is a reincarnation of John Calvin. His message, *in nuce*,[75] is the Sinaitic sovereignty of God."[76] This is, of course, a rhetorically overdetermined claim, since even in his 1922 lectures on Calvin's theology Barth makes it very clear that one cannot repeat the witness of another. "Only a Christian and a theologian who has learned in Calvin's *Institutes* to pursue the truth with which he is concerned by using his own eyes and ears can be a 'Calvinist.'"[77] And yet Horton has noticed something important, at least arguably from Barth's perspective: that Barth is attempting to follow the *message* of Calvin. In critiquing the Reformer's treatment of predestination, especially but not only in terms of the form his account of double predestination took, Barth does not feel that he is being inconsistent with the insight of the Reformed tradition, an insight into the grounding of all things in the activity of the graciousness of God. What Barth's reparative work does to the integrity of the Reformed tradition, then, may well remain a live issue. But one thing is for sure: Maury and Barth do not regard themselves as radically departing from Calvin and the (actually quite interestingly complex) set of Reformed traditions. Rather, they

---

72. EF 42.

73. Barth, *Knowledge of God*, 72.

74. Barth, *Knowledge of God*, 73. This argument forms the heart of Barth's criticism of the Lutheran development of the doctrine of predestination (cf. Barth, *Knowledge of God*, 78–79).

75. In English idiom "in a nutshell."

76. Horton, "God Lets Loose Karl Barth," 101.

77. Barth in Busch, *Karl Barth*, 439.

understood a "christologicalisation" of the doctrine to be an outworking of key theo-*logical* commitments from the work of Calvin, among others, especially the Triunity of the Self-communicative God.

Just such an approach animates the Swiss theologian's criticism of Brunner's appeal to Calvin in 1934 as a "natural theologian," or one who affirms "an 'unrefracted *theologia naturalis*[78]' with which sin 'has as it were nothing to do,' a system of natural theology, a self-sufficient rational system, detachable from the *theologia revelata*[79] and capable of serving it for a solid foundation."[80] Accordingly, Barth (and Maury, too, in "*Election et Foi*")[81] develops the Reformers against themselves in order to enable the heart of their message, or "the substance of the Reformers' theology which is quite unequivocal" to be more consistently heard.[82] "If we really want to retain the Reformers' position over against that of Roman Catholicism and Neo-Protestantism, we are not in a position today to repeat the statements of Luther and Calvin without at the same time making them more pointed than they themselves did."[83]

This is the reason Hans Urs von Balthasar famously gives for treating Barth with such theological respect:

> Cutting back through all the distorted developments of neo-Protestantism, he has gone back to the root sources of Protestantism, Calvin and Luther, and has even refined and purified these sources. He has modified or dropped certain points in Luther's doctrine, and he has done the same with Calvin. Calvin's doctrine is thought through to the end, spelled out more fully and corrected where necessary.[84]

More specifically, Barth attempts to solve the problem not by dispensing with the concept of double predestination, or by making it a feature of each one who is elect *and* reprobate in Christ as Emil Brunner does. Rather, Barth locates the doubling specifically in Christ alone, something he claims to have learned from Maury: a "treatment

78. Natural theology.

79. Revealed theology.

80. Karl Barth, "No!," 95.

81. The Scripture "will lead us in some points to not follow what Calvin heard in it [on election]. But that will not be being unfaithful to him; on the contrary, that will be truly Calvinist." EF 43.

82. Barth, "No!," 104.

83. Barth, "No!," 101.

84. Von Balthasar, *Theology of Karl Barth*, 19.

of Jesus Christ as the original and decisive object of the divine election and rejection."[85] So he declares that "Predestination means . . . the non-rejection of man"[86] precisely because Jesus Christ takes our place in the condition of reprobation.[87]

Here another question arises from Barth's treatment of election where the scholarship on Barth does not find accord. The issue is that of the eschatological implication of his reconfigured account of election in *CD* II/2. I do not have the space to address this matter in any detail at this point, but suffice it to say that commentators have not agreed on whether Barth's position does indeed lead inexorably to an *apokatastasis*, and even if it does, whether that indicates a boon or a bane with his reconception of election. This does not necessarily entail that more work needs to be done in order to achieve scholarly consensus, and certainly not if that requires explicating Barth's logic from a vantage point above his texts, as tends to occur among many of his Reformed critics. Given the plethora of studies on the matter, the issues are reasonably clear. What still requires a more adequate treatment, though, is the fact that Barth himself consistently theologically denied the *apokatastasis* as anything more than a *hope*. It is certainly easy to excuse this when the *logic* of his doctrine of election is read as apparently clearly necessitating a universalist claim. And yet a

85. *CD* II/2:154.
86. *CD* II/2:167.
87. There is an issue here of whether to understand this as requiring a certain type of retributivistic soteriology "in which revenge is even for God a 'necessary' part of righteousness" or an eternal anticipation of the historical infliction of creatures' sinful action on Christ (Gockel, *Barth and Schleiermacher*, 183). A suggestion of the latter comes in Barth's Gifford Lecture on Article 8 of the Scots Confession. Here Barth announces the theme of "the curse" and the "boundless affliction of this curse which lies upon us" by casting an historical eye on the narrative of Jesus: "Our burden [is] the fact that we cannot live with Him," and it is this which "becomes His burden" (Barth, *Knowledge of God*, 76). The language that follows takes a more expiatory form as a consequence. Gockel also regards divine reprobation as a concept belonging to Barth. He is correct that "Maury nowhere says that Jesus Christ was elected for damnation or reprobation or that he actively chose it for himself" (Gockel, *Barth and Schleiermacher*, 162n14). This is because Maury does not develop in the same way the agency of Christ in electing. The closest he comes is in providing his own type of parallelism, that it is on the Cross that election is realized: "[God] strikes Him [Christ] while welcoming us; He causes Him to die while letting us off." That Maury continues to eschatologicalize reprobation is clearer from the succeeding claim that Gockel does not cite in support: "There *are not* elect and reprobate, there *will be* elect and reprobate." In *La Predestination* Maury draws the contrast between "man as the elect . . . [and] as the non-elect, as rejected." EF 43.

more generous attention to these marginal notes, and therein a reading of the texts as having their own integrity that the reader cannot simply impose herself on, might offer a crucial hesitancy. Presumably Barth was not being theologically stupid, and it would take an almighty argument to entertain that he was being deliberately duplicitous here. Barth himself simply did not feel that his account of God's election obliged him to provide an eschatologically predictive *apokatastasis*, unlike Brunner, for instance, whose more actualistic account of election results in his confident announcement that "the Bible teaches that there *will be* a double outcome of world history, salvation and ruin, Heaven and Hell."[88] The "difficulties" with the *apokatastasis*, if one wants to regard it in such negative terms, are far from solved by any appeal to Barth's "other," or actualistically conceived earlier account of election.[89] Could this not be an issue illuminated by the role that wickedness or disobedience plays in Barth's account, so that, despite the election of all by, in and for Christ, *das Nichtige*[90] continues to incomprehensibly blight creaturely relations with God, others and self? Perhaps before he is lambasted further for his logical inconsistency, or naïvely for his causal impact on the recent theologies of the *apokatastasis* (causalities are both difficult to historically discern, and are part of a complex range of influences on really quite theologically diverse sets of eschatologically universalist commitments), scholars might want to work a little bit harder in the activity of understanding what is theologically going on in Barth's writing at this point.

Appropriately, nay necessarily, an "afterword" can witness not only *to* but also *away from* the studies and the debates that have emerged over recent years. To speak to the first of these, it is distinctly arguable that the divergences in the scholarship, the multiplicity of voices and readings (as long as they are respectful of the texts' own particularities and not flush with the self-interested power of a reader-response type of

---

88. Brunner, *Christian Doctrine of God*, 1:326 (cf. 348).

89. For instance, it is inappropriate to suggest that Barth can be saved from the *apokatastasis* by developing his pneumatology in such a way that would lead him back into the bind of double predestination—since not all receive the gift of the Spirit not all are predestined to salvation—and that he cannot permit in the name of the freedom of the gracious God to be gracious *ad extra*.

90. *CD* III/3.

hermeneutical solipsism), are testimony to the complexity of a theologically rich set of works.[91] Even the more heated disagreements, when they are at least tempered by the humility of the scholar and the generosity of grace, indicate the rude health of Barth-scholarship.[92] To the theological world the passion of the disputants may be a puzzle, but it is distinctly a refusal to evade the seriousness of reading and understanding theological texts with as much precision as the theological scholar can provide. Barth himself recognized and lamented the way his style had manifestly led to considerably problematic handling of his writings.[93]

But there is more, and this is the second of the tasks an afterword has to offer, in encouraging not merely thinking about Barth, but non-repetitive theological work that can be conducted through and beyond him. As McCormack argues, "Karl Barth was the greatest theologian since the Reformation. But we do him no service if we simply repeat him. For his interest lay in the subject matter to which he bore witness. And it is to that subject matter that we must direct our attention, not to Karl Barth as an end in himself."[94] Doing theology through and after Barth may involve occasions of turning Barth against himself, as Barth certainly did with Calvin.

In other words, in order to do justice to Barth's own theological temperament, one would need to permit this particular twentieth-century theologian to function as something of a John the Baptist-like figure. Barth admits in the Preface to the second edition of *Der Romerbrief*: "All human achievements are no more than prolegomena; and this is especially the case in the field of theology."[95] Therefore, it comes as a matter of

---

91. It is arguable that Michael Dempsey has not done the relations between the scholars a good service by opening his summary of the issues on the contested readings on election with Barth's claim that "those who are at loggerheads here . . . not only speak another language . . . [but] have a different faith" (Dempsey, *Trinity and Election*, 1).

92. It is, however, an unfortunate sign of the state of the disagreements that someone like Philip Carey has to use conflictual language in order to describe the condition of relations between Barth scholars at Princeton: "Rumors of war persist in Princeton" (Carey, "Barth Wars"). Cf. McCormack, *Orthodox and Modern*, 277.

93. On September 20, 1939, Barth bemoaned that "I have not always succeeded, in former times and also today, in expressing myself in a manner comprehensible to all is a part of the guilt which I certainly impute to myself when I see myself surrounded by so much anger and confusion" (Barth, "How My Mind Has Changed," 686).

94. McCormack, *Orthodox and Modern*, 137.

95. Barth, *Epistle to the Romans*, 2.

concern that "recent commentators confine themselves to an interpretation of the text which seems . . . to be no commentary at all, but merely the first step towards a commentary."[96] This, as his comments on Calvin in the lectures of 1922 indicate, is actually not to do good theological or historical work at all:

> We cannot stop at establishing that four hundred years ago Calvin said this or that. . . . To stop there would be to deny that history is life's teacher, and, I would add, it would be to deny the immortal Spirit of God whom Calvin heard speaking through Paul even though Paul was long dead. . . . The historical Calvin is the living Calvin who, as he did say this or that, wanted to say something specific, one thing, and who, insofar as his works are preserved, still wants to say it, perhaps in a way he could not do in his lifetime and to earlier readers of the works. . . . Calvin's theology is historical because, through every transparency and means of communication, it is teaching by the immortal Spirit of God.[97]

An example of where he was heading by this point can be found in his lectures on *John* 1 from 1925 and 1933 in which Barth embarks on a practice of reading that from Augustine's *De Doctrina Christiana*[98] clarifies what makes for a good reading of the scriptures. Here he recognizes that the Word cannot be replaced by the words, cannot be left behind as in, for example, its reduction to the gaze of historical curiosity. Nor can it leave behind the words since it speaks *in and through* them. As a consequence, the words are crucially not, in an important sense, their own. "They are in some sense from the very first its prisoners."[99] "From the very first" is seemingly a temporal reference, and would accordingly introduce a successiveness. But this is not the import of Barth's reference which is instead a statement of theological provenience, constitution, and regulation. So he adds a note of authority: "A word, no, *the* Word has been spoken which in principle, as the Word of the Creator, precedes and is superior to all that is."[100]

What matters for Barth in theological work, in other words, is the next step beyond revering the historical sense of the text, even beyond

---

96. Barth, *Epistle to the Romans*, 6.
97. Barth, *Theology of John Calvin*, 3-4.
98. On Christian Doctrine.
99. Barth, *Witness to the Word*, 12.
100. Barth, *Witness to the Word*, 12.

an attempted ossification or foreclosing of any tradition of interpretation of that text, and that is the witness the text provides to the *Sache* (that is for him at this early stage the *krisis* Word of God made flesh for us and our salvation). *After* this Word, if by that is meant a post-Word successiveness that leaves the *Logos* behind in the *logoi*, there is not theology, *theos-logia*. Rather, there is nothing(ness). But from, in and through this Word there is life, and that life is abundant with the radiance of God's grace, a theology in which the walls that separate the twentieth-century Swiss theologian and the various readers of the early twenty-first century become somewhat kerygmatically transparent. And so, "The Word ought to be exposed in the words."[101] This is why Barth, with his radically reconceived account of God's Self-determination to be faithfully "for man . . . the One who loves in freedom," remains a valuably profound theologian of the joy of the Gospel, even though that be a Gospel irreducibly bound up with a story of crucifixion, and of a theologian of hope who thinks and speaks with what Hunsinger calls "a *hilaritas* informed by *gravitas*, but which never succumbs to it" nor arrogantly takes itself "too seriously."[102] It is this service to the Word of the Gospel, the God of Israel and all things that enables Barth to remain theologically interesting not only to the Reformed tradition but also to the church catholic.[103]

---

101. Barth, *Epistle to the Romans*, 8.

102. Hunsinger, "Introduction," vii–viii.

103. "Only by overlooking or forgetting the truth in Christ which has broken into the world of Adam, could we judge the truth in Adam to be absolutely without light" (Barth, *Christ and Adam*, 61).

# BIBLIOGRAPHY

Asbill, Brian D. *The Freedom of God for Us: Karl Barth's Doctrine of Divine Aseity.* London and New York: Bloomsbury, 2015.

Barth, Karl. *Christ and Adam: Man and Humanity in Romans 5.* Translated by T. A. Smail. New York: Collier, 1962.

———. *The Epistle to the Romans.* Translated by Edwyn C. Hoskyns. 6th ed. Oxford: Oxford University Press, 1968.

———. *God Here and Now.* Translated by Paul M. van Buren. New York: Routledge, 2003.

———. "How My Mind Has Changed in this Decade: Part Two." *Christian Century* (1984) 684–86.

———. *The Knowledge of God and the Service of God According to the Teaching of the Reformation: Recalling the Scottish Confession of 1560.* Translated by J. L. M. Haire and Ian Henderson. The Gifford Lectures, University of Aberdeen 1937–1938. London: Hodder and Stoughton, 1938.

———. "No! Answer to Emil Brunner." In *Natural Theology*, edited by Emil Brunner and Karl Barth, 65–128. Translated by Peter Fraenkel. Eugene, OR: Wipf & Stock, 2002.

———. *The Theology of John Calvin.* Translated by Geoffrey W. Bromiley. Grand Rapids: Eerdmans, 1995.

———. *Witness to the Word: A Commentary on John 1. Lectures at Münster in 1925 and Bonn in 1933.* Edited by Walther Fürst. Translated by Geoffrey W. Bromiley. Grand Rapids: Eerdmans, 1986.

Brunner, Emil. *The Christian Doctrine of God.* Vol. 1 of *Dogmatics*. Translated by Olive Wyon. London: Lutterworth, 1949.

Busch, Eberhard. *Karl Barth: His Life from Letters and Autobiographical Texts.* Translated by John Bowden. London: SCM, 1976.

Carey, Philip. "Barth Wars: A Review of *Reading Barth with Charity*." *First Things*, April 2015. http://www.firstthings.com/article/2015/04/barth-wars.

Dempsey, Michael T., ed. *Trinity and Election in Contemporary Theology.* Grand Rapids: Eerdmans, 2011.

Gockel, Matthias. *Barth and Schleiermacher on the Doctrine of Election: A Systematic-Theological Comparison.* Oxford: Oxford University Press, 2006.

Gorringe, Timothy J. *Karl Barth: Against Hegemony.* Oxford: Oxford University Press, 1999.

Hector, Kevin W. "God's Triunity and Self-Determination: A Conversation with Karl Barth, Bruce McCormack, and Paul Molnar." In *Trinity and Election in Contemporary Theology*, edited by Michael T. Dempsey, 29–46. Grand Rapids: Eerdmans, 2011.

Horton, Douglas. "God Lets Loose Karl Barth." In *The Christian Century Reader*, edited by Harold E. Fey and Margaret Frakes, 101. New York: Association, 1962.

Hunsinger, George. "Election and the Trinity: Twenty-Five Theses on the Theology of Karl Barth." In *Trinity and Election in Contemporary Theology*, edited by Michael T. Dempsey, 91–114. Grand Rapids: Eerdmans, 2011.

———. "Introduction to the Routledge Classics Edition." In *God Here and Now*, by Karl Barth, vi–xvi. New York: Routledge, 2003.

———. *Reading Barth with Charity: A Hermeneutical Proposal.* Grand Rapids: Baker Academic, 2015.
Lossky, Vladimir. *Orthodox Theology: An Introduction.* Translated by Ian Kesarcodi-Watson and Ihita Kesarcodi-Watson. Crestwood, NY: St. Vladimir's Seminary, 1978.
Maury, Pierre. *Jésus Christ, cet inconnu: six allocutions pour le carême 1948.* Strasbourg: Oberlin, 1948.
———. *La Prédestination.* Geneva: Labor et Fides, 1957.
———. *Le Grande Œuvre de Dieu.* Paris: Je Sers, 1937.
———. *Predestination and Other Papers.* Translated by Edwin Hudson. London: SCM, 1960.
———. *Trois Histoires Spirituelles.* Geneva: Labor et Fides, 1962.
McCormack, Bruce L. "Election and the Trinity: Theses in Response to George Hunsinger." In *Trinity and Election in Contemporary Theology*, edited by Michael T. Dempsey, 115–37. Grand Rapids: Eerdmans, 2011.
———. "Grace and Being: The Role of God's Gracious Election in Karl Barth's Theological Ontology." In *The Cambridge Companion to Karl Barth*, edited by John Webster, 92–110. Cambridge: Cambridge University Press, 2000.
———. *Karl Barth's Critically Realistic Dialectical Theology: Its Genesis and Development 1909–1936.* Oxford: Clarendon, 1995.
———. *Orthodox and Modern: Studies in the Theology of Karl Barth.* Grand Rapids: Baker Academic, 2008.
Molnar, Paul D. "Can the Electing God Be God Without Us? Some Implications of Bruce McCormack's Understanding of Barth's Doctrine of Election for the Doctrine of the Trinity." In *Trinity and Election in Contemporary Theology*, edited by Michael T. Dempsey, 63–90. Grand Rapids: Eerdmans, 2011.
Reymond, Bernard, ed. *Karl Barth—Pierre Maury: Nous qui pouvons encore parler: Correspondance 1928–1956.* Paris: Symbolon, L'Age d'Homme, 1985.
Torrance, Thomas F., ed. *The Incarnation: Ecumenical Studies in the Nicene-Constantinopolitan Creed.* Edinburgh: Handsel, 1981.
Von Balthasar, Hans Urs. *The Theology of Karl Barth.* Translated by John Drury. New York: Holt, Rinehart, and Winston, 1971
Webster, John. *Karl Barth.* 2nd ed. London: Continuum, 2004.

# Subject Index

abandonment, of Christ Jesus, 48–49, 105–6
Abraham's election, 86–87
absolute decree, 92–93, 104, 112
  see also decretum absolutum
absolute love, 71–72, 169
actualistic election, 127–28, 130–31, 142, 153, 221, 246, 253
Adams, Damon, x, xv, xix, 11, 172, 191
*After Fundamentalism* (Ramm), 3
apokatastasis, 11, 173n5, 177n23, 179n34, 181–90, 225–26, 231, 252–23
Arianism, 243
assurance of salvation, 9, 85, 101, 117, 119, 169, 179, 219
Athanasian formula, 245
atonement, 150n22, 154, 175n14, 178n31–79, 188, 200n40, 2018n99, 226
authority
  Bible as, 76–78
  of Christ, 71–74, 76–78

Barth, Karl
  doctrinal revision, 125–34
  Göttingen doctrine, 125–29
  letter to Finet, 16–17
  letter to Thurneysen, 134
  on Maury, 4n9, 7, 13–14
  Maury's influence, 129–30, 134, 142, 237–38
  Münster dogmatics, 128n25
  political context of doctrine, 134–36
  on Scots Confession of 1560, 9, 240, 252n87

  on theology, 235–36, 238, 240, 241n32 254

Bell, Rob, 187
Berkouwer, G. C., 6n17, 176–77, 225n49
Bible
  as authority, 76–78
  election presented in, 85–87
  sole source of knowledge, 81
Bloesch, Donald, 3, 12 n32, 33
Busch, Eberhard, 123n2, 3, 126n12, 134n51, 139, 140n72, 160n7, 229n66, 231n73, 235, 236n2, 237n14, 250n77
Bosc, Jean, xi, 10, 28n1

calling of the elect, 103–4, 116
Calvin, John
  absolute decree, 92, 93, 104
  covenant of life, 126
  *decretum absolutum*, 131, 150, 198, 218–20, 243
  divine election, 46–47
  double predestination, 147n5
  election as a labyrinth, 41–42, 116, 95
  grace, 55
  *Institutes of the Christian Religion*, 5, 2n2, 42, 54, 81, 126, 172, 243n44, 250
  joy of election, 49, 164
  mortal labyrinths, 109
  personal predestination, 116
  rejection or reprobation or two separate and fixed groups 127

## SUBJECT INDEX

Calvinist theology, 53, 85, 92n4, 146n1, 147n5, 149, 160, 243, 250
*The Cambridge Companion to Karl Barth* (McCormack), 245
Capper, John Mark, ix, xv, xix, 11, 159
choice
    to accept or refuse, 50–51, 63–64
    commitment to Christ, 63
    election and, 41–42, 46–47
    God's supreme choice, 108
    human agency, 66–67, 162–63, 169, 229–30
    of God, 97
chosen
    to be Jesus Christ, 83–85
    meaning of, 108
Christ, Jesus
    abandonment of, 105–6
    atonement, 150n22, 154, 175, 178–79, 200n40, 208n99, 226
    divine election, 46–47, 133–38, 144–45, 159
    as "the elect," 130
    election, presence of, 46–49
    election of God by God, 88–92
    giving of self, 69
    He who chooses us, 69–70
    the place of eternal election 100–101
    pre-existence of, 101–3
    rejected, 104–5, 112–14, 130–31, 131n37
    relationship with the Father, 97–98
    relationship with us, 74–75
*Christianity and Barthianism* (Van Til), 2, 8n21
*Christology in Cultural Perspective* (Greene), 6
"Christomonism" (Barth), 6n17, 174, 239–40 n22
commitment, 63
cyclic time of Greek metaphysics, 84n2

*decision of faith*, 77, 153, 227, 228n63, 229, 232
*decretum absolutum*, 131, 150, 198, 218–20, 243
*Der Romerbrief* (Barth), 230n72
destiny, 42, 45, 71, 73, 74, 77, 83–84, 91, 102–3, 117, 161, 204, 209, 227n54
*deus absconditus*, 240, 245
Devil, works of darkness, 93
discursive resistance, 137, 142
*Disruptive Grace* (Hunsinger), 2n3
divine election, 46–47, 133–38, 144–45, 159
divine favoritism, 237, 250
divine preferentialism, 245
divine righteousness, 156
double election, 109–11
double predestination
    an alternative concept, 129–30
    Barth of the Göttingen years, 127–29
    Barthian critique of Reformers' understanding, 219, 250–51
    election in Christ and, 49
    new man and, 52–54
    supralapsarian view, 92n4
double-minded Christians, 62, 166

the elect
    Abraham, 86–87, 98, 114,
    Christ as, 130
    distinguished from the condemned, 7n20, 52–53
    grace and rejection, 115–16
    Jesus, 103–4
    residing in Christ, 98–100
    unfaithful elect, 108–9
    who they are, 47, 51, 57–58, 116
election
    accomplished by God, 44–45
    actualistic, 128, 131, 142, 153, 221, 246, 253
    Barth's doctrine of, doctrinal revision 125–32
    calling of Christ, 103–4
    demonstrated, (the marks of election) 57–58

## SUBJECT INDEX   261

in Christ, 45–49
faith and, 44
as free act of God, 44, 47, 54,
  80, 84, 86, 89–91, 94–95,
  97, 129, 142, 152, 198, 209,
  219n23, 247
of God by God, 88–93
grace and, 132n40
historical fulfilments of, 114
human or divine notions, 83
injustice of, 42–43, 49, 55–56,
  110, 149, 156, 249–50
of Jesus Christ, 150–55
joy of, 56, 164–65, 170
as a labyrinth, 33–34, 80, 95, 101
opus Dei ad extra externum
  (external work of God directed
  outwards) 132n40
opus Dei ad extra internum
  (external work of God directed
  inwards) 132n40
as paradox, 47, 149, 152, 156,
  183
pastoral ministry, 117–19
philosophical standpoint, 81, 83,
  119, 159, 160, 215, 243–44
political resistance (as), 123,
  134–37
sovereignty, 54
theological not anthropological
  doctrine, 6, 88–93
  See also Maury-Barth
  comparison of election
  theology; predestination
encounter, the divine/human,
  163–64
eternity, 83–4n2
evangelical, 1, 32, 125, 156, 163,
  178n31, 180, 186n68,
  189n83 & 84, 214n8

faith
  election and, 41–59, 11n32, 43–
  4, 49–50, 52, 54–58, 61–64,
  119, 149, 153, 159, 196, 205,
  223n41, 225n48, 226n51,
  from hearing, 64–65
  justification by, 55–56

forgiveness, 34, 51, 94, 99, 115, 117,
  118, 215–16
freedom, human, 11, 41, 43, 57, 197,
  205–10
free grace, 97, 106, 231–33

Gockel, Matthias, ix, xv, xix–xx, 10,
  129, 146–58, 172–73, 178,
  191–92, 184n53, 227n54,
  252n87

God the Father
  chooses to be Jesus Christ,
    83–85, 161–66
  immutable counsel, 147n5
  as love, 91–92
  as omnipotent Will, 240,
  relationship with Christ, 97–98
  repentance of, 113–14
  secret counsel, 42–43, 54, 113,
    148
Gorringe, Tim, 243n41
Göttingen Dogmatics, Barth's, 8,
  125n9, 128, 129, 131, 133,
  136, 142, 146, 147n3, 152,
  153, 156, 221n31, 238
grace
  acceptance of, 51
  free grace, 97, 106, 231,
  frightening aspect, 47–48
  positive grace, 49, 52, 109–11,
    112, 217
  rejection and, 115–16
  salvation by, 55
  sheer grace, 93–94

Hattrell, Simon, ix, xx, 1–19, 25n2,
  28n2, 41n1, 60, 80n1
Heppe, Heinrich, 126
Hitler, Adolf, 123–24, 135, 137, 138,
  138n63, 241
Holy Scripture. *See* Bible
Holy Spirit the, 11, 12, 58, 77, 81, 89,
  99, 136, 157, 175n14, 197,
  201–5, 208–10, 230–32, 248,
  249n70
homiletical orientation, 11, 165,
  213, 214, 215, 221

homoousion doctrine, 243n43,
human justice, 43
human freedom, 11, 41, 43, 57, 197, 205–8
human response, 153, 164, 288
humanity, as co-humanity, 16
Hunsinger, George, 2n3, 128n22, 129n29, 133, 133n48, 150n22, 173n4, 201, 202n54,58 & 59, 247, 248n60, 249n67, 256n102,

immutable counsel, 147n5
incarnation, 70, 97–98, 100, 129, 132, 151, 241–42, 243n43, 248
*Institutes of the Christian Religion* (Calvin), 5, 41n2, 42n3, 4 & 5, 54, 81, 126n16, 172, 195n2, 243n44, 250,

*Jesus is Victor* (Bloesch), 3, 11n32, 12n33, 176n20
*Jesus is Victor* (Greggs), 182n46 & 47
Jewish people, 137–41
joy, ix, xix, 11, 29, 34, 43, 49, 54, 56–57, 58, 67, 72, 75, 77–78, 114, 116, 117, 119, 159–70, 198n24, 210, 218, 256,
judgment, 8, 45, 51, 53, 54, 72–73, 101, 113, 155n55, 169, 178, 183n50, 222, 228
Jüngel, Eberhard, 132n40, 164n29, 229n65
justice, 43, 48, 56, 105, 106, 149n17, 152n38, 227n54, 237,
justification, 55, 118, 125, 151n30, 176n20 & 31, 215n13, 216,

*Karl Barth's Critically Realistic Dialectical Theology* (McCormack), 3, 19, 144, 158, 211, 234, 258

*La Predestination* (Maury), 19, 35n1, 80n1, 236, 239, 244n49, 250, 252n87, 258
labyrinth, election as, 41, 42, 116,
Last Judgment, 72, 94, 104, 138, 154

Lindsay, Mark, ix, xx, 10, 123–45, 124, 136, 137, 140, 144, 159
linear time of biblical thought, 84n2
*Logos asarkos*, 247
*Logos enarkos*, 132
*Logos incarnandus*, 133, 243, 245
Lutheran development of predestination doctrine, 125, 243, 250n74

Mackie, Robert, ix, xi, 10, 30–34, 213
Maury, Pierre
  Barth's forward to *Predestination*, 28–30
  Barth's friendship, 12–16
  biographical information (Mackie's overview of his life), 31
  character of, 30–34
  Gustave Monod's tribute, 25–27
  Jean Bosc's tribute, 28–29
  letter from Kirschbaum, 60–61
  letters from Barth, 2n2, 7–8n21, 6n18, 7n20, 60n1, 147n7, 156n58
  letters to Barth, 60–61
  Jacques Maury's tribute to, 23–24
  on Ultimate Decision (*See* "The Ultimate Decision")
Maury, Pierre, writings
  "Election and Faith" (*See* "Election and Faith" ["Election et Foi"])
  *La Predestination*, 19, 35n1, 80n1, 236, 239, 244n49, 250, 252n87, 258
  "The Ultimate Decision," 5, 11, 60–79, 159–71, 200n39, 217n18, 227–28
Maury-Barth comparison of election theology
  on divine election, 133–38
  double predestination, 109–11, 146–47
  translation interpretations, 148–50, 156

## SUBJECT INDEX 263

Maury-Barth post reflections
   Balthasar's commentary, 251n84
   Barth on, 238–44
   God as omnipotent Will, 240n26
   Gorringe's commentary, 243n41,
   Hunsinger's commentary,
      247–49
   McCormack's commentary,
      244–49
   Molnar's commentary, 247–49
McCormack, Bruce
   Barth reflections, 237–38,
      239n22, 245–49
   *The Cambridge Companion to Karl Barth*, 245
   Christ as subject of election, 132–33
   *Karl Barth's Critically Realistic Dialectical Theology*, 3, 19, 144, 158, 211, 234, 258
   locus of predestination, 125n10
   Trinity, 132n43
McClymond, Michael, 174n12, 178, 179n33, 181n40, 42, 43, 184n52, 186n68
McDonald, Suzanne, xiii-xiv, xxi, 4, 4n11, 213, 221n32, 224n44,
McDowell, John, x, xv, xxi, 12, 235
mediator of election, 244n49
*Mein Kampf* (Hitler), 138
mercy, 34, 52, 55, 95, 110–11, 113, 115, 117–19, 130, 141, 161, 182n48, 250
Migliore, Daniel, 5n13
Molnar, Paul, 132n43, 133n47, 247n57, 249n70,
mortal labyrinths, 109
movement of faith, 115
Münster dogmatics, Barth, 128n25
mystery and of revelation, 83

National Socialist dogma of election, 139
natural theology, 7, 243, 244, 251
Nazism, 124, 136–39
negative election, 49, 101, 110, 149, 216
new man, 51–54, 209, 241

obedience (of the elect), 58
object of election, 244n49
O'Neil, Michael, x, xxi-xxii, 11, 12, 198, 200, 213

Pascal, Blaise, 50n14, 51n16, 64n6, 76, 112, 156n59, 166, 236
paradox, election as, 147–48
particularism, 129–30, 129n29
patience, divine, 114, 161, 186, 226n52
Pelagianisms, 245
politics and religion, 134–36
positive election, 109–10, 149–50
positive grace, 49, 52, 109, 111, 112, 217
prayer, 58, 71, 91
preaching, xiv, 11n32, 24, 29, 36, 104, 117, 118, 182, 183n49, 213, 214, 215n13, 216
predestination
   Abraham's election, 74–75
   actuality of, 86
   assurance of salvation, 117
   Barth on, 126–34
   biblical context, 82
   calling of the elect, 104-4, 116
   chosen in Christ, 98–100
   Christ's election, 88–92
   double (*See* double predestination)
   double election, 109–11
   election of God by God, 88
   election without Christology, 112
   eternal election of Christ, 100–101
   God's supreme choice, 106–7
   historical fulfilments of election, 114
   human or divine notions, 83
   incarnation, 97–100, 129, 132, 151, 242, 243n43, 247, 248
   Jesus Christ, the elect who elects, 103–4
   Jesus Christ, the one rejected, 105–6, 112–14

opinions on, 81
overview, 85–87
pastoral ministry and, 117–19
philosophical notions, 83
revelation, mystery of, 83
time and eternity, 83
total love, mystery of, 105–6
unfaithful elect, 108–9
witness of the elect, 117
Word, who was in the
    beginning, 101–3
*See also* election
pre-existence, of Jesus, 101–3
proclamation 11n32, 85, 95, 124,
    198, 200, 204, 205n70, 213,
    214n8, 215–18, 221, 223–27,
    227n54, 231–33
"prodigious audacity," 66, 167
*Prolegomena* (Barth), 124
*Protestant Biblical Interpretation*
    (Ramm), 3n4, 11n32
Protestantism, in France, 1n1
punishment, 48, 105, 178, 191

*Reformation Thought*
    (McGrath),126n17
*Réforme* (journal), 4n9, 10, 13n36,
    16, 28n1&2
*Reformed Dogmatics* (Heppe), 126
Reformers the 24, 53, 148n13,
    156n58, 165, 239n32,
rejection
    Barth on, 150n23
    of Christ, 105, 112–14
    grace and, 115–16
relationship with Christ, 64–65
repentance, 114, 115, 159
reprobation, 53–54, 92n4, 127, 129,
    132, 140–41, 152, 177–78,
    183, 199, 252n87
Resurrection, 84, 87, 105, 151–52,
    182n47, 226n52
revelation, mystery of, 83
revenge, 252n87
Reymond, Bernard, 2n2, 4n9, 5n14,
    6n18, 7n20, 13, 14n37,
    15n44, 17n48, 60n1, 129n27,
    147n4 & n7, 148n9, 156n58,
    157n64, 235n1
righteousness, 116

salvation, eternal, 55–56
Scots Confession of 1560, 9, 240,
    252n87
secret counsel, of God, 42–43, 54,
    113, 148n12
self, giving of, 70–71
self-contradiction in God, 147
Self-determination by God, 133n47,
    216, 220, 242, 247, 249n71,
    256
sovereignty, irresistible, 111
sovereignty, divine, 82, 142, 190,
    230, 237, 240, 250,
sovereignty, of God's Word, 229,
Stossich, Leo, x, xv, xxii, 11, 12, 195,
    230n69,
*The Student World*, 33
supralapsarianism, 92n4
systems distinguished from the
    Good News, 179, 239n20

theogony, 90n3
theology
    Barth on, 235, 238, 249–53
    natural theology, 7, 243–44, 251
*The Theology of the Reformed*
    *Confessions,* (Barth), 8
Thurneysen, E., 13n36, 126n13,
    134n52, 143
Torrance, Andrew, 207n89, 90,
Torrance, Thomas, 243n43,
Trinity, 82, 89, 91, 97, 102, 132n41,
    42 & 43, 133n44, 46 & 48,
    157, 202, 248
"two monotheisms," (Lossky),
    237n10
two separate choirs, 147n3

"The Ultimate Decision" (Maury)
    Bible, as authority, 76–77
    commitment to Christ, 63
    decision, to choose Christ,
        66–67
    eternal life, 68–69

faith from hearing, 166–67
God in Christ, 64–65
Joy, as it relates to election, ix, xix, 11, 67, 72, 75, 77, 78, 159, 161, 162, 163, 165–65, 167, 169, 170, 198, 210, 218, 256
Lenten series "The Great Work of God" (1937), 6
revelation of God, 61–63
unbelievers, 154–55
universal salvation, 110, 155n55, 175–186, 197n19, 199n29,37, 200, 225n49
universalism, x, 11, 12, 54, 155n55, 172, 173, 177n23, 178, 178n30, 179n34
universalism, Christian (influence of Barth), 180–90
universalism, (rejection by Barth), 225–26n50

Van Til, Cornelius, 2n3, 8n21
Visser't Hooft, Willem, 13–14n38,39, 16, 31, 33, 34
vocation, 45, 50, 58, 100, 116, 159, 204, 224n44,

von Kirschbaum, Charlotte, xiv, 11, 60n1, 129n27, 148n9, 157n64, 235n1, 238
Von Balthasar, Hans Urs, 3n7, 183n50, 51, 184n52, 251n84,

Ward, Graham, 3n8
Weber, Otto, 123n2
Webster, John, xv, 205n72, 235n18, 240n28, 29
Weimar Republic, 134

worship, 26, 42, 49, 56, 93, 109, 217

zeal, 163

www.ingramcontent.com/pod-product-compliance
Lightning Source LLC
Chambersburg PA
CBHW071241230426
43668CB00011B/1537